HORIZON

NOVEMBER, 1958 • VOLUME I, NUMBER 2

Horizon
A Magazine of the Arts

NOVEMBER, 1958 • VOLUME I, NUMBER 2

PUBLISHER
James Parton

EDITOR
Joseph J. Thorndike, Jr.

MANAGING EDITOR
William Harlan Hale

ASSISTANT EDITORS
Margery Darrell
Hilde Heun
Ada Pesin
Jane Wilson

EDITORIAL ASSISTANTS
Robert C. Agee, Caroline Backlund,
Gertrudis Feliu, Mary Ann Pfeiffer,
Nancy Teass, Martha Thomson

ART DIRECTOR
Irwin Glusker
Assistant: Richard B. Browner

ADVISORY BOARD
Gilbert Highet, *Chairman*
Frederick Burkhardt   Oliver Jensen
Marshall B. Davidson   Jotham Johnson
Alfred Frankfurter   Richard M. Ketchum
J. H. Plumb

CIRCULATION DIRECTOR
Richard V. Benson

HORIZON is published every two months by
American Horizon, Inc., a subsidiary of American
Heritage Publishing Co., Inc., 551 Fifth Avenue,
New York 17, N. Y.
Single Copies: $3.95
Annual Subscriptions: $18.00 in the U.S.A.
$19.00 elsewhere

Second-Class postage paid at New York, N. Y.

HORIZON welcomes contributions but can assume
no responsibility for such unsolicited material.

COVER: On his rearing charger, Jean de Bruges, the Lord of Gruthuyse, has lowered his visor to meet the Lord of Ghistelles in the famous tourney held at Bruges in 1392. In memory of this event, King René of Anjou created his magnificent *Livre des Tournois*, whose illustrations are here presented with an article beginning on page 92. Fortunately the book was preserved for posterity by Louis de Bruges, a descendant of Jean, who ordered two copies made and personally presented one to Charles VIII, King of France, in 1489. Other copies were subsequently made, and the reproductions here used are from the parchment pages of French Manuscript No. 2692 in the Bibliothèque Nationale.

FRONTISPIECE: One of the loveliest miniature paintings of the Italian Renaissance is this "Adoration of the Magi" by Girolamo of Cremona. The swirling dolphins, fruits, and vines that surround the holy scene almost obscure the fact that the whole work is an illumination of the letter *O*. It is part of a choir book now in the Piccolomini Library at Siena, and appears in *Italian Miniatures*, published by Harry N. Abrams, Inc.

The face of Akhnaton (left) in this Middle King-dom colossus is not that of the real Pharaoh but that of a demigod, half Egyptian, half Eternal.

The sacred art of the ancients, which disappeared in Hellenic times, was reborn with rising Christianity in mosaics like that of a zealot at Ravenna.

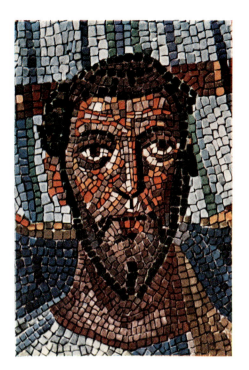

THE GODS IN ART

ANDRÉ MALRAUX IS SEEKING THE KEY TO MAN'S FATE BY

A PHILOSOPHICAL STUDY OF ALL THE WORLD'S ART. IN

HIS NEW VOLUME, "THE METAMORPHOSIS OF THE GODS,"

HE PURSUES THIS DARING VENTURE OF THE INTELLECT

By HENRY ANATOLE GRUNWALD

"The greatest mystery is not that we should be tossed by chance amongst the profusion of matter and the welter of the stars; it is, rather, that within this prison we are able to draw from ourselves images powerful enough to deny our nothingness."

MALRAUX: The Walnut Trees of Altenburg

Once, during a visit to the United States, André Malraux was asked whether he agreed with the famous statement by Rebecca West that "the railroad stations are the cathedrals of America." "No," he replied, "the museums are the cathedrals of America."

The remark may or may not say much about America; it says a great deal about André Malraux, an agnostic who worships art and whose private cathedral is that vast and dizzying intellectual structure he calls the "Imaginary Museum." During most of his career, Malraux was better known as a novelist and a dabbler in politics who had moved from left to right. He lived his own legend—that of a brilliant intellectual passionately committed to action, who had made the grand tour of his era's better wars and revolutions —China, Spain, the French *maquis*. His adventures in art did not become widely known, at least in the United States, until the publication here five years ago of *The Voices of Silence*, his monumental and passionate survey of man's art in all regions and all ages.

Actually, this was no new departure for Malraux. Art has been his lifelong avocation. "I am," he has said, "in art as other men are in religion."

His name first made headlines in France during the 1920's when he went digging for lost Khmer statues on the Royal Road of Cambodia, found them, and ended by fighting the French Government for their possession. Over the years, no war was too rough, no journey too fatiguing to keep him from museums, churches, or temples, where he exchanged stares with strange idols, measured man against his monuments, and recorded innumerable shapes and colors on the film of an apparently indelible memory. Between travels, he spent years editing art books. He is currently supervising a giant, forty-volume series spanning all art history. Yet his concern with art is even deeper than these biographical facts suggest; it is above all a philosophical concern. "Malraux's anguish was born the day his catechism ceased to express the truth for him," a friend of his has written. Malraux himself has declared that he would never bow to religion in order to gain the peace it offers the weak. But he is intelligent and sensitive enough to know that this by itself is not a tenable position. Other men have been able to settle down within commuting distance of the void, more or less snug in a universe empty of meaning, purpose, or hope. Not Malraux. As the French critic Jean Onimus puts it: "He is one of those modern atheists who has finally consented to go to the limit of atheism without stopping at the lazy and hypocritical level of smiling irony . . . Malraux cannot resign himself to the Death of God. He cannot dwell in nothingness; the absurdity of it catches him by the throat."

To escape this absurdity, Malraux decided long ago, man must defy his fate. Though the human condition be basically intolerable—blind life quickly staggering toward death— man can nevertheless be great. Against all odds, he must assert dignity and heroism. One way to do so is in action— politics or war. Another, more lasting way is in the creation of "images powerful enough to deny our nothingness"—art. Malraux explained this in *The Voices of Silence*. "True arts and cultures relate man to duration, sometimes to eternity, and make him something other than the most favored denizen of a universe founded on absurdity," he wrote. "Each

The transition from the sacred to the purely human is clearly seen in Greek sculpture. The statue on the left half of the opposite page, the Kouros of Milo, of the sixth century B.C., is already recognizably Greek, with its smile and its graceful equilibrium, but still not of this world. Only half a century later the Kore of Euthydikos (at right on this page) is serenely human but idealized in what Malraux calls the Divine spirit of the high classical period. In the fourth century B.C. the transition is completed with the purely human, exactly representational Apoxyomenos by Lysippus, shown at far right, opposite page. Illustrations accompanying this article were taken from Malraux's newest book, so far published only in French as La Métamorphose des Dieux.

6

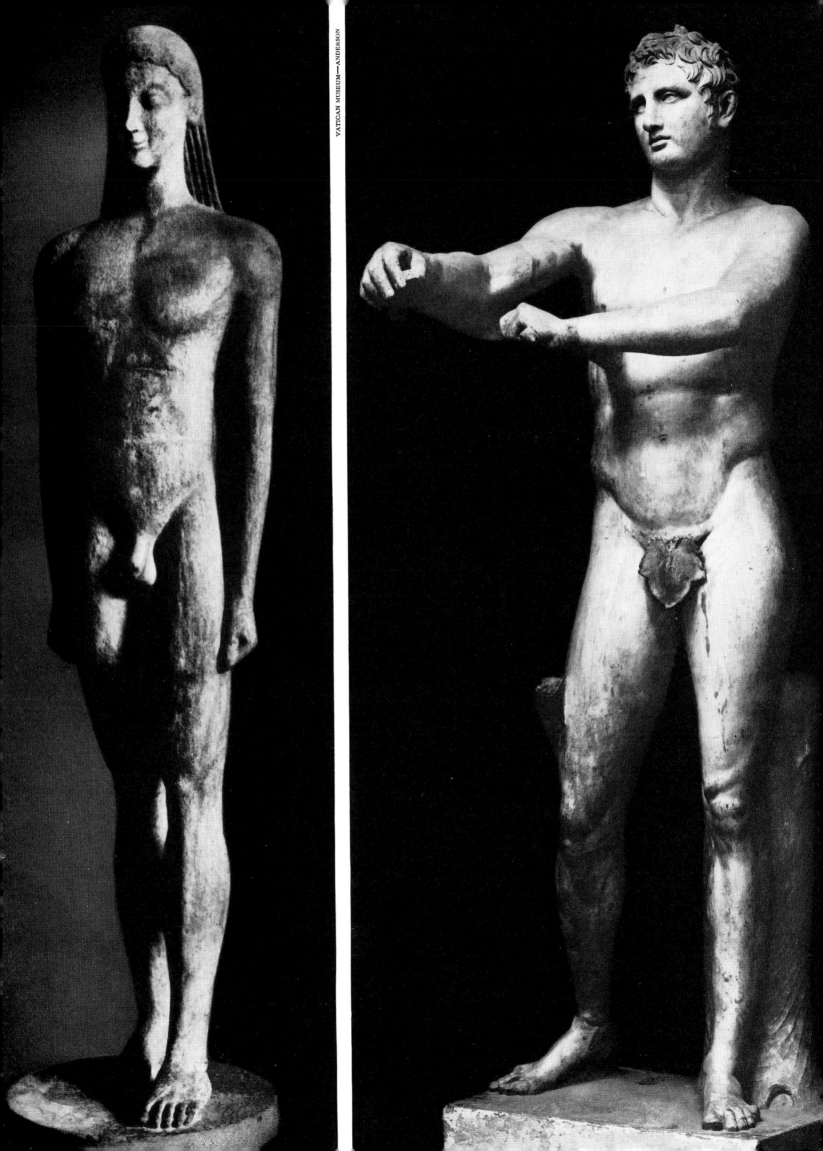

At the end of the Middle Ages, with the waning of religious fervor, sculptors strove less for the spiritual beauty of their subjects and more for the aesthetic beauty of their statues. Saint Paul (above) glories in a beard of elaborate curls, while Saint Mary the Egyptian (below) is robed in a single, long cascade of stylized hair.

of the masterpieces is a purification of the world, but their common message is that of their existence and the victory of each individual artist over his servitude, spreading like ripples on the sea of time, implementing art's eternal victory over the human situation. All art is a revolt against man's fate." Elsewhere he has said: "Art is an antidestiny."

THE IMAGINARY MUSEUM

In which the art of every age is at last brought together and searched for its deepest meaning

Malraux's latest devotional study of this antidestiny is a remarkable work entitled *La Métamorphose des Dieux*. The book, so far published only in French (Paris: La Galerie de la Pléiade), is in a sense a continuation of *The Voices of Silence*. But it is also a self-contained work and a fresh beginning. Most of the basic ideas contained in the new book can be found in the earlier one, but there they are scattered amid a staggering profusion of sights and insights. In *The Metamorphosis of the Gods*, Malraux has pulled together a number of these insights—chiefly those concerning art as an expression of the otherworldly—and arranged them in what, for him, is almost order. The resulting work is breathtaking, irritating, beautifully but densely written, repetitious, humorless, fascinating, and unquestionably brilliant. Every page glows with a rare passion for art—and, considering the author's agnosticism, it displays a longing sensitivity and an almost professional knowledgeability about religion. As the title accurately suggests, it is concerned with the changing shapes of faith at least as much as with the changing shapes of art.

The setting is still the Imaginary Museum, or, as it is also known, the Museum without Walls. By this concept, as he explained at length in *The Voices of Silence*, Malraux refers to the fact that, thanks to photography and modern reproduction techniques, mankind can for the first time have all the world's art before its eyes. The spectator is no longer limited to isolated masterpieces or to truncated museum collections assembled by chance. He can see art as it has never been seen before, not only in all its vastness but in all its detail: for lens and light can show him, larger than life, the remotest corners of otherwise inaccessible façades, the faintest smiles on otherwise invisible faces.

As the chief curator and guide of the Imaginary Museum, Malraux recalls Toynbee and Spengler. For one thing, he shares their infatuation with the past, their conviction that it can speak to us, that stones have tongues. For another, he shares their mental habit of imposing patterns on the universe. He, too, is obsessed with the contemporaneity of everything. As Toynbee might compare certain aspects of the Egyptian Middle Kingdom to the modern American

EGYPTIAN MUSEUM, CAIRO—HASSIA

This funerary painting from a late Egyptian sarcophagus marks the return of a mysterious, otherworldly spirit after centuries of representational art. The weird figures and lurid colors reflect the disintegration of the whole Mediterranean world as the Roman Empire neared its end. This work is contemporary with the earliest Christian art of the catacombs.

Middle West, Malraux glories in placing a Buddhist statue of 500 B.C. alongside a late medieval crucifix. As he writes in *La Métamorphose:* "The art worlds hitherto known to mankind were exclusive, like religions; our art world is an Olympus where all the gods, all the civilizations, address themselves to all men who understand the language of art."

From the heights of that Olympus, Malraux observed the works of man and produced in *La Métamorphose* a personal confession of aesthetic faith, which, by virtue of its style and its poetic vision, comes close to being itself a work of art.

THE "OTHER WORLD" OF ART

The rediscovery of primitive painting and sculpture helps modern eyes to see that art has a deeper mission than visual beauty

The story goes that the painter Théodore Rousseau once set up his easel before a tree. A peasant walked up to him. "Why do you paint this oak tree," asked the peasant, "when it is already there?" The answers that different painters might give to this excellent question would categorize their consciously or unconsciously held aesthetic theories. "I paint this tree to show others, who have never seen it, exactly what it is like," one painter might say. Another: "I see things in this tree you do not see, and I paint it to tell you what I feel." Another: "I do not paint this tree at all, but my vision of it. I paint to express myself." Another: "I paint for the greater glory of God." Another: "I paint for the same reason I might play or dream—to escape." Another: "I paint because I must." Another: "I paint to teach you the appreciation of excellence—first in physical things, then in things spiritual." Another: "I paint to teach you goodness."

All these answers, and innumerable other possible ones, share the notion that art is meant to express beauty and to delight the senses or the mind. Most share the view that the artist paints by his own volition. Many—by no means all—share the view that art is primarily concerned with reflecting the physical world of shape and color, filtered through the artist's personal vision. With all these propositions Malraux disagrees. In his view, beauty and delight are not the chief

Saint Luke was painted with mystical fervor in the Gospel of Ebbo, an illuminated manuscript of ninth-century France. Such painting was meant not to depict reality but "to express what cannot exist on earth."

aims of art; the artist is not a being free to "express himself" but an instrument of a more or less mysterious force; and the aim of the true artist is not to paint the visible but the invisible world. These are some of the aesthetic assumptions underlying *La Métamorphose des Dieux*.

Writing almost continuously in the breathless, historical present, Malraux begins by reporting a fact: the discovery during the last hundred years of countless ancient and exotic works, most of them religious in character. In the West, these works brought about an aesthetic revolution. A hundred years ago, they were looked on—if looked on at all— as archaeological curiosities. They were fetishes, icons, idols—exactly what they had been to their creators, who were "artists for whom the idea of art did not exist." Now they are regarded as art, and they are teaching men to see in a new way. "Europe discovered Negro art when looking

at African sculptures placed between Cézanne and Picasso, not when looking at fetishes placed between coconuts and crocodiles." Malraux finds it remarkable that our civilization—"the first agnostic civilization"—should be so busy "resurrecting sacred works." But busy it is, and with the attention to this sacred art "which nobody had ever admired in a body before, and which nobody admired at all a century ago," men's feelings about all art began to change.

"Europeans," Malraux writes, "by the tens of thousands crowd thousands of expositions of Mexican and Etruscan art; by the hundreds of thousands, they crowd the expositions which bring together the monastic treasures of Vienna and the works of Rembrandt; just as many Japanese file past the pictures of Braque, and millions of Americans past those of Van Gogh and Picasso. Pilgrims to the cities of art are more numerous than those who came to Rome during the Holy

In a Breton Gospel, Saint Luke appears in even stranger form with the head of an ox, his traditional symbol, which denoted both the spirit of sacrifice and the patient bearing of the yoke for the good of others.

Year. Faced with the figures of Florence and Venice, these pilgrims may mix the idea of art with happiness, beauty, pleasure of the eye; but they do not so mix it before the figures of Chartres or Luxor, before Mexican or Etruscan statues. It is not in the name of happiness, in the name of the traditional ideas of beauty or visual pleasure, that the movies make a hero of Van Gogh . . . people from all countries, scarcely aware of their community of feeling, seem to expect the art of all ages to fill an unknown void in them."

All of these people are touched by "that enigmatic power which unites for us in a common presence the statues of the most ancient Pharaohs and those of Sumerian princes, those sculptured by Michelangelo and by the masters of Chartres; the frescoes of Assisi and the cells of Nara, the pictures of Rembrandt, of Piero della Francesca, and of Van Gogh—

the paintings of Cézanne and the bisons drawn on the walls of the prehistoric caves of Lascaux." What is that "enigmatic power?" Its key lies in the fact that the sacred arts "reject or scorn the submission of images to the testimony of our senses. For the sculptors of Moissac as for those of Ellora, for the fresco painters of Ajanta as for the mosaic makers of Byzantium, appearance and reality have the same meaning: all human reality is merely appearance in the view of that world of Truth which their art aims to manifest or to suggest. . . .

"These gods and ancestors, heroes and priest-kings, immortals and obscure dead—art had the mission to express their deliverance from the human condition, their release from time. . . . The power by which they reach us, and which for us is the very power of artistic creation, was initially the power that *gave form* to that by which man became man, by

11

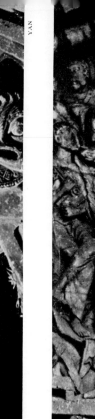

YAN

ARCHIVES PHOTOGRAPHIQUES

which he escaped chaos, his animal life, and animal instincts. . . . If man had not raised his successive worlds of Truth against external appearance, he would not have become a rationalist but a monkey. . . . 'Men give names to the gods,' an Indian saying has it, 'but the gods may accept them or ignore them.' The greatest artists gave images to the gods, but the gods accepted them only if men recognized them. Thus began the reign of style."

Sacred art—and in a sense all art—"imposes the presence of another world. Not necessarily an inferno or a paradise, not only a world after death; a world beyond, rendered present. For all these forms, in various degrees, the real is appearance; and something else exists, which is not appearance and which is not necessarily called God."

This "other world," this "something else" beyond appearance, is the criterion by which, in *La Métamorphose*, Malraux judges and classifies art. Of course there are different kinds of "other worlds" (for example, the worlds of the pagan gods and of the Christian God). But in each category, art moves between two poles—faithfulness to the "other world" and surrender to the human world. In short, Malraux's history of art is a series of ups and downs between what David Riesman might call the other-world-directed and the man-directed, between the vision of Truth and the copying of truths.

The critic Clive Bell, though he would scarcely have appreciated Malraux's prolonged brooding about the other-worldly, or the dialectic zigzags of his style, nevertheless

sketched some ideas in his famous essay, *Art*, that make for an interesting comparison with Malraux's. Up to a point, at least, Bell too saw in art an antidestiny: "Art and Religion are two roads by which men escape from circumstance to ecstasy." The road of art, as Bell saw it, moves in a succession of slopes. By a slope he meant "that which lies between a great primitive morning, when men create art because they must, and that darkest hour when men confound imitation with art." Malraux himself would reject as patronizing and misleading the concept of the "primitive" beginnings. But Bell's image of the slope, though Malraux does not explicitly use it, clearly fits his theory and helps to summarize a work that resists summary as does a poem, a theological treatise, or an encyclopedia.

SACRED ART IN ANTIQUITY

It united mortal man with Eternity—but Greece brought the gods into daylight and Rome let them die

The high ridge of Malraux's first slope is what he calls the Sacred—the art of the ancient Orient up to and including Egypt. Malraux's view of the function of that art is perfectly expressed in this remark about the Sphinx and the Pyramids: "These giant forms rise together from the small funeral chamber which they cover up, from the embalmed corpse

In Romanesque and Gothic sculpture the figure of the Savior changes as Christian faith loses its mystical fervor. At left is the awesome, Biblical Christ of the Moissac abbey church and next, the Christ of outstretched arms at Beaulieu. The third figure, from the royal portal at Chartres, is still Christ in Majesty, but greatly softened in aspect. In the statue at far right, done half a century later for the south portal, He is completely metamorphosed into the loving Jesus, "who speaks not to all men but to each."

which it was their mission to unite with eternity." In short, the art of the Sacred was predominantly funereal, its aim being not to show man in the here-and-now but to ease and express his transition to the beyond. The practitioners of that art for the most part shunned realistic representation, not because they were incapable of it, but because it was forbidden by the strict conventions of their religion. The most celebrated "realism" in all the Orient was that of Tell el-Amarna, yet its colossus of the great Akhnaton (see page 4), when compared to Akhnaton's death mask, shows a human face transformed into the elongated, mysteriously smiling countenance of a demigod. Like Akhnaton's colossus, the statue of the Pharaoh Zoser of the Third Dynasty represents the face of the Sacred. "Nothing remains of the power that caused Egypt to emerge from prehistoric night; but the power that caused the statue to emerge from it speaks to us with a voice as strong as that of the masters of Chartres, or of Rembrandt. We no longer have anything in common with the creator of that statue, not even the sentiments of love or of death—perhaps not even a way of looking at his work; but when we are faced with this work, the accent of a sculptor who was forgotten for five thousand years seems to us to be as invulnerable to the rise and fall of empires as the accent of mother love."

Malraux's next slope, considerably lower because considerably closer to the world of man, is that of Greek art. It is the art of what he calls the Divine—meaning the pagan divinities. He places the transition from the Sacred to the

Divine between 550 and 500 B.C. At the beginning of that period, "all art was hieratic. The preachings of Buddha, the work of Lao-tse, the Upanishads had been known for a century. Western Europe was at the end of the Iron Age." Half a century later, in Greece, the serenely human Kore of Euthydikos (see page 6) had been created. "Fifty years were enough to reject the art of three millennia. During those fifty years, man for the first time unlearned the Sacred."

What caused the change? Not, as some art historians used to think, an improvement in technique that brought artists closer to "illusionism"—that is, representation giving an illusion of reality. The figures of Greek sculpture for the most part were not realistic at all, but idealized. "The cleverest forger could not insert a realistic face in the Parthenon frieze. The Ergastines are beautiful, not like their models but like columns—or music." What caused the change was a shift in man's concept of the "other world." The gods

13

changed before art did. "In Greece we hear for the first time, through the voice of Euripides: 'I do not like the gods who are worshiped at night.' Thus begins the fragile art of those gods who must die with the sun. . . .

"Ulysses still prostrated himself before Earth; we cannot imagine Pericles prostrate before Athena, nor praying with his *hands folded*. The gesture of worship that symbolizes Greece is the offering of the sacrifice. The interventions of the gods are as unpredictable as their oracles. No book of revelation sets down their law. The temples do not dispense religious instruction, and the Greeks do not have a priestly caste. [They are] without clergy, without theocracy, without Creator, without supreme Judge, and without eternity."

Under this dispensation, the existence of Pallas Athena or Aphrodite "was no less self-evident to everyone than the existence of the libido was to Freud, who resurrected Aphrodite. Cultivated Athenians did not believe in that existence in the same way a Christian believes in the existence of Christ—but perhaps in the way a Christian believes in the existence of the Devil. They recognized that existence within themselves." And so, "the sacred is replaced by the sublime, the supernatural by the marvelous, Destiny itself by tragedy."

The result was an unprecedented freedom for artists. "Greek art was still tied to Egypt when it discovered the smile, and with it also a new equilibrium of the human body. One could not confuse the Kouros of Milo [see page 7], even if it had no head, with an Egyptian statue. Its elongation, its thinness from waist to arms to spindle-shaped legs, its neck that is twice as long as that of a Memphis scribe and much more vertical, give the statue the lightness of a pottery vase that was unknown to even the most fluid Egyptian figures." In contrast, "there is in Oriental sculpture an invincible heaviness. . . . The Orient, which invented winged beings, could not make them fly." What Greek art achieved was not simply movement, as is sometimes said, but the independence of the person, of the human being.

At the same time, Greece invented the work of art. "The people whose gods were only immortals, and who knew no afterlife except a life of shadows, invented the immortality of great human creations." Egyptian or Sumerian statues, without their consecrated purpose, were merely stone. But for Greece, any statue, consecrated or not, representing mortals or immortals, could become part of the divine by virtue of the creator's talent, "because for Greece, talent is nothing but the expression of the divine. The gods take shape through art as the light takes shape through the object on which it falls."

With the waning of the Middle Ages, painters lost their touch for myth, fable, and anything supernatural. The Venus who appears beside the tree in this scene in Les Echecs Amoureux *at the end of the fifteenth century is so obviously only a naked woman that the artist felt he had to identify her with a label.*

14

Pluto's realm, as illustrated in Les Echecs Amoureux, *is no longer a nether world of terror but a court scene peopled by figures of artificial fantasy. The mythological king of the underworld and his wife, Proserpine, are here attended by lute players together with the fabled three-headed watchdog, Cerberus.*

Greek art remained faithful to the divine so long as its people remained faithful to the gods. But when the old Olympians were "no longer gods of a religion but gods of a culture," the " 'makers of gods' became makers of statues." Praxiteles still saw artistic creation as "a break with preceding forms, the discovery of an unknown world or a divine image." After him, the slope lowers more and more toward mere representation. With Lysippus, "the creation of the divine ceases." As representation, his Apoxyomenos (see page 7) is clearly superior to much that came before. Lysippus "tried to conquer the resistance of bronze and marble by suggesting the unattached state of all movements—life itself." But only mortal life. "One cannot imagine a god of the Sacred—or an Olympian—resembling the figures of Lysippus: they would have lost their divinity."

Roman art continues the process. "Rome conquers Greece and Olympus; she does not conquer the divine. She invents without realizing it, the parody of divinization. . . . She is superstitious, but superstition can adapt itself to atheism as well as to faith; she offers sacrifices to unknown powers but knows nothing about communion with them. . . . Henceforth, everyone considers art the imitation or idealization of appearance. . . . For the first time, appearance has become *reality*." Finally, "under a sun now menaced by Roman pomp, nothing remains of Greece, Egypt, and the Orient but a rumbling of gods neither sacred nor divine. [But] in the approaching night, once again the eyes of the Sacred begin to glow."

That glow is everywhere in the "vast religious ferment that corrodes the empire." Egypt, for instance, once again finds its old funereal genius in the shroud portraits of the Fayum. Colors that were totally unknown in the art of the ancient world appear, notably salmon and violet, which dominate "the frenzied figures of the last sarcophagi." Not only in color but in shape there is rebellion everywhere against "illusionist" representation, for men once again refuse to accept external reality as anything but appearance. By about the fourth century A.D., Christian art seems to be merely one among these many rebel movements—but its rebellion is victorious.

Thus Malraux arrives at his third great slope, which he calls Faith. Along that slope moves the long, haunting procession of images through which Christian artists have offered up a visual and ever-varying *Te Deum*.

THE RETURN OF THE SACRED

Byzantium rises in jeweled gloom—the apostle pictured with the head of an ox—Christ in Majesty turns into the loving Jesus

At the beginning of Christian art stands, in jeweled gloom, Byzantium. The radiance of the sun beating upon the Acropolis has been replaced by the candle flickering in the shadows. The sanctuary has reappeared, a "resurrection in glory of the catacombs." The dominant image in that sanctuary is the mosaic, an art form that once again serves the supernatural. Light, space, and movement in the old Greek sense are eliminated as sternly as they were in Egypt

15

—again not because of the artists' lack of skill, but in order to make clear that their art is not of this world. The deep blue backgrounds of the Ravenna mosaics (see page 5), the unreal gold backgrounds found in mosaics all over the Christian world, suggest—but do not represent—the light of God. Once again art serves the world of Truth. Byzantine art "is not an illustration of the life of Jesus, but a theological affirmation of the nature of Christ . . . a defense and illustration of God in His ungraspable majesty." Like Byzantine theology, Byzantine art fights the Aryan heresy that separates the Son from the Father and tends to slide "toward a man named Jesus." That is why sacred scenes are not so much scenes as symbols, and why the Virgin, even when she holds a child on her lap, is not the mother of a child but of God.

The Byzantine spirit survives the centuries of iconoclasm, the centuries of barbarian invasion. When the next major impulse of Christian art is felt during the Carolingian renaissance of the ninth century—the art of the illuminated manuscript and the miniature—it is certainly not Byzantine; but like the Byzantine, it is Augustinian in its theological emphasis. And like the Byzantine, it does not know external realities. It is an immensely diverse art, with innumerable different schools, ranging in a relatively short time from the Gospel Book of Charlemagne, which could be the imitative art of some western province of Byzantium, to the Kells and Saint Gall Gospels in which Christ, the Virgin, and the apostles are "Biblical hieroglyphics," and to the "frenzy" of the Gospel of Ebbo. Yet all, including the strangely fascinating Gospel books of Brittany, "express what cannot exist on earth." The artist who painted the Saint Luke of Ebbo (see page 10) did not intend to represent a flesh-and-blood apostle any more than the artist responsible for the Saint Luke of Brittany (see page 11), "who signifies the saint *because* he is not a man." Luke is pictured with the head of an ox because this sacrificial animal is the saint's traditional symbol—standing for the true sacrifice of Christ as well as for the patient bearing of a yoke.

For all its evocative magic—"akin both to the stained glass window and the totem pole"—the miniature remains an art that clings to the book. It is made by monks for monks. This does not change until the great, almost spontaneous surge of religion in the eleventh century, when the civilization of the monastery turns into the civilization of

CONTINUED ON PAGE 112

The figure of the Virgin underwent a remarkable change. In the Coronation of Notre Dame Cathedral, Paris (below), she is Queen of Heaven, crowned at Christ's side. Two hundred years later, in a statue from Krumlov, Bohemia (far right on this page), she is the loving Mother of the Child. Religious art puts increasing stress on the representation of suffering, as in the Mater Dolorosa at Liège (right).

EGLISE DE SAINT-JEAN, LIÈGE—DESSART

ROUBIER

KUNSTHISTORISCHES MUSEUM, VIENNA—GALLERY PLÉIADE

THE VIRGIN AND CHANCELLOR ROLIN, *by Jan Van Eyck.*

By HESKETH PEARSON

My uninvited collaborator GBS

When, in October, 1938, I managed to get Bernard Shaw's consent to write his Life, it didn't occur to me that I would also get his full collaboration. What I expected, and what I wanted, was his permission to use copyright material, his authority for all the facts, and his verbal answers to questions that would arise in the course of my investigations. But as the work progressed he became more and more interested in it and wrote me many letters and post cards between the periods of our talks. Whenever he was staying in his London flat I used to call about once a week and we conversed for an hour or two at a time. I always had plenty of questions to ask and he always had plenty to say in reply. But when either of us was in the country the business was usually conducted by correspondence. He was unceasingly generous with help and advice. Though the busiest writer of his age, he never failed to see me when I wanted an interview, and he dealt with all my letters fully, mostly by return of post. Sometimes when we were in different parts of the country he would delay answering a question until we met. Once I wanted to hear about his voyages to different parts of the world when he was past seventy. "As to my travels," he replied, "any account of them would be like a Canadian Pacific or Hellenic Travellers prospectus, to be avoided carefully. We must talk about them some day. Writing would take a year." In due course he talked about them, very amusingly too, as will be seen in my book.

One of his main characteristics was perseverance with whatever he had promised or undertaken. From the moment that he accepted me as a biographer he gave me, so to speak, the freedom of his company; and to assure my position he wrote this letter for the benefit of the English and American publishers and press:

> 4 Whitehall Court, S. W. I.
> 2nd December 1938.

Dear Hesketh Pearson,

Unfortunately I cannot prevent anyone from writing about me, from the briefest scurrilous paragraph to the most pretentious biography.

But no sane publisher will touch a biography or essay unless (a) he has some assurance that I am not going to be unpleasant about it, and (b) the author's name is a guarantee of readability.

So you may go ahead with my blessing. There is no one else in the field.

> (signed) G. BERNARD SHAW

He gave me a word of advice at the outset. I told him that in certain respects he would have to be debunked. His comment was: "I need inbunking, not debunking, having debunked myself like a born clown." He talked like one of his own prefaces and, as in those, dropped scraps of reminiscence and autobiography into a disquisition on some favorite theme. For example, he was speaking about the Nature Cure for apparently incurable diseases, and suddenly said: "My sister Agnes developed a goiter, to our amazement, when she was a small girl. She was sent to the seaside, and it went away as it had come. The Nature Cure acted." Again, when he was holding forth on marriage, he disclosed this: "Acting on behalf of a friend I was once compelled to blackmail his wife into divorce proceedings by threatening her that if she didn't agree she'd get nothing, but that if she did she'd get a decent income. I don't know which of us cut the worst figure, but I do know that the divorce laws were responsible for our shame."

In the postscript to my *G.B.S.: A Full Length Portrait* I have already recorded his denials of certain actions attributed to him and many stories told about him, and he advised me to say in my preface that the chief merit I claimed was to have omitted all the lies that had accumulated from biography to biography during the last sixty years. But as I had heard several of the episodes which he repudiated from the actors concerned in them, their veracity being further guaranteed by witnesses, I came to the conclusion that his memory for whatever seemed to him trifling was shaky. However, what is stupid to a sociologist is often revealing to a biographer, and I am as certain as it is possible to be about anything that some of the anecdotes he described as "the silliest Green Room gossip" were authentic.

For instance, the actor concerned and three other members of the company vouched for the truth of this:

"Why not come on the stage singing some topical song, say 'Another Bit of Sugar for the Bird?'" Shaw suggested at a rehearsal. The actor seemed at a loss, and Shaw promptly obliged by making an entry on the stage and warbling the popular ditty. "Surely you know that?" he said. "Of course I do," replied the actor, "but I couldn't miss the chance of hearing you sing it." Shaw joined heartily in the laughter against himself, and the incident captures the atmosphere of informality and friendliness which he generated at rehearsals.

Then, too, I am fairly certain that the account Lady Astor gave me of what she said to Stalin during their interview at the Kremlin was accurate, because H. G. Wells, who had discussed the matter with Stalin, declared that "his memory of her rankled." But when I showed her report to Shaw, he spoke emphatically: "This is what Lady Astor now imagines she said. Not a word of it actually passed. Obviously we could not have asked Stalin for an interview to insult him in his own house." Yet the odd thing is that in Shaw's own account of what happened, given in my book, Lady Astor's behavior "rocked the Kremlin to its foundations," for she told Stalin that on the subject of the treatment of children he didn't know what he was talking about. This was probably more insulting to a fellow like Stalin than her remark which Shaw asserted she couldn't have made: "When are you going to stop Czarist government . . . shooting your opponents?" After all, the shooting of opponents was a mere matter of routine, but the Soviet prided itself on the way little children were cared for and brought up to be good Communists. One of Stalin's complaints, reported by Lady Astor but denied by Shaw, struck me as highly characteristic of a disgruntled dictator: "People want so many things. They even seem to want silver watches."

I finished my biography of Shaw early in 1940 and wrote to ask whether he wished to see it before it went to the printer. His reply convinced me that it could not go to the printer until he had seen it. I took it to his flat in Whitehall Court and asked whether he could finish it in a few weeks.

"That depends on how much there is to correct," he said.

"As you are my authority for most of it, the job won't take long," I said.

"That depends on your other authorities," he said.

"Oh, they are all trustworthy!" I assured him.

"They may be perfectly honest but wholly inaccurate," he rejoined.

"Well, suppose a third of the book needs correction in places, how long will you take?"

"Say five years?"

"Please be serious."

"I promise to be."

"You mean five weeks, I suppose?"

"Good heavens, no! It takes me more than that to write a play. Shall we say six months?"

I groaned.

"Now go away and start your next book at once," he ad-

vised. "Nothing is more amateurish than to be unable to do this. I don't know how long I shall be. Besides, there is this filthy war upsetting everything. I am interrupted every day by demands for articles about it, not all of which can be refused."

He spent a year correcting and adding to my book, and even then he only finished the job under constant pressure from me. "You've no idea how long this takes," became the burden of his song whenever I tried to rush him. He returned the manuscript in bits and pieces. His secretary, Blanche Patch, told me that she came across chapters strewn all over the house. With the last installment he assured me that he could have written three plays in the time he had spent arguing with me and correcting the errors of my so-called authorities. I replied that posterity would be grateful to me. His comment on that lacked restraint.

His early corrections and interpolations were made in pencil, so that I could rub them out, he told me, and rewrite them in my own words. But gradually he warmed to the work and made his contributions in ink, using red ink for unpublishable comments. I may as well confess that in this way he provided me with all the material for his socialistic activities. "Here is the Fabian chapter!" he said, handing it back to me with countless erasures and additions. "Your attempt at it was heroic; but nobody who had not been personally through it could possibly have done it. What a job!" My interest in politics has always been confined to an interest in the personalities of a very few politicians; and economics, the pumped-up partisanship of reds, blues, buffs, etc., and all the other political games that fascinate so many people leave me cold. So I had to depend on Shaw for everything of that nature, condensing the pabulum with which he provided me into as clear and concise a narrative as possible.

Our disagreements on innumerable matters were manifold, and I have recorded most of them in the postscript to his Life. But our debate on his support of Russian Communism was one of the few things I didn't chronicle therein. In my manuscript of the Life, I prefaced an account of his trip to Russia with several quotations from his works which, taken together, made an unanswerable case against Stalin's police state. Here is one: "Progress depends on our refusal to use brutal means even when they are efficacious." Here is another: "Civic education does not mean education in blind obedience to authority but education in controversy and in liberty, in manners and in courage, in scepticism, in dis-

CONTINUED ON PAGE 134

Shaw loved to write about Shaw, even to the extent of rewriting whole passages of Hesketh Pearson's biography of himself. This page is typical of Pearson's manuscript as it left Shaw's hands with scrawled interpolations, extensions of remarks, and comments to the biographer. Shaw spent as much time on this book as if it had been one of his own.

This quoted description is Almroth Wright, the original of Ridgeon, not myself.— Bennett was not envious: quite the opposite, I should. I fancy my way of handling his own opinions took him out of his depth a bit.

is really a description of himself: "He has the off-handed manner and the little audacities of address which a shy and sensitive man acquires in breaking himself in to intercourse with all sorts and conditions of men. **Bennett's** feeling of constraint was simply the vanity of a man who did not like to be forgotten and was not generous enough to revel in another **man's** innings; but one of **his** most lovable charac-teristics was his consideration for younger men who felt shy and out of it. Frank Swinnerton never forgot how as a youngster of no account he arrived late, hot and dishevelled for a luncheon party given by H.G.Wells, and how everyone bowed distantly to him except Shaw, who walked right across the room, shook hands and went into lunch with him.

Another of his characteristics, admirable if not lovable, was the unexpectedness and rapidity of his repartees. Lady Astor gave me an instance. Over breakfast at Cliveden she remarked "I hate killing for pleasure", a sentiment with which she knew Shaw was in hearty agreement. "Do you hate killing for pleasure?" one of her children asked Shaw. "It depends upon who you kill", he replied. Another example. *A strange lady giving an address in Zürich wrote him a proposal, thus.* ~~The famous dancer, Isadora Duncan, once addressed him~~: "You have the greatest brain in the world, and I have the most beautiful body; so we ought to produce the most perfect child." Shaw asked: "What if the child *inherits* my body and your brain?" *This story has been foisted on* ~~He illustrated~~ *to Isadora Duncan, who was not the lady. (NB Shaw illustrated)* for me the difficulty of giving pleasure without pain: "I was staying with Lady Chudleigh, a devout Roman Catholic, when a *Prussianized foreign* ~~German~~ visitor made the appalling gaffe of describing how his brother had been imprisoned merely for saying that the doctrine of the Immaculate Conception was all rot. Lady Chudleigh *a saintly Catholic, did not know what to say.* ~~looked pained~~. I at once

Houselights up for the curtain call: a traditional ceremony at New York's Met as seen by a latter-day arrival from China, the water-colorist Chen Chi, whose work

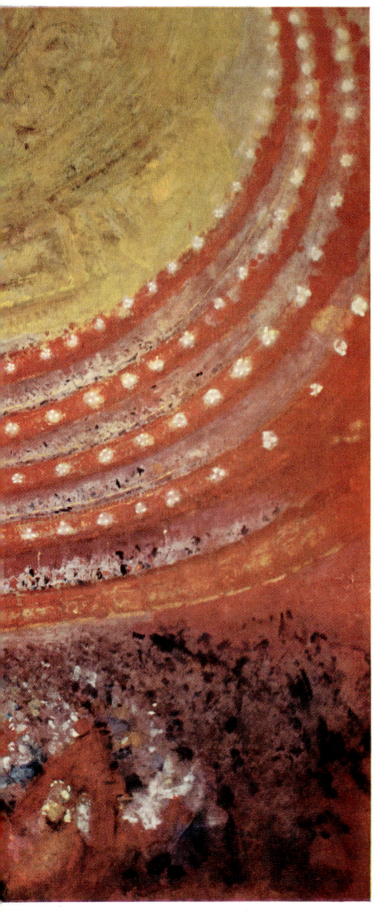

BEHIND THE GOLDEN CURTAIN

By JOSEPH WECHSBERG

Grand opera, often declared dead and buried, is much alive and more popular than ever. Handicapped by absurd libretti and implausible acting, harassed by financial difficulties and production problems—no opera house on earth ever breaks even or gets all the good singers it needs—grand opera gladdens the hearts of its addicts and continues to win new ones. So many divergent experts and artists—poets, dramatists, composers, conductors, coaches, singers, musicians, dancers, painters, designers, technicians, producers, and extras—are involved in an operatic production that standards are often precarious and the costs staggering. Pompous aesthetes call opera a fraud; cold fish call it a bore. But anyone dead to the divine beauty of Mozart's *Le Nozze di Figaro* misses as much in life as one who doesn't enjoy the first touch of spring in the air, the colors of a Renoir, the sight of a lovely woman, the aftertaste of a fine claret, or the afterthought of a good book.

Grand opera is now performed in over a hundred opera houses and theaters all over the world. Some have a short season of a few weeks; others play ten months. Germany and Italy lead with thirty-nine and eighteen opera houses respectively. In Western Europe and in the countries behind the Iron Curtain even medium-sized cities have permanent opera companies. Among the world's great opera houses, Milan's La Scala, Vienna's Staatsoper, and New York City's Metropolitan Opera House are the Big Three. As runners-up, I have picked London's Covent Garden, Bayreuth's Festspielhaus, and the German Staatsoper in East Berlin, a

has won many prizes in his adopted Western home.

23

major opera company in the Communist world today. The Paris Opéra, ornamental as it is, is not in their class.

La Scala

In Italy grand opera is the national religion and the country's leading opera house, the Teatro alla Scala ("Theater at the Stairs") in Milan, a national shrine. The government and the city offer suitable sacrifices on its altar—subsidies as large as La Scala's entire revenue from ticket sales.

La Scala is a genuine national theater. Elegant first nights, *prime*, at fifteen dollars, for well-heeled opera lovers, are followed by about forty *serate per i lavoratori*, at half a dollar, for working-class opera lovers who hear the same casts and conductors. That has been a sacred tradition since Toscanini, whose life's passion was La Scala; the conductors are in absolute charge of musical matters and conduct all performances with the originally rehearsed casts. The *stagione* system has always worked well here.

The house was bombed out during the war, rebuilt and reopened in 1946—a square, brown, not particularly inspiring building from the outside, with a magnificent gilded auditorium and about the finest acoustics on earth (although some performers prefer Bayreuth). The orchestra's tone is full and beautiful, its chorus first-rate, and the staging always interesting, although the sets are often strangely unimaginative. The quality of the performances is uneven—a weakness

FPG

La Scala shares with all other leading opera houses—but even ordinary evenings are distinguished by a sense of unity and precision, even though there may be occasional lapses in taste and style. Improvisation is rare; most performances are well rehearsed. Small armies of chorus members and extras execute carefully planned movements across the vast stage, knowing exactly what they are doing, and individual acting mannerisms are the privilege of the stars only. The singing isn't always as beautiful as one would expect in the world's *bel canto* cathedral, but the average is very high and even the secondary parts are well sung, which is the real test of an opera company. La Scala is the only opera house in the world that has a full-time, professional school for gifted young singers who draw small salaries during years of training. Part of the large house is La Piccola Scala, where a dream of Toscanini has come true: operas are performed there for a small, intelligent, appreciative audience.

La Scala performs about two hundred nights a year, most of which are sold out. The opera season runs from early December to mid-June, and there are shorter ballet and symphony seasons. Scala audiences are sure of their opinions and express them without restraint. Ladies and gentlemen in evening dress sometimes get into violent arguments; no holds are barred in the gallery, and a few years ago a tuxedoed gentleman in a box threw a shoe at the stage in a moment of disapproval. The audience is often carried away by its flair for melody and sense of drama, and your neighbor may start to hum the melody being sung by the tenor; that would be impossible in the colder emotional climate of a German opera house. But the Italian *brio* is infectious and after a while the disciplined visitor from the northern latitudes finds himself humming too. Except during some modern works, of course, which were written with the brain and not with the heart, and whose composers had no ear for melody and inspiring lyricism.

The Vienna State Opera

At the end of the last war, after a decade of misery and fear, the people of Vienna began to rebuild their bombed, burned-out Staatsoper. The job took ten years and ten million dollars. In the meanwhile the State Opera Company gave memorable performances at the old Theater an der Wien, where Beethoven's *Fidelio* had had its *première* in 1805. During the cold, hungry postwar years, Vienna's famous ensemble here developed its inimitable Mozart style that has influenced opera singing all over the world.

The Staatsoper's reopening, on November 5, 1955, was Austria's greatest postwar event and a national housewarm-

Late eighteenth-century building taste, faultless acoustics, and an unmatched operatic tradition mark Milan's La Scala, where elegant first nights alternate with top-cast performances for workers.

ing party. Few citizens could afford $200 for a ticket, but thousands stood outside their beloved opera house in a cold drizzle, and millions listened to the broadcast of *Fidelio*. The performance was mediocre but the excitement was terrific.

Many Austrians never go to the Staatsoper but all have a warm, personal feeling about "their" opera house. There are lots of people in Vienna who have never heard *Figaro* but few who don't know what happened at last night's *Figaro*. Life and the musical theater are inseparable in the music capital of the world, with its constant interplay between stage and realism (many elderly Viennese remember the pompous old gentleman who gave Hofmannsthal the idea for the character of Baron Ochs von Lerchenau in *Der Rosenkavalier*), and probably there is a house down your street where either Gluck or Haydn, Mozart, Beethoven, Schubert, Wagner, Richard Strauss, or Alban Berg lived. The private lives of the famous artists are public property, the feuds of the divas make the front pages, and the appointment of Herbert von Karajan as the new opera director, after the stormy departure of his predecessor, Karl Böhm, caused far more excitement than the election of Austria's new president.

The Staatsoper is always sold out—some people queue up all night long to get a ticket—but the deficit is always high. The Austrian government puts up almost six million dollars a year to subsidize its state theaters, and most of the money is spent on the Opera, but the taxpayers don't complain. Performances are given every night from the first day of September to the last day of June (and during July and August at the Salzburg Festival). On many evenings a second company performs Mozart, Rossini, or a modern work at the beautiful but acoustically inferior Redoutensaal of the Imperial Palace, and in summer sometimes a third cast performs *al fresco* in front of Schönbrunn Palace. The Vienna Staatsoper has the best opera orchestra on earth, a superb ensemble of sensitive musicians with a feeling for beautiful sound, which has always been considered more important locally than brilliant precision. The standards of the performances are erratic. On a sloppy evening the State Opera can be pretty bad. On a great night it tops every other house for tradition and taste when all operatic components—music, singing, staging, lighting, conducting, acting, dancing—are blended into a magnificent entity.

Contact between stage and audience that stimulates both performers and listeners is strong in Vienna's auditorium, which holds only two thousand people. Strict aesthetic controls are exercised by old-timers in the parquet who have heard earlier performances of the same works under Gustav Mahler, Franz Schalk, and Richard Strauss, and by youth-

Built at the height of Napoleon III's splendor, the Paris Opéra was designed to display its audience no less than the musical talents of the Empire, and its grand staircase is a spectacular stage in itself.

ful *aficionados* in the Fourth Gallery, home of future geniuses where many artists (the last and the present director, among others) have served their apprenticeship. "The Fourth" was long the headquarters of the famous claque that could make or break a star. Their judgment is not always considerate but rarely wrong. Score-reading is so common that small reading lights have been installed over certain seats.

Going to the Opera in Vienna is always a little like going to church. Since the time of Mahler's rule, no one has been permitted to enter during the acts. The ushers are never permitted to use flashlights. Candy-munchers and whisperers are immediately identified as barbarians from abroad, even though they may hail from the Austrian provinces. The Vienna audience is appreciative and critical, prejudiced and nostalgic. Favorite singers are judged not by how they perform tonight, but by how they used to sing at their best. Even on dull evenings there is a certain atmosphere about the place that gives the performance a few moments you will remember many years afterward.

New York's Met

Not so long ago opera enthusiasts in Europe would talk condescendingly about the Metropolitan in New York (where most of them have never been), and today some operatic America-Firsters in turn like to run down the European houses. These ignorant chauvinists on both sides of the

Banners of the liberated and reconstituted Austrian Republic fly over the Vienna Staatsoper, show place of Emperor Francis Joseph, on its reopening night in 1955 after wartime bombardment. During its ten years of reconstruction, in which every displaced stone was put back in place, the State Opera also made efforts to scale new heights in performance despite occupation and poverty. The ghosts of past directors Richard Strauss and Gustav Mahler overhang the building, the special citadel of the performing of Mozart.

Atlantic overlook the growing *Gleichschaltung* between European and American opera houses, which now have the same repertory, the same singers, the same conductors and stage directors. There are less than a hundred first-rate singers in the world today, and all opera houses compete for their services; it isn't unusual for an artist to perform in America and in Europe the same week. (Good for his pocketbook, bad for his voice.) Europeans think of the Met as a "rich" house. Actually the Met's management spends a great deal of time and energy on collecting dollars from rich patrons or from radio listeners. Of all the world's great opera houses the Met is the only one that gets no public subsidies whatsoever. With its lack of funds, the high cost of unionized labor, and the demand for expensive voices, the Met is always on the brink of financial disaster and rarely in the mood for costly experiments. Between 1943 and 1957 it performed no world *première* of any new work. Unpopular works are rarely revived. The repertory consists of sure-fire box-office favorites that everybody has heard for years and wants to hear again. Of late, however, cautious forays into virgin territory have been made, less popular works have received splendid productions, and this season the Met is to stage Alban Berg's *Wozzeck*, after numerous expensive orchestra rehearsals. The time may yet come when *Die Meistersinger* will be given without cuts or when difficult, beautiful works such as Strauss's *Frau ohne Schatten* will be performed, and the old subscribers be damned.

The Met is a house of many extremes, like everything in America. Performances vary bewilderingly from dull to brilliant, from improvisation to near-perfection. The sets may be wonderful or terrible. The orchestra plays beautifully—under a good conductor. Vocally, the Met is tops: no other opera house, not even La Scala, can afford so many fine voices at the same time. The Met gets the best singers from the Continent and collects great American voices, of which there are more every year. But a sense of unity is lacking in many productions, and there is still no ensemble art.

Management and performers are often blamed for the shortcomings of the Met, but it is really the audience that deserves most of the blame. New York's operagoers do not "live" opera the way people do in Milan or Vienna. For many Americans a night at the opera is still a social duty or just an evening's entertainment. But grand opera is a demanding art that gives itself only to those who give much to it. So long as many people continue to come late, spend half an act at the bar, and leave early, the Met will lack that certain aura indispensable to the true opera lover.

Covent Garden

London's Royal Opera House, Covent Garden, is handicapped by lack of adequate rehearsal and storage space, a shortage of seats in the gallery and the amphitheater, high costs, and insufficient state subsidies. The present contributions by the Arts Council are barely enough to support a relatively short ballet and opera season, and there is always some sort of crisis at Covent Garden. But as long as there is opera, there will always be a crisis, and opera enthusiasts learn to live with it. Covent Garden is a feudal house with many memories but few traditions, where liveried footmen hold open the curtain while the artists take a bow. It stands in London's fruit-and-vegetable market, and boxes with oranges and carrots are often placed against its walls. The English are not as opera-crazy as the Austrians or Italians. They frankly consider Covent Garden a liability, but they agree it must be preserved like an old castle in the country.

Covent Garden's orchestra does not compare with the great English symphony orchestras; the wood winds and brass are good, but the strings lack color and warmth. The staging is often very good, but the singing is rarely distinguished except when foreign singers are imported, or English artists are performing under a prominent foreign conductor. The audience never seems to grow very excited, no matter whether a performance is very good or very bad. Performers often complain that it is hard to establish contact with their listeners, and the lukewarm British temperament is blamed for this lack of enthusiasm. On the other hand, London audiences are extremely well-mannered and overlook shortcomings that would cause grave headshaking in Vienna and loud invective in Milan. English opera lovers seem to reserve their temperamental outbursts for performances outside of England, where they often drop their national reserve and lustily cheer or boo with the rest of the crowd. Score readers are a little suspect at Covent Garden, and minor cuts are accepted graciously. But there is also much to be said for English audiences. They listen with quiet concentration, don't unwrap candies during a *pianissimo* and don't tell each other the story of *Rigoletto* while Gilda sings her aria. The applause and the room temperature are lukewarm by Continental and American standards. Put on some warm underwear before you go there.

Bayreuth

This Bavarian house offers, I think, the richest experience in the contemporary musical theater. The climate is humid, the Festspielhaus is a styleless, red brick building, the performances are not always perfect. Wieland and Wolfgang Wagner have the problems of managers elsewhere—rising costs, uncertain subsidies, strong competition, and a growing scarcity of robust Wagnerian voices able to execute Richard Wagner's inhuman vocal demands. Everything is exaggerated at Bayreuth: endless performances, long intermissions, wonderful acoustics, terrible seats. But the artistic climate is invigorating, the enthusiasm contagious, the tension happy. There is no routine whatsoever—and routine is the archenemy of good opera. Everybody is excited and performs a little better than usual, which makes the difference between a good performance and a great one. Some people say Bayreuth could not exist if its annual festival lasted longer than a month, after one month of rehearsals; the tension just couldn't last. But while it lasts, it's wonderful. Where else could you find an orchestra that does not grumble when the final rehearsals of *Die Meistersinger*, *Tristan und Isolde*, and *Parsifal* start on three successive nights at 7 P.M. and end at about two-thirty in the morning?

The four "Ring" evenings, still the most important pro-

ductions of the festival (which also features *Parsifal* and two other Wagner works) are stunning. From the opening scene in *Das Rheingold*, when stage and auditorium seem flooded by the blue-green waters of the Rhine, to the closing scene in *Götterdämmerung*, there are moments of great beauty. What Wieland Wagner does with an empty stage, a cyclorama, and a few lights in *Parsifal* is sheer magic and an impressive lesson to stage designers and producers elsewhere who clutter up their stages with props and people but fail to create the spirit of a work. The Wagner brothers have not only achieved Grandfather Richard's dream of the *Gesamtkunstwerk*—"total theater"—but have given a new lease on life to Grandfather's work, which showed dangerous symptoms of becoming slightly passé.

Compared to the monotonous, silly *Parsifal* productions elsewhere, Wieland Wagner's production — simple and straight and aimed at the people of our generation—is a revelation. Bayreuth is precision per se. The slightest gesture is planned, trained, and executed with accuracy; the performers' movements are synchronized with the beautiful sound of the covered orchestra. Neo-Bayreuth has to be heard and seen to be believed.

The Paris Opéra

This is the most ornamental and least important of the world's great opera houses, a noble edifice with little musical meaning. Opera in France has never become a national art. The Théâtre National de l'Opéra contributes nothing by way of literary, political, or gastronomical discussion, and many Frenchmen think of it as a sort of musical museum—a pretty stuffy one. As a palatial building, it is one of the sights of the capital. Jean Louis Charles Garnier, the architect of the Second Empire, put everything into the Opéra that was good and expensive, maybe a little too much. In spite of all the pomp and marble, the sculptures and staircases, you feel a little cold when you finally sit down in the magnificent auditorium, and nothing that happens between stage, orchestra, and listeners will warm you up.

French oboists and horn-players are famous all over the world, and there are first-rate orchestras in Paris, but not at

CONTINUED ON PAGE 133

A tradition very different from Vienna's surrounds London's Royal Opera House at Covent Garden, a structure of Victorian colonnades and red plush that stands amid the city's old flower, fruit, and vegetable market—once the site of a medieval convent garden. Here Queen Elizabeth and her Consort attend this year's gala performance marking the building's centenary, and in honor of its surroundings the royal box is festooned with local market produce. In an earlier theater on the same ground, many of Handel's operas had their premières.

LONDON DAILY EXPRESS

Grand Tier box holders of the Gilded Age would never recognize their opera's new home, yet their Diamond Horseshoe remains

By NELSON LANSDALE

When New York's present Metropolitan Opera House was projected at about the time of the inauguration of President Garfield, the architect whose plans were selected over those of three competitors, Josiah Cleaveland Cady, had never heard an opera up to that time or designed even so much as a small theater. By contrast, the man chosen to design the long-awaited new home of the Metropolitan, due to open in the fall of 1961, is the highly knowledgeable Wallace K. Harrison, senior partner of the firm of Harrison & Abramovitz, who among other things has been designing auditoriums for the past thirty-five years—including both the Radio City Music Hall and the General Assembly of the United Nations.

Unlike Cady, moreover, Harrison is an *aficionado* of opera who has sought out performances both here and in all the major houses of Europe and who has his own strong preferences among works (Richard Strauss's *Der Rosenkavalier* being his favorite). The circular living room in Harrison's house in Huntington, Long Island, is elaborately equipped with high-fidelity equipment that enables him to tinker with acoustics in his spare time. He is not likely to decorate his new proscenium arch as Cady did the old one, namely by plastering it with cartouches bearing names of half a dozen composers apparently chosen at random—two of

CONTINUED ON PAGE 117

Three generations separate the design of New York's first Metropolitan Opera House from that of its second, and only the use of arches in the façades would seem to link them. As against the old house, wedged in on once-fashionable Broadway, the new (seen here in model) is to rise as part of a co-ordinated civic development— the Lincoln Center for the Performing Arts. Yet despite radical departures in appearance, the new Met will cling to old traditions.

28

OUT OF THE

OLD MET, THE NEW

By WILLIAM HARLAN HALE

In Revolt Against Togetherness

Promoters of a passion for unanimity would like to make of America one big happy In-Group from the cradle to the grave. Ultimately the individual rebels

Some of America's most inescapable outdoor billboards, located across the country from the strategic corner of New York's Fifth Avenue and 42nd Street to the "Miracle Mile" of Hollywood's Wilshire Boulevard, recently have displayed a religious rather than a commercial message. A personable young father, his well-coifed young wife, and their equally personable and well-coifed three (sometimes four) young children are shown grouped in attitudes of devotion, and beside them runs the slogan, "The Family That Prays Together Stays Together."

The posters, put up in numbers approaching one thousand by a religious group-activity organization called "Family Theater" and sponsored among others by the General Outdoor Advertising Company, do not identify themselves with any particular denomination. Nor do they show any of the conventional symbols of faith. Pray for whatever you choose to whichever God you will, they seem to imply; the main thing is that you do your praying together.

Some churchmen have taken offense at this well-intentioned message as confusing individual faith with sheer sociability and "grouping." "A while ago," one minister adds, "we also had a popular song called 'Let's Hold Hands in Church'—and that's a form of Togetherness, too." But whatever the theological objections, the Family Theater's posters at least suggest the extent to which America has been pervaded by a lay religion unique to our times.

This faith is unique, for one thing, in that it is the first one ever to be patented by one of its chief sponsors. In 1954, as the world knows, the popular monthly *McCall's* christened itself "The Magazine of Togetherness." The word "Togetherness" caught on so well that the management soon felt it had to take steps to protect it. The term, Assistant Publisher George H. Allen has declared, "is something which cannot be used commercially without our

permission." So when Macy's in New York last year launched *its* promotion campaign for Togetherness, with such texts as "Have you ever realized that the earliest example of Togetherness in the United States is the United States itself? . . . You can't have an effective nation . . . or a family . . . without Togetherness," it was careful to specify at the foot of its advertisements, "Togetherness is a word, practically invented by *McCall's*, the great family magazine, and adopted by Macy's, the great family store."

As "practically invented" by *McCall's* (although the word was in fact used earlier by writers as various as the philosopher Alfred North Whitehead and the novelist D. H. Lawrence, who fortunately are not around to see the uses to which it has been put), Togetherness means that more and more men, women, and children are doing more and more things together. The corollary to this is that they are doing fewer and fewer things separately and individually. The implication is that it is right and proper that this should be so. "A Man's Place Is In the Home," was the heading of the first article published by *McCall's* on promulgating its new design for American life, and it told about a "typical" father cavorting with his children, feeding and dressing them, washing the dishes, paneling a cellar game room for them, attending P.T.A. meetings with his wife, and projecting a barbecue and a play yard—almost all of them, *McCall's* pointed out, things which he wouldn't have dreamed of doing in the less communal and less happy days of a quarter of a century ago. No doubt *McCall's* lady subscribers were delighted at this information as to how swiftly and completely their husbands had been tamed and domesticated. As for male readers, no immediate poll was taken. But then, American males have been submitting to so much grouping and to playing so unexceptionally the part of a good Organization Man, saddled with his ranch-type in Winnetka, his Cape-Codder in Levittown, or his split-level in Shaker Heights, that there was really little ground for protest against this revelation of their final indignity.

In fact, as time and Togetherness went on, there were many males who came forth to endorse without qualification the gospel according to *McCall's*. It meant "feeling together," said one; it meant "sharing," said another; it meant living according to "the Eleventh Commandment—the Golden Rule," said a third. It even meant such things as dieting together. "Together we got rid of 77½ pounds and loved it," ran one joyous couple's testimonial in the magazine, citing the way they were helped by Knox Gelatin. *The New Yorker*, usually inclined to be skittish about popular enthusiasms, has itself been invaded by Togetherness in the form of a whole series of advertisements on that theme, ranging from pictures of people toasting each other in Cocomalt and root beer ("to Togetherness") to families photographed by Bachrach in poses of excruciating mutual doting. Under Togetherness, as advertised across the nation, we are also encouraged to dress alike, parents and children, all donning ourselves for instance in matching bright-red pajamas and bathrobes. We should all drive the same cars; live in the same Togetherness-breeding, communal, split-level, picture-window developments alike; and (this hardly needs to be stated explicitly) think alike. On a higher level, says *McCall's*, Togetherness (registered in the U.S. Patent Office) also means "the need for interdependence in world affairs, in community activities. . . ." It is, in fact, "the hope and trend of our times. . . . Togetherness is here to stay."

Yet there are also an increasing number of people who, faced with the prospect of wearing red pajamas like their children's, are saying they wish Togetherness would please go away, and who are dreaming of an American brand of *apartheid*.

For Togetherness, for all its jejune implications, is more than a word "practically invented" by a smart magazine promotion department. It *is* a philosophy—even though it is often presented as the notion of having no philosophy at all save that of making up a team and doing all things

On their higher levels, Togetherness and Grouping take the form of proliferating committees. A White House surrounded by councils, boards, and panels now also has this body of Special Assistants for Cabinet Co-ordination. President Lincoln reached decisions alone.

the same way. It is one thing to reduce the male (and the female too) from the status of self-determining adult to that of cog in an in-group, wearing a fixed smile. The next step is to say that the group is right, the individual who does not blend with it, wrong. As the father becomes the joyous family dishwasher, so the once independent observer is invited to become a fellow subscriber to unanimity. We are in the presence of a mystique of "belongingness" which holds that the group—any group—somehow simply by virtue of being a group produces better citizenship, sounder behavior, and more virtuous and creative ideas than individuals acting and thinking on their own.

In popular education, Togetherness is "life adjustment," "group-defined standards," and what some progressive high-school teachers call the "We feeling." In business and government, it is the proliferation of the committee system as a means of achieving uniformity and dividing responsibility, culminating in such advanced devices as "brainstorming" sessions to "organize group creativity" and in the experiments with "leaderless groups" being conducted by the National Training Laboratory in Group Development at Bethel, Maine. In the special field of psychometrics, it produces such instruments as the Harwald Group Thinkometer, a device for measuring the degrees of unanimity achieved in discussion, the top point being a kind of nirvana of unanimity.

In housing, it is the similar assumption across the country by forward-looking architects and hard-shelled developers alike that the stock American, whom they know so well, doesn't want such old-fashioned things as privacy in his house, but really just wants lots of glass, lots of intrafamily communication (which saves on partitions, and then you can save some more by putting the stairway right up through the living room), and is in love with the idea of picture

windows, even when they frame nothing but the neighbor's back yard.

Educational Togetherness, as purveyed by the massed legatees of the late John Dewey, holds that the main object of schooling is not to instruct a pupil in a body of knowledge but to bring about his adjustment to the group. It is this approach that has made dominant "educationists" in our high schools abhor competition or even the giving of class grades, since this might inhibit the summit aim of co-operation, and to stress instead "group dynamics" and "group psychological engineering" that will keep everyone happy. The teacher becomes less and less a teacher and more just an elder pal or playmate—a "resource person" who "sparks sharing," as *The Clearing House*, a magazine for high-school teachers, recently put it, and who should tread lightly since he "may interfere with group dynamics if he attempts to communicate opinions, attitudes, ideas, and so on."

The Soviet Union imposes collectivism and conformity from the top; American progressive educators have imposed it from the bottom. In their mythology of the common man and their fear that too much learning may be a dangerous thing, they have shied from giving special attention to the gifted on the ground that this might create the specter of an educated elite. Of the ten "real life" needs of students, a study of the National Association of Secondary School Principals argued some time ago, only one or two actually involve the intellect. Under such a rationale, we find our schools teaching such subjects as "Clicking with the Crowd," "How to be Liked," and "How to Get Closer to Dad." And, if Dad is not as close to you as he should be, there is the "Standard Bell Adjustment Test," under which a pupil is asked such questions as, "Do you feel your parents have been unduly strict with you?" and "Is either of your parents very nervous?" The father, like the teacher, evidently should be brought down from his position of authority and made to conform with the child.

What "group dynamics" performs in education, "brainstorming" or "braining a thing around" provides on Madison Avenue. This communal technique was first evolved nearly two decades ago by Alex F. Osborn when, as a partner in the advertising agency of Batten, Barton, Durstine & Osborn, he found himself anxious to stimulate his fellow executives to a greater output of selling ideas. The theory on which he worked was that men thrown together in a group will spontaneously produce ideas, whereas the individual alone might not: in short, a group thinks better than one man. At brainstorming get-togethers, criticism and any form of debate are ruled out, and men are encouraged just to throw in as many notions on a given subject as fast and impulsively as they can, under the stimulus of a sort of group hypnosis. "When I can make my brainstorming team feel they are *playing*, we get somewhere," one executive to whom Osborn taught his technique has reported; to which master-brainstormer Osborn himself adds, "A good device is to create the atmosphere of a picnic."

Far from being dismissed outside of Madison Avenue as zany, the Osborn method of Groupthink has been adopted, according to *Fortune*, by a majority of the firms listed in that magazine's directory of the 500 largest U.S. industrial corporations as well as by the Army, Navy, and Air Force, and several civilian government departments—which may help explain some of the odder eruptions of policy in recent years. But here, too, dissidence has reared its head. A study made early this year at Yale University, using 96 students as guinea pigs to test the brainstorming theory, has come up with the insurgent finding that an individual may actually be more creative than a group. "Those who worked in groups," Yale reported of its experiment, "did not do as well as those who worked alone, not only in terms of total number of ideas, but also in terms of number of original and good ideas." And Yale's president, A. Whitney Griswold, even before the findings had come in, asked rhetorically in a baccalaureate address, "Could *Hamlet* have been written by a committee, or the *Mona Lisa* painted by a club? Could the New Testament have been composed by a conference report?"

To see Togetherness in fullest flower, one cannot do better than to make a trip to one of the summer sessions in "Group Development" that have been conducted for several seasons under the auspices of the National Education Association at Bethel, Maine. There, bodies of a hundred or more assorted people drawn from many walks of life gather to form into groups without a leader, without an agenda, without any instructions at all, simply to observe how they themselves function as a group. "When the pressure that an agenda imposes on a group is removed," one summary of the Bethel Laboratory's work has it, "it is possible to see more clearly how behavior develops among group members." This of course poses the question, If you have no agenda—in other words, nothing specific to talk about—why gather as a group at all? Why not go fishing or maybe read a book?

While Bethel proceeds with its T-Groups ("Diagnostic Training Groups"), S-Groups ("Skill Practice Groups"), and C-Groups ("Community Groups"), the Harwald Group Thinkometer ticks on, and in the offices of the Educational Testing Service in Princeton, New Jersey,

CONTINUED ON PAGE 146

DAVID E. SCHERMAN

GENE HEIL

John Greenleaf Whittier withdrew into this quiet Massachusetts homestead to ponder legends and write Snowbound. *But in architect Philip Johnson's house in New Canaan, a pace-setter of contemporary style, living is communal and there is hardly any place to withdraw to.*

33

Frost in the Evening

At eighty-four, the poet

holds audiences that cherish him

and know his works by heart

Once twenty years ago I had been asked to call on Robert Frost when he came to Harvard to give the Norton lectures. He was then living in a house off Brattle Street. As I walked up there from Harvard Square in the late spring afternoon, I found myself racing a thunderstorm. The wind swirled dust clouds across Cambridge Common—where on a similar afternoon General Washington had assumed command of the Continental Army—and a few drops of water fell on me, but the real rain held off until I reached Robert Frost's porch. Then it came down in a sudden needling flood. Abruptly, even before I could ring the bell, the door opened and a slight young man without coat or jacket darted out past me and down the steps with a bale of manuscripts under his arm. He dog-trotted toward Brattle Street, oblivious of the rain pelting through the new chestnut leaves. Robert Frost, white-haired and avuncular, stood in the doorway looking after him for several seconds before he turned to me.

"That boy just wrote an epic," he said finally, indicating the drenched retreating figure. Then the thinnest of smiles broke across his face. "He's a Lowell, too," he added.

The Robert Frost of those days—he was then in his sixties —much resembled W. B. Yeats. There was the same shape of head, the same profusion of white hair, the same fine-cut jaw and high forehead—only Frost's face was homelier and had none of Yeats' rather theatrical arrogance. Yeats on the platform looked as if he might have been carved from marble; Frost's unposed features seemed chiseled from New England granite. That was my only meeting with him, though I have heard him read at various times. What I remember most clearly of that wet afternoon is a story he told of a kitten that fell down a cesspool but managed to climb out even though it wore its hind claws off.

"You see," he said, "that kitten was determined to get out. I've often thought of writing a poem about it."

Robert Frost is unique in that for two generations now ordinary people who do not read poetry have been reading his. Such general aliterary acceptance is, I think, the thing he values most. Americans read and recite and know his poems for the joy and awareness they derive from them. Frost's poems became a shared experience between himself and his readers. This hearty attitude plus his rural themes made him suspect in the social-minded thirties. The intellectuals were not quite sure they accepted him—until Auden, across the water, gave the go-ahead signal.

The other evening I went once more to a Robert Frost reading. It was the first time I had seen him since World War II. The granite features had begun to erode, to sink into themselves. His hair was thinner and cropped short, and the resemblance to Yeats was gone. Somehow he appeared more solid than in my recollection and slightly incongruous in one of the new narrow-lapeled suits. The flesh about his jaw was heavier. His eyes seemed to have become enormous—that was what I noticed at once, the blue depths to them.

In spite of the decades that have carved his features, an evening with Robert Frost has not changed at all. I don't suppose that any literary figure in the English-speaking world has the same rapport, the informal give-and-take with an audience that Frost has. His audience comes knowing exactly what it wants and what it will get. It doesn't expect to hear anything new or learn anything it didn't know before. It has come to see an affectionately familiar face and to hear the poems it already knows by heart.

Robert Frost always engages in a mock battle with his audience in which he always loses. Armed with his *Complete*

By FRANCIS RUSSELL

IVAN MASSAR

Poems he maintains that he wants to read some of his newer ones, the ones he himself doesn't know by heart. That is not why the hall is filled. The people are there to hear the earlier poems from *A Boy's Will* and *North of Boston* and *Mountain Interval*. They will listen politely to the later verses, but there always comes a point when Frost will look up from his *Complete Poems* and say apologetically, "Well, that was kinda long. But I don't get a chance to say it much. What do you want now?"

They know exactly what they want. Voices call out from all over the hall: "Mending Wall"; "Birches"; "The Runaway"; "Stopping by Woods on a Snowy Evening"; "Fire and Ice"—those poems that half the people there could probably recite themselves. Between poems, Frost makes any wry comments on life that occur to him. He never prepares for one of his evenings. Even his Norton lectures were impromptu.

Under the oak stalactites and Victorian gargoyles of Harvard's municipal-Gothic Sanders Theatre, I sat and listened to Robert Frost's familiar voice recite—he prefers the word *say*—the familiar lines. Watching his slow sturdy figure, I remembered with regret that he was in his eighty-fifth year—that in the cycle of things we might not see him many times again. How well his poems had weathered time and wars and poetic revolutions. But I too, I must admit, preferred the old ones. In between poems, he told of a high politician he had met in Washington a few weeks before who complained of the confusion of the world.

"Let's play the confusion game," Frost said. "Are you confused?"

The politician said that he was.

"Now ask me that same question," Frost told him.

So the politician asked him, "Are you confused?"

"No, I'm not," said Frost. "I win!"

At the end of that quick hour Frost took out his key-winding pocket watch.

"It looks like I've kept you too long."

"No," the audience called back at him.

"Well," he said, "I'll say three more, any three you want. But then no encores, it's too far to walk back up here again. What do you want?"

" 'The Road Not Taken!' "

" 'The Tuft of Flowers!' "

I cupped my hands and shouted, " 'Reluctance!' "

So he ended, his head held back a little, his eyes half closed, his voice as casual as if he were just talking:

> *Ah, when to the heart of man*
> *Was it ever less than a treason*
> *To go with the drift of things,*
> *To yield with a grace to reason,*
> *And bow and accept the end*
> *Of a love or a season?*

Then he tucked his book under his arm and started for the stairway at the rear of the platform under the Harvard seal. But at the third step he turned, his head just above the foliations of the Gothic banister, and waved to us. We waved back, as one would wave to a relative on the deck of a ship. So between waving and clapping we held him fixed. And in spite of his final remark, Robert Frost came back up the stairs and said four more poems.

Francis Russell, who lives in Massachusetts, has published in magazines ranging from American Heritage *to* The Country-man, Time & Tide, *and* Irish Writing, *and is the author of* Three Studies in Twentieth-Century Obscurity.

A Chance Meeting on the American Road

By OLIVER JENSEN

HENRY I: What in tophet is that contraption, Henry?

HENRY II: An Edsel, Grandpa.

HENRY I: An automobile?

HENRY II: Yes.

HENRY I: Glad you told me. What do you call that color?

HENRY II: "Sunbrite Red," or "Flamingo Pink," or something like that. I haven't got the chart here.

HENRY I: Looks like a hootchy-kootchy dancer's tights. What do you charge?

HENRY II: Well, it lists at $4,121.

HENRY I: I mean with the wheels, and doors, if it has doors, and all that.

HENRY II: Well, with white walls, armrest, heater, manicure set, radio . . . this one here would come close to $5,500, about.

HENRY I: You see this little Model T? Cost $290 in 1924, with the crank. Got twenty miles a gallon. You know how many Model T's I sold? Fifteen million, that's how many. How many you sold of these Edsels?

HENRY II: About 55,000, but you see the whole automobile business is off a third. Things are tough.

HENRY I: Anyway, it's nice of you to name it for your Pa.

HENRY II: We did a lot of research on that, Grandpa. Got in over 18,000 names. We even got a poetess named Marianne Moore to think up more. She suggested *Mongoose Civique*, and *Pastelogram*, and *Pluma Piluma*, and . . .

HENRY I: Lucky you came to your senses. I never had any use for poets except maybe Stephen Foster. I bought the house where Foster was born and stuck it in my museum. It looks real nice there.

HENRY II: Grandpa, the experts say you bought the wrong house.

HENRY I: I suppose you got experts who told you to build a squashed-out firecracker like this?

HENRY II: As a matter of fact, we have. We had only one car in the medium-priced field to General Motor's three and Chrysler's two, so Market Analysis called in Styling, and they contacted Motivational Research, and they started running interviews in depth and thematic apperception tests to determine what kind of car personality we ought to . . .

HENRY I: Speak plain English, boy.

HENRY II: All right, we wanted a car to fit in between the upper lower-priced car and the lower medium-priced car. For the young executive family on its way up.

HENRY I: I was afraid something like this would happen ever since your father started running around with all those society people in Grosse Pointe. What are you selling—transportation or social position?

HENRY II: We're selling dramatic Edsel styling; we're selling exclusive Teletouch Drive; we're selling getaway push, and Cruise-O-Matic, and thrust-boost, and fluid-torque. We're selling Magic-Circle steering.

HENRY I: Magic circle steering? You mean a wheel instead of a tiller? We put that on when your Pa was a boy. What's magic about that?

HENRY II: It turns easier—but look, you have to talk that way these days, Grandpa. You find out what the consumer thinks he wants, and you give it to him. We call it "*you* ideas."

HENRY I: Maybe you'd better get some "*me* ideas," Henry. I made what I wanted. People could take it or leave it. I said they could have any color as long as it was black.

HENRY II: We have psychology now. We tell people that their car reflects their taste, that the Lincoln look is their look.

HENRY I: Looks like every other look on the road.

HENRY II: You have to create desire. Listen to this Ford ad: "Experts in such world style centers as Paris and Rome examined Ford's classic, deep-sculptured silhouette. They studied its Power-Flow hood, its new Honeycombed grille, its massive one-piece bumper. They looked at the Sculptured rear deck and Slipstream roof with its seven front-to-rear grooves. And they pronounced it all 'Magnificent'!"

HENRY I: Don't pay any mind to foreigners, Henry.

HENRY II: Take the Thunderbird, Grandpa. We call it the "most wanted, most admired car in America!"

HENRY I: You got figures to prove that?

HENRY II: We don't have to. We use floating figures.

HENRY I: Floating figures?

HENRY II: Well, maybe people don't really care much about fuel consumption, for instance, but they think they do. So we tell them the new Ford saves 15 per cent on gas.

HENRY I: Fifteen per cent of what?

HENRY II: We don't say. That's what makes the figures float.

HENRY I: How many horsepower has this thing got, boy?

HENRY II: We have them in 303 and 345.

HENRY I: Good glory, Henry, what for? You ain't pulling a train of cars. Twenty horse was enough for the Model T and she moved along real smart. You got a whole regiment of cavalry hitched up there.

HENRY II: People want it. They want getaway. They want to pass the other guy. The car is a prestige symbol in America, that's what our sociologists say.

HENRY I: I had a Sociology Department here once, right after we put in the five-dollar day. Got a preacher to run it. He used to send investigators around to our workmen's houses to see that they didn't spend their money foolishly.

HENRY II: I'd like to hear what Reuther would say to that.

HENRY I: These investigators would see if there was any boozing or borrowing money or hanky-panky or any kind of misbehaving, and if there was, we sure straightened *them* out. But people didn't like it. Didn't know what was good for them. Lay off sociology, Henry. You've been letting too many people get at you. Nobody could get at me, excepting Harry Bennett, and Charlie Sorenson, and—that's long ago—Jim Couzens.

HENRY II: We don't operate that way any more, Grandpa. We have a lot of executives now, in every echelon.

HENRY I: Chair warmers. Worse than bankers.

HENRY II: We have a "management team." We have a new philosophy, "Ford is People!"

HENRY I: (impolite noise)

HENRY II: I don't see why you're down on us, Grandpa. I don't see why everybody's down on us. Even the President of the United States took a crack at Detroit. At least, we think he did.

HENRY I: They almost made me President once, back in 1924, until they found a fellow who talked even less, name of Coolidge. And you know why they wanted me? I gave Americans a cheap car that was better than walking, or riding in a buggy, better than what they had before. Changed the country around considerable, too.

HENRY II: But we make a better car now. As it says in the ad, the Edsel is "the most beautiful thing that ever happened to horsepower." Why, every year we do something better!

HENRY I: Maybe it ain't so much better as different, Henry. You make too many kinds of cars, and that goes for all Detroit. You got six makes, and three price classes in each make, and there's about twelve or fifteen models in each class, and there's all kinds of bodies and paint jobs inside of each model. It's worse than Heinz's pickles. Make one or two cars, make 'em good, make 'em cheap. Didn't I explain mass production to you boys?

HENRY II: We have to compete, Grandpa.

HENRY I: Maybe a low price would compete better 'n a lot of shiny gewgaws and ad-man talk. I kept on making the same old Model T year after year. Same tools, same parts, just a few models. I sold cheap and I made a billion dollars. I remember, once, the ad men were complaining about the car being just the same as the year before. They couldn't think up anything to say, but I told 'em. The ads read: "We just couldn't build a better car."

HENRY II: You can't sell a simple little car like yours nowadays, Grandpa.

HENRY I: I don't know about that, boy. I see a lot of little European cars buzzing around the roads.

HENRY II: They're just a fad. Limited market.

HENRY I: That's what the carriage makers said once. Henry, that thing of yours is too long for the roads, and too long to park. It's so low you're going to make everybody hunchbacked. A lady can't step into it. She's got to wiggle in like Little Egypt.

HENRY II: Our Styling Department would faint dead away if they could hear you.

HENRY I: If Harry Bennett was around, I'd have him run those people out of the Rouge. How long since you sold a car for under a thousand dollars, Henry?

HENRY II: Now, Grandpa, you know that's impossible nowadays.

HENRY I: How do you know if you don't try? I see that Wrigley the gum man kept his prices down. Didn't fancy his product up either. Maybe you could build a plain sort of car with a square corner here and there, and a running board for the kids to ride up the driveway on, something that doesn't look shot out of a gun. You could stick on fenders so that a fellow don't have to rebuild the whole side of the car if something hits him.

HENRY II: You can't do anything revolutionary in Detroit now, Grandpa.

HENRY I: Well, you use that word enough out here. Every time you invent a new ash tray it's "revolutionary." But if I was young again, I'd show you what a revolution *really* is.

HENRY II: But history doesn't repeat, Grandpa.

HENRY I: History is bunk. Well, goodbye, boy. Keep your weight down.

(*Exit, rattling*)

*"Are three hundred and
sixty-five rooms at Knole
in Kent really necessary
even for a duke?
Two hundred yards, or
six hundred and six feet
to be precise, seems
excessive for the front of
any house; the Marquess
of Rockingham thought
his dignity required it;
and an entrance hall
sixty feet square
and forty feet high
put his visitors
in a suitably humble
frame of mind.
But did Mylord of Exeter
require four huge
billiard rooms in which
to disport himself?"*

The NOBLE Houses

OF EIGHTEENTH-CENTURY ENGLAND

Longleat, in the rolling Wiltshire hills, is the seat of the Marquesses of Bath. This painting by the Dutch artist Jan Siberechts shows the house as it looked in 1676, with a coach and six pulling up to the gate, townspeople passing on the road outside the wall, and a lady and gentleman strolling in the garden; behind the great Tudor house, huntsmen pursue deer across the park. The owner at the time was Sir Thomas Thynne, known for his wealth as "Tom of Ten Thousand." Longleat was begun by his ancestor, Sir John Thynne, in 1547, and its first royal guest was Queen Elizabeth, who paid a visit some time before the year of the Spanish Armada when "O'er Longleat's towers, o'er Cranborne's oaks, the fiery herald flew." Two centuries later, another Thomas Thynne entertained George III at a mammoth party during which the royal visitors, parading on the roof, were cheered by a throng. It was George who created his host the first Marquess of Bath. Longleat today is the home of the 6th Marquess.

From the year 1200, slowly and not at all steadily, trade, the lifeblood of civilization, began to flow through the veins of barbarized Europe. In spite of war, pestilence, famine, depression and recession, the volume grew. Setbacks there were in plenty: prosperous markets vanished; wild inflation and gluts of gold and silver brought the society of Europe to the brink of disaster; the deep-rooted institutions of its primitive past, jealous of power and privilege, frequently thwarted its rapid expansion. Yet gradually a tide of wealth swept over the old noble warrior society—the world of feudalism with its great stone fortresses and their mailed retainers, a world of steel and war and bleak virility in which wealth was locked in gold and silver plate, barbaric jewelry, and gem-encrusted reliquaries.

Not all was submerged, even if feudal institutions suffered a sea change. Nobility remained, and kingship and priesthood still worked their magic; these, as we shall see, gave their own strange twist to the wealth that each passing century brought to Europe's shores. By 1750 the Western world had captured a vast commerce unequaled in man's history. The riches derived

By J. H. PLUMB

The planning of a great estate was a passionate interest of many English aristocrats. This picture, Lord Hervey and his Friends, *painted by Hogarth about 1736, shows the master of Ickworth in Suffolk displaying the design for an ornamental temple. Except for the Vicar of Isey, who gazes through a telescope from the tilting chair at left, all those present were figures of some political importance in the Whig government of Sir Robert Walpole. Left to right from the Vicar, they are: Stephen and Henry Fox, later Lords Ilchester and Holland; Lord Hervey; the Duke of Marlborough; and the Right Honorable Thomas Winnington. The painting hangs in the library of Ickworth, the seat of the Hervey family, Earls and later Marquesses of Bristol.*

Almost every country house embodies the dream of some ambitious man or woman. Wentworth Woodhouse (above, left) is the result of a building competition between the 1st Marquess of Rockingham and his kinsman, Lord Strafford. Its 606-foot façade made it the largest country house in England and a fit home for the 2nd Marquess, who was twice prime minister. Hardwick Hall in Derbyshire (center) is the monument of Elizabeth, Countess of Shrewsbury, the most determined house-builder

from it, or from the stimulus that it brought to industry and to the land, enabled men of property to live in a sophisticated luxury previously enjoyed only by the aristocracy of ancient Rome, the satraps of Oriental despotism, or the mandarins of China. Nowhere are the changes from barbarism to sophistication so clearly mirrored as in the houses, the furniture, the clothes, and style of life of the rich.

Venice led the way. Safe within its lagoon, it knew neither feudal aristocracy nor the fortified dwelling, and its most ancient palaces, open to the sun and sky and built for comfort and not security, were an augury of the future. Wealth for Italy followed quickly; its tiny city-states bred a jealous competitive rivalry; the monuments of its ancient glory spurred ambition; finally, the contraction of economic opportunity due to the failure of Byzantium stopped up new outlets for investment and permitted an extravagant self-indulgence in competitive living. The fifteenth and early sixteenth centuries witnessed an astounding efflorescence of architecture, painting, sculpture, indeed of all the arts and crafts that adorn the life of man. It was a curious blend of noble and bourgeois which combined grandeur with comfort, display with domesticity; aristocratic extravagance gave a panache to the delights of middle-class existence. Above all, it created new standards of architecture for all who could afford to build in the grand manner. The baths and villas of Imperial Rome provided models for a series of brilliant architects from Brunelleschi, through Michelangelo, to Palladio, whose *I Quattre Libri dell' Architettura* most strongly influenced the aristocracy of eighteenth-century England.

In the series of splendid villas that Palladio built about Vicenza and Venice, he achieved a combination of proportion, magnificence, and brilliant decoration of incomparable quality. These and the palaces of Rome, Florence, Venice, Genoa, and Milan set a new standard for luxurious living hitherto unknown in Europe. The fashion quickly spread—indeed much more quickly than the technical knowledge or skill in craftsmanship—and great palaces, often overblown and barbarous in concept, were built in northern and western Europe long before a detailed knowledge of the new architecture had been assimilated. Some of these great houses, modified and purified by later generations, still exist; a few which responded, as it were, to the distant echoes of the new style captured a sense of proportion that adds distinction to their barbaric charm. Of these the great English Tudor houses of Hardwick Hall, Longleat, and Burghley are the most famous.

The great age of building came to France in the sixteenth century, the time when many of the fabulous châteaux of the Loire were built, creating a tradition of palatial architecture which, modified and refined, lasted until the Revolution. England's turn followed a century later. What Inigo Jones started, Christopher Wren and the eighteenth century completed. Yet the great age of English domestic architecture is brief, stretching from 1660 to 1830. During that time, as in France, a mania for building seized all who could afford it.

"Every man now," wrote an Englishman early in the eighteenth century, "be his fortune what it will, is to be doing something at his place, as the fashionable phrase is, and you hardly meet anybody who, after the first compliments, does not inform you that he is in mortar and heaving of earth, the modest terms for building and gardening. One large room, a serpentine river, and a wood are become the absolute necessities of life, without which a gentleman of the smallest fortune thinks he makes no figure in his country."

of Tudor England. Of "Building Bess" it was said that "she had been told she would never die as long as she was building, and she died in a hard frost when the men couldn't work." Audley End (right), built by Thomas Howard, Lord High Treasurer of England, brought from his sovereign, James I, the remark that it was "too large for a king though it might do for a Lord Treasurer." Howard poured his fortune into the house and ended up in Star Chamber, charged with misappropriating public funds.

Millions of pounds sterling were poured into bricks and mortar and plaster to give Britain the splendid architectural heritage that is forever associated with the Four Georges— the Hanoverian kings who ruled from 1714 to 1830. In every town or village, the Georgian houses—so easily recognizable with their mellow red brick, sash windows, elegant white porticoes and fanlights—demonstrate how aristocratic taste spread quickly down into middle-class society. And not only down. This taste for light, airy, well-proportioned, elegant rooms speedily leapt across the Atlantic to New England and to the southern states, to give the same gracious setting to their growing wealth.

These houses are still eagerly sought, still lived in and loved, but the great Palladian mansions that inspired them have fallen on harder times. As wealth ebbs from Europe, roofs are stripped of lead, marble chimney pieces are wrenched from their sockets, gilded paneling is torn out, and finally the hammer blows of demolition men echo across the deserted parks. Other buildings, more fortunate, are turned into schools, nunneries, homes for the sick and aged.

TEXT CONTINUED ON PAGE 46

Sir Robert Walpole, Earl of Orford (facing page), was the glorified embodiment of the country squire, with his bluff good humor, his John Bull appearance, his love of dogs, horses, hunting, and landed estates. The master of English public life for more than twenty years and the chief architect of the office of prime minister, he preferred to be painted by John Wootton as Master of the King's Staghounds in Windsor Forest. Walpole's family seat, Houghton Hall, was his greatest pride. There each fall his political supporters gathered in the "Norfolk Congresses," to eat, drink, hunt the fox, and make their plans for the government of England.

The Cholmondeley Family (below), painted by Hogarth in 1732, portrays Mary, Robert Walpole's daughter, seated with her husband, George, later 3rd Earl of Cholmondeley, three of their children, and George's brother, in a scene of aristocratic domesticity. The picture gallery behind the children reflects the taste that made fine private museums of many houses. When the Orford title died out with Horace Walpole in 1797, Houghton Hall passed to the Cholmondeley branch, and is now the home of the 5th Marquess.

COLLECTION OF THE MARQUESS OF CHOLMONDELEY

43

THE
CHAPEL

THE NORTHERN FRONT

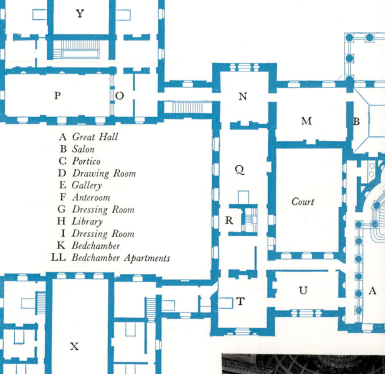

A Great Hall
B Salon
C Portico
D Drawing Room
E Gallery
F Anteroom
G Dressing Room
H Library
I Dressing Room
K Bedchamber
LL Bedchamber Apartments

THE SOUTHERN FRONT WITH FOUNTAIN

THE
GREEN
STATE
BEDROOM

THE
BROWN
STATE
BEDROOM

THE GRAND HALL

PHOTOGRAPHS *Country Life*

THE
SALON
(*TWO VIEWS*)

THE LIBRARY

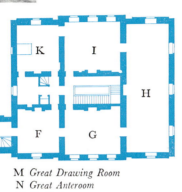

M *Great Drawing Room*
N *Great Anteroom*
O *Vestibule*
P *Chapel*
Q *State Bedchamber*
RS *Dressing Room and Closet*
T *Bedchamber*
U *Dressing Room*
W *Dining Room*
X *Kitchen Offices*
Y *Laundry*

THE SCULPTURE GALLERY

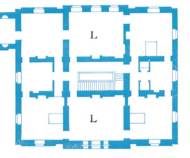

THE PLAN OF HOLKHAM HALL

Holkham Hall was designed as a central block with four wings, as shown in this plan. This Palladian mansion was built for Thomas Coke, Earl of Leicester, on the Norfolk salt marshes which he reclaimed from the ocean. William Kent, the chief architect, outdid himself in the grand hall, with its noble staircase and alabaster columns. The design derives from the Italian Renaissance architect Palladio and, through him, from the ancient Roman architect Vitruvius. Hannah More, who visited Holkham in 1777, after the estate had passed to Leicester's nephew, was most impressed by the fine paintings which the Earl had bought on the Continent. She thought the grounds depressingly flat and noted that Lord Coke was being "universally condemned" for spending £10,000 on a new garden, but found herself enchanted by the 100-foot-long grape house, "the most elegant thing I ever saw in my life . . . all of stone and plate glass . . . a graceful little Paradise."

CHIMNEY PIECES IN THE SOUTH-
WEST AND NORTH-WEST WINGS

TEXT CONTINUED FROM PAGE 42

Many are handed over to the State-sponsored institutions for preservation. Most of those that are still lived in, open their doors to an eager public whose shillings and half-crowns help to patch the crumbling stone and keep the rot at bay. A few, locked securely in their vast parks, still witness the traditional life that has always been lived there; but each year the number diminishes, each year sees another fabulous home, replete with pictures, statues, furniture, all culled from the far corners of the world, open to public display.

To most visitors it is a strange, unreal world that opens before their eyes, and questions crowd in. Are the 365 rooms at Knole in Kent really necessary even for a duke? Two hundred yards, or 606 feet, to be precise, seems excessive for the front of any house; the Marquess of Rockingham thought his dignity required it; and an entrance hall sixty feet square and forty feet high put his visitors in a suitably humble frame of mind. But did Mylord of Exeter require four huge billiard rooms in which to disport himself?

Parks were in proportion to houses. A series of landscape gardeners—Bridgeman, Kent, "Capability" Brown—taught the English nobility to remodel the surrounding countryside. Rivers were diverted, lakes dug, so that the house might be reflected in a peaceful stretch of water, sometimes decorated with gilded barges from which a private orchestra could entertain the guests with the latest airs of Handel or Mozart. No one balked at planting vast woods that could not possibly mature for two centuries. Fifty miles was not an unusual circumference for a park, and Sir Robert Walpole, King George I's prime minister, used fifty men, women, and boys merely to weed his plantations. Doric temples, "Gothick" follies, Chinese pagodas, often exquisitely decorated and furnished with the same luxury as the house, garnished a vista or, carefully concealed, caused delight by surprise.

The Duchess of Bedford had been in Paris when Madame

COPYRIGHT *Country Life*

The Chinese Dairy at Woburn Abbey was built during the vogue for Oriental design that flourished in the late eighteenth century.

A French Noble's View

However grand the English country houses seemed to Anglo-Saxon eyes, they made quite a different impression on a noble visitor from the Continent. The Comte de Mirabeau, who traveled to London in 1784, left this account of his journey:

"From Lewes, we traversed the finest country in Europe, for variety and verdure, for beauty and richness, for rural neatness and elegance. It was a feast for the sight, a charm for the mind, which it is impossible to exaggerate.

The approaches to London are through a country for which Holland affords no parallel (I should compare it to some of the valleys of Switzerland), for, and this remarkable observation seizes immediately an experienced mind, this sovereign people are, above all, farmers in the bosom of their island; and that is what has so long saved it from its own convulsions. I felt my mind deeply and strongly interested as I travelled

de Pompadour, Louis XV's mistress, started a rage for dairies—built exquisitely, of course, and often lined with Sèvres porcelain. In these the great ladies of the Court could ape the dairymaid. Not to be outdone, the Duchess built her own dairy at Woburn—larger, finer, more exquisite still—red and black, very à la mode in its *chinoiserie*, and mirrored in its own lake. The same reckless expense, the same lavish use of the finest materials, the same sense of building for eternity pervade even the stables. Those at Woburn are the size of a small village, beautifully designed and planned, built regardless of cost. The stalls for the horses at Houghton are made of the finest oak, exquisitely carved with a crispness of detail that argues the highest standard of craftsmanship.

Within, of course, the houses showed the same prodigality. There can be found the best marbles of antiquity; masterpieces of art of all times and countries—Rembrandt, Holbein, Velazquez, and a hundred others; French furniture of a quality and distinction hard to find in France itself; porcelain that graced the palace of the Celestial Emperor cheek by jowl with the finest china of Meissen and Sèvres; illuminated manuscripts, plate of gold and silver, Renaissance bronzes and jewels, rock crystal; tapestries and carpets from Aubusson and the great factories of the East; books by the million and family portraits—

through this well cultivated and prosperous country, and I said to myself, whence this new emotion. Their castles, compared to ours, are but pigeon houses. Several cantons in France, even in the poorest provinces, and all Normandy, which I have just visited, are finer by nature than these fields. Here we find in this place, and that place, but every where in our country, fine edifices, proud buildings, great public works, the traces of the most wonderful works of man; and yet this contents me more than those things astonish me. It is that nature is here ameliorated and not forced . . . that the high state of cultivation here announces the respect for property; that this care and universal neatness is a living system of well being; that all this rural wealth is in nature, by nature, according to nature, and does not disclose that extreme inequality of fortune, source of so many evils, like the sumptuous edifice surrounded by cottages; it is that here everything informs me that the people are something; that every man has the development and free exercise of his faculties, and that thus I am in a new order of things."

Reynoldses, Gainsboroughs, Romneys—by the ton. As room follows room, blazing with gilt and shining with marble, the perceptive sight-seer asks himself time and time again: why such magnificence? why such ostentation? why did any class of men feel the need for such a wanton and public display of their wealth?—for public it was.

The thousands who now troop through the salons and boudoirs of the great houses of England are treading in the footsteps of generations of sight-seers. From the moment they were built, the houses were open to visitors; they needed to be gentlefolk and they were expected to be generous to the housekeeper. In the eighteenth century the curious and the *cognoscenti* designed for themselves summer tours and took their fill—sometimes admiring, sometimes critical—of the grandeur of their times. Few would have comprehended Dr. Johnson's meaning when he said to Boswell after viewing Lord Scarsdale's great house at Kedleston: "Nay, sir, all this excludes but one evil—poverty." None bothered to ask themselves the questions that spring so insistently to the mind of the modern visitors. Why was this necessary? How much did it cost? What number of servants were required? Just how did people live in palaces as vast as these?

Although commerce diversified and fructified the wealth of Europe, it may be likened to the yeast rather than the substance of riches. The solid basis of Europe's economy

remained, right up to modern times, the land and its products—foodstuffs, wool, hides, timber, minerals—and, of course, the rents that men were willing to pay either to wring from it a wretched livelihood or to exploit it like any other commercial activity. But in whatever way the land was used, its ownership conferred, as the long centuries passed, more than wealth. It conferred status—power—greatness. From the wide, harsh steppes of Russia to the wild, sea-lashed coast of Galway, men were measured by their acres. The law, the army, the Church, the service of the State might confer gentility, even nobility, on those who were successful in the practice of these professions, but such short cuts to social greatness were comparatively rare. The political power in all European states—except for a few merchant oligarchies such as Venice, Genoa, and Amsterdam—rested on land ownership.

England, at the time when the great country houses flourished, was covered with a network of landowning families, some aristocratic, most belonging to the gentry. Every fifteen or twenty miles in the south—and fifty or so in the north—there would be the great park belonging to a nobleman or to someone rich enough to vie with the nobility. Seeping into the interstices of the large estates were the manor houses of the lesser gentry. Many of these families stretched back to that first great expansion of agrarian wealth which took place in the twelfth and thirteenth centuries; few, even among the nobility, derived from the great baronial aristocracy of the Middle Ages who had battered themselves to death in the Wars of the Roses. Most families had risen slowly, by prudence, by lucky marriage, by ability in law, commerce, or the Church; a few by the luck of a sovereign's favor. Usually it was a matter for generations rather than individual men, so the roots of families went deep into their neighborhoods: intermarriage so that estate could be joined to estate was exceptionally common. As families grew in wealth, so they grew in standing, and natu-

TEXT CONTINUED ON PAGE 50

*T*he Orangery at Heveningham Hall enabled its owner, Sir Gerard Vanneck, to have oranges grown under glass through the winter.

The

Delights

of

Country

Life

Fox-hunting

Cock-fighting

Shooting

Fishing

Card-playing

Racing

Dicing

Bathing

49

The Chinese Closet at Syon House in Middlesex was designed by Robert Adam to delight a noble lady in her hours of frivolous elegance. The exotic birds on mythic branches, which surround each of the fine mirrors, made this a retreat of supreme fascination.

TEXT CONTINUED FROM PAGE 47

rally enough the offices of local government fell into their hands. The same families in Norfolk—the Walpoles, the Cokes, the Townshends, Astleys, Pastons, Hollands—provided the deputy lieutenant, the justice of the peace, the colonels of militia, the members of Parliament decade after decade, century after century.

Land equaled power: that simple equation was quickly grasped and men set about deliberately extending their acres. They looked for heiresses of wide lands; they stopped providing estates for their younger sons, turning them out into the professions (law, Church, army, navy, or, if need be, commerce); they devised strict legal settlements so that the heir to great territories became merely the tenant for life—for they hoped by these strict entails that their agglomerations of wealth and power might be protected from the dissolute, the incompetent, the mad. Naturally, the well-endowed succeeded at the expense of the lesser gentry. They had the resources or the credit to buy up what became available; they could make better bids for heiresses; they could afford more specialized advice, legal or practical, take risks and win profits from more experimental farming or indulge their fancy in more industrial enterprises. Coral-like, their wealth grew. Sometimes the disasters of life—lack of heirs, civil war, insanity not in one but several generations

—pulled a great family down, but when it did it usually enriched the few that remained, or scattered opportunities to the lesser gentry. Furthermore, the greater the family and the wider its local social and political power, the more certain it could be of playing an important and lucrative part in national life; and from this came titles, honors, sinecures, pensions, the great offices of Church or State.

In 1711, young Thomas Pelham-Holles, aged eighteen, succeeded his relative the Duke of Newcastle in estates (although not in title) and became the possessor of thousands of acres in a dozen counties of England, enjoying a rent-roll of more than £30,000 a year (multiply by 12 for modern pounds; by 36 for dollars). At twenty-one he was made Viscount and Earl and Lord Lieutenant for two counties, a year later Marquess and Duke, two years later Lord Chamberlain and Privy Councilor, and a year after that Knight of the Garter, and so on and so forth. He could personally influence the election of a dozen members of Parliament. Nottinghamshire and Sussex knew him as their master. The great houses that he built or adorned—Nottingham Castle, completely remodeled, high on its cliff above the town; Haughton, his hunting lodge in The Dukeries; Claremont, his uncle's vast new Vanbrugh palace for which he redesigned the landscape; the old family mansions of his father, Halland and Bishopstone, both gutted and re-created—these were the necessary symbols of his territorial greatness. Like the gold plate that loaded his table and the hordes of servants that attended him on every journey, they were necessities of his social status. Vast palaces, extravagant living, profusion in every act of life were compulsive in a world that equated wealth with power.

Nor was the Duke of Newcastle exceptional. The Dukes of Bedford enjoyed an income equally large from the vast estates their ancestors had acquired from loot of the monasteries Henry VIII had destroyed. In addition, the Bedfords acquired by judicious marriage great areas of London, principally Covent Garden and Bloomsbury. Docks at Rotherhithe cradled their own fleet of East Indiamen. It is not surprising that magnates such as these should require three or four palaces (among them the huge house at Woburn that now draws hundreds of thousands of visitors a year and whose enormous park and chain of lakes comfortably absorb a great zoo and numerous pleasure grounds).

The Devonshires were richer still, and grew richer with each passing generation. Hardwick Hall, Chatsworth, Bolton Abbey, Lismore Castle and Compton Place and Devonshire House—all vast, all costly, all crammed with pictures, statuary, furniture, and teeming with servants—gave them security and comfort in their peregrinations. At one time the Dukes of Buccleuch rejoiced in eight country houses (five gigantic) and two London houses (both palaces).

In themselves, or rather in their titles, these men symbolized great accretions of social and political power as well as wealth. They were heads of great clans of families who had served them or depended on them or allied with them for generations. These were thickest where the estates lay; these clients they needed to visit, to entertain, and to impress. The great palace, abbey, or castle in which they passed a few weeks each year remained after their departure as a symbol of their greatness. Furthermore it provided work, hospitality, and sometimes protection, for the estates of these men were the centers of great economic enterprises.

Hidden behind the great rooms of state were the offices of stewards and bailiffs, the meeting grounds of merchants, attorneys, agents who drew up the leases, bargained for the timber, farmed the land, let out the mineral rights, and in one of the Duke of Bedford's houses even sold cloth at the back door. A host of upper servants—stewards of the household, housekeepers, keepers of the chamber, clerks of the kitchens, chaplains, librarians, tutors, governesses, personal servants—all required a host of minor servants to attend to their wants. Many a noble household required five or six great tables to feed the servants; three was quite normal.

Labor was plentiful and in general cheap in England from the sixteenth to the twentieth century. Sixty, seventy, or even a hundred indoor and outdoor servants were nothing unusual on one estate; if the owner had a passion for gardens and hothouses the number might be doubled. For such hordes not even Blenheim nor Castle Howard nor the stupendous pile of Wentworth Woodhouse were big enough, and the attics were as crowded with servants as the dormitories of army camps. This profusion of servants, like the enormity of the house, was a part of the necessary display, a piece of conspicuous consumption that proclaimed the wealth of the owner. And as grandeur bred grandeur, so servants bred servants. Tasks were fabulously differentiated: one man and one man alone might fill the oil lamps or replenish the candles; even the clocks had their own winder. The servants' hall became as hieratic as an Oriental despotism, as finely graded in precedence as a state banquet. In order therefore to keep the estate working and to provide the domestic setting that society thought requisite, the servants' quarters and offices in a noble house doubled the size required for show.

Diverse as were the economic enterprises and huge as the domestic staffs came to be, yet these things do not explain entirely why men built such vast palaces. The need to maintain their social and political status by the prestige won through ostentation lies nearer to the truth. This certainly is why many a nobleman built beyond his means—as the Suffolks beggared themselves in creating the monstrous pile of Audley End. Yet there was a more subtle factor involved. The British aristocracy, like the Kwakiutl Indians of the West Coast of Canada, found their egos, the whole idea of themselves as a class and as persons, involved in wanton display: the greater the man, the more absolute his

The Velvet State Bedroom at Houghton Hall, built by Robert Walpole for royal guests, contains perhaps the finest bed in England. The gold braid alone cost £1,219 3s. 11d., a sum that was itemized to the last fringe and flower in the decorator's bill.

disregard for thrift. Whims, moods, any mania, whatever the cost, could be indulged without guilt, without remorse, without any sense of betrayal of the standards of a class, even if it ended in bankruptcy and ruin. And it was the combination of these factors—political, social, economic, and one might almost say anthropological—which led to the profuse extravagance of aristocratic life over three centuries of English history. Yet it gave to Britain an exceptional artistic heritage.

As one walks through the great rooms of state one can sense some of the symbolism of these vast houses. Such rooms, of course, were not lived in; they were rooms for reception either on formal or semi-formal occasions, rooms to be strolled through to the more intimate private apartments where daily life was lived. In the seventeenth century this was usually the bedroom (frequently the bed was fenced off by a rail), but by the eighteenth century smaller, cosier sitting rooms, cabinets, or boudoirs became at first the fashion, then the rage. The great state rooms usually consisted of a vast hall (one of the most spectacular is at Holkham, derived by William Kent from designs by Palladio), one or two salons and drawing rooms (those at Wilton, the famous "double-cube" room, and at Petworth, remarkable for its Grinling Gibbons carvings, are exceptional), a state dining

A fine pack of hounds was the pride and joy of every fox-hunting English squire. This magnificent pack, belonging to Peter Beckford of Stepleton House, was painted with its two huntsmen resplendent in their beige coats on the grounds of his Dorset estate. Of Beckford, an admirer once wrote: "Never had fox or hare the honor of being chased to death by so accomplished a hunter from the time of Nimrod to the present; never was a huntsman's dinner graced by such urbanity and wit and never did the red wine of Oporto confuse the intellect of so politic a sportsman."

room and at least one state bedroom, used only by visitors of extraordinary distinction.

For these rooms no expense was spared. The finest plaster workers were brought in from Italy; tons of mahogany and other rare woods were imported from the East and West Indies; gold leaf was squandered (at Chatsworth the window frames are gold-leafed *outside* as well as within); and Europe was ransacked for paintings and sculpture, furniture and marble. The cost is rarely known. Sir Robert Walpole at Houghton spent £1,219 3s. 11d. on the trimmings alone of his fabulous green velvet state bed, especially designed for him by William Kent (multiply by 12 for modern pounds; by 36 for dollars). This bed alone cannot have cost far short of a hundred thousand dollars, at present rates. The cost of Blenheim, without furniture or pictures,

was rather more than a quarter of a million pounds. Eastbury, also by Vanbrugh, which only existed for twenty-five years, cost £125,000. Houses that were very modest by these standards, such as the delightful one at Ombersley, built by the first Lord Sandys, quickly devoured £30,000 or £40,000. Yet so essential to greatness were these houses that men would load themselves and their descendants with debt rather than deprive themselves of the glory of ownership. Lord Sandys, a man of moderate means but inordinate ambition, mortgaged his estate to the tune of £23,220 in order, doubtless, to impress the citizens of Worcester whom he represented in Parliament. By the middle of the eighteenth century such monuments to a family's importance were *de rigueur*—cost what it might.

And, of course, the contents needs must match the scale

The first cricket match played north of the Tweed is commemorated in this painting of the Cathcart family by David Allan. Lord Cathcart (center), who made a gallant record as a British officer in the American Revolution, has put up a tent borrowed from his regiment of the Coldstream Guards. All over England, at the matches on Sunday afternoon, nobles and villages played as equals. "If," wrote the historian George Macaulay Trevelyan, "the French noblesse had been capable of playing cricket with their peasants, their châteaux never would have been burnt."

of building and the sumptuosity of its decoration. To form his great picture collection (now, because his bankrupt grandson sold it to Catherine of Russia, housed in the Hermitage at Leningrad—save for those pictures that a bankrupt Soviet Government in turn sold to Andrew Mellon), Sir Robert Walpole employed not only the ambassadors of the Crown to scour the dealers but also spies and secret agents to discover what might be extracted from the houses of the European nobility. Naturally prices soared; Sir Robert himself frequently broke his own records, like a Greek shipowner today after a Renoir or a Gauguin. Usually this hardheaded statesman, to whom suspicion was as natural as breathing, bought well; but many vain, arrogant young noblemen became easy dupes for the fakes and copyists. Yet even so, the artistic collections of the English

TEXT CONTINUED ON PAGE 56

*O*VERLEAF: *The entrance hall at Syon House is the work of Robert Adam, eighteenth-century England's greatest architect. The room is a double cube and is entirely white except for the black and white marble floor.* ON THE FACING PAGE: *This famous painting of* The Honorable Mrs. Graham *by Thomas Gainsborough represents the eighteenth-century ideal of feminine loveliness. Mary Graham was the sister of the 10th Lord Cathcart, who appears in the painting shown above. Gainsborough painted her shortly after her honeymoon with Thomas Graham, later Lord Lynedoch. When she died at thirty-five her husband was so grief-stricken that he stored his painting and never looked at it again.*

TEXT CONTINUED FROM PAGE 53

nobility, even after the enforced sales of the last fifty years, remain of exceptional quality and worthy of the most distinguished museums of Europe.

As with paintings, so it was with all that was rare, exotic, and costly: nobleman vied with nobleman over jewels, pictures, books, plants, animals. The world was ransacked to give distinction to an English house and garden. Here are a few exotics that poured into the household of the "Princely Duke of Chandos": Captain Massey of Carolina sent him rice, kidney beans, pineapples, a Mexican squash, or little beaver and flamingos; Chiswell of Virginia sent mockingbirds; Stephens of Cape Coast, a tiger that mauled a servant; Ashley of Barbados, pineapples, cinnamon, coffee trees, avocado pears; from Jamaica, pawpaws, star apples, custard apples, guavas, tamarinds; Harriman of Leghorn, broccoli seed, fennel, *agro di cedro*, orange-flower water, capers, *muscatello di Castello* vinegar, preserved citron, anchovies, Lucca oil, olives, and evergreen-oak acorns; Oporto provided Lamiego hams; Lisbon, sugar, raisins of the sun, Malaga raisins, currants, lemons, oranges, musk and watermelon seeds. By 1739 Chandos boasted of the finest and largest collection of fruit in Europe. And his rare birds were equal to his fruit. They poured in from the four quarters of the globe: storks from Rotterdam, wild geese from Barbados, whistling ducks from Antigua, redbirds from the Gold Coast, blue macaws, Muscovy ducks, parakeets, a crown bird, ostriches, an eagle—all grotesquely expensive.

Chandos also loved music; so he created an orchestra of about thirty instrumentalists and vocalists, conducted by the famous Dr. Pepusch. "His concert," as he called it, lived in his house and provided background music to his dinners. It cost him nearly £1,000 a year in wages, but this was less than his wine bill, which ran at about £1,500 a year, roughly the same as Sir Robert Walpole's, whose household in 1733 returned 540 dozen empties.

For those who did not relish artists or menageries, furniture or gardens, there were the hounds and the horses, the women and the gaming tables. Lord Stavordale, scarcely beyond adolescence, lost eleven thousand guineas at cards only to regain them the next evening in a single bid when he cursed himself for not playing for really high stakes! Even generosity could grow as wanton as a weed. Lord Egremont, the owner of Petworth, disdained to pay his servants wages. If they greatly pleased him, he would give them £1,000 or at times £2,000 worth of stock; for little kindnesses they got £50 in the local savings bank. Guests at Petworth were always welcome; they stayed weeks, months, even years. He celebrated special occasions—victories, coronations, royal birthdays, and, of course, his own—with vast public entertainments that amazed even his own time. Here is a description of the feast he gave when he reached his eighty-third year:

"A fine sight it was; fifty-four tables, each fifty feet long, were placed in a vast semi-circle on the lawn before the house. Nothing could be more amusing than to look at the preparations. The tables were all spread with cloths and plates and dishes. Two great tents were erected in the middle to receive the provisions which were conveyed in carts like ammunition. Plum puddings and loaves were piled like cannon balls and innumerable joints of boiled and roast beef were spread out, while hot joints were prepared in the kitchen and sent forth as soon as the firing of a gun announced the hour of the feast. . . . They think 6,000 were fed."

Yet, lavish as this life was, it had its curious shortcomings, its little weaknesses, and even its darker side. The plumbing in these great mansions was almost nonexistent. Houses that had a bathroom, like Chatsworth, were famed for them. One lavatory was thought to be sufficient for the huge house at Harewood. And we find Chandos writing urgently to Jamaica for bitterwood in order to line his daughter's cradle to keep out the bugs. The absence of drains and the presence of parasites bred diseases. Chandos himself buried two wives and eight of his children. In all great households death was a constant visitor, and perhaps this gave a keener edge to their appetite for life; and perhaps in their need to build on a scale fit for eternity, we can discern their sense of life's transience, a hint of tragedy, and a challenge to death. That is as may be. TEXT CONTINUED ON PAGE 60

The Duke of Newcastle's Cook

One of the chief concerns of a fashionable lord was to keep a good table, and the key to a good table was a French cook. The cartoon at the top of the facing page shows the Duke of Newcastle remonstrating with his famous chef, Cloué: "Oh! Cloué, if you leave me I shall be starved." But Cloué has been reading King George's proclamation against Papists, and is not staying in England. After struggling along for a while with an English cook, Newcastle addressed an appeal to Lord Albemarle, the British ambassador to Paris, who had taken Cloué into his service. After consultation with Cloué, Albermarle recommended a man named Hervé, taking care to warn the Duke that "a cook of greater reputation may be got, but then most of them are very impertinent . . . none of that class chuses to leave Paris without they are attended by an Aide, *a* Rotisseur, *and a* Patissier." *Hervé did not satisfy, and within the year Newcastle was back with his problem. This time Cloué undertook to set his old master straight: "My Lord Duke, at the moment I know of no cooks available such as your Grace requires; it is indeed very rare to find one who is both a good cook and a good* rotisseur. *In most of the best houses in France a cook never makes the roast." Fortunately, Newcastle in the meantime had become prime minister and his Paris correspondents were able to find him a cook named Fontenelle who suited his taste. The kind of meal that the Duke's cook served up on a grand occasion may be studied on the opposite page. The menu for the First Table (i.e. the Duke's own guests, as opposed to various hangers-on who showed up but got a simpler meal) offers 109 items and ends with a galaxy of Gallic confections.*

LONDON, THURSDAY JUNE 4TH, 1761

HIS GRACE THE DUKE OF NEWCASTLE'S DINNER
FIRST TABLE

(4 hoggs feet	Beef Hodge-Podge a la Flamande	Terrein 3 Pulletts
4 hoggs ears	Soup a la Reine	Leg Lamb boyled
1 sweetbread)	Soop Green Peas	1 pullett Collyflower
	Terrein 4 Ducks	

2 Pulletts in Scollops	Twenty Pigs Feet au blanc
Combs, Eggs and 12 lambs Sweetbreads	4 Chickens a l'aspic
Turtle	Turtle
Rump of beef glasse	Squabbs with Crawfish

Soop Sente	Soop Clair
4 Peepers a la poelle	Fricandeau of veal au Lettue
Turtle	Turtle
2 Bt. Lamb in Jelly	Marbre of Cow Heels
24 Lambs Ears hollandaise	8 beef pallates au sausome

Filletts of Mackrell	Filletts of Soles
Pattys Baraguel	Pattys Spagniole
Filletts of Turbot	Filletts of Saumon
Filletts of Lobsters	Filletts of Turbot
Pattys of Mutton	Pattys Bashimell
Filletts of Smelts	Filletts of Gudgions

4 REMOVES	4 REMOVES
8 Mackrell boyld	Haunch venison
Sturgeon	Chynes mutton
Trouts	Cold meat
8 Mackrell broyled	Cold meat

SIDE BOARD

2 venison pastys	Bt. Veal	2 Necks Lamb
Pye beef	2 shr. Mutton	2 Shr. Lamb
Beams and bacon	2 Hch. Mutton	1 Loyn Lamb
	2 Breast Mutton	4 Rabbits
	2 loyns Mutton	

2ND COURSE

Patty of pidgeons cold	CROCANT—Bridge with a Temple	2 Leveretts	3 Peepers
Crawfish	Jelly	2 Pheasants	7 Pidgeons
12 calves feet, Blancmange	Prawns	1 Goose	1 Capon
	Gateau d'Amande	10 Quails	2 Leveretts
		2 Turkey	4 Rabbitts
			and 12 sallads

3RD COURSE

Pease	Lettue farce	Orange Jelly	A Chinese boat	Crocant	Egg Basket
Rhenish cream	Eggs au citron	Pastry a Cherry Tree	Hen and Chickens	6 Flower potts	Pyramid
Artichauts	Beans	Ext Jelly	Basket	7 Lambs	Basket of Apricots
peaches in jelly	French Beans	Sparagras	A Hagg	7 Boats	Dogg Chained
Pastry à Wagon	Coffee Cream	Rhenish cream			
Marbre	Collyflowers	Pease			
		and 12 plates pastry			

A VIEW OF THE CAIN & ABEL BIRD-CAGE AND THE GRAND TEMPLE WALKS

The Grounds at Chiswick

Rippling cascades, marble statues, and high yew hedges delighted Richard Boyle, 3rd Earl of Burlington, as he strolled about the gardens of Chiswick House. As a leader of national taste and a patron of classical architecture, Burlington had commissioned his protégé, William Kent, to model Chiswick after Palladio's Italian Villa Capra at Vicenza. Kent's principle of garden design was "to follow nature

A PROSPECT OF THE CASCADE AND PART OF THE HOUSE

A VIEW OF THE GARDEN FROM THE TOP OF

A VIEW OF THE BACK PART OF THE CASSINA AND THE SERPENTINE RIVER TERMINATED BY THE CASCADE

even in her faults." His great trees supplied large areas of light and shade, while numerous paths rendered no spot very far from an idyllic knoll along the canal which ran through the gardens. Visitors could amuse themselves by boating, fishing, or watching peacocks strut along the walks leading to temples and aviaries. On the pedimented gate by Inigo Jones, Alexander Pope wrote the following fanciful epigram:

Passenger: "Oh gate, how cam'st thou here?"
Gate: "I was brought from Chelsea last year
Battered with wind and weather;
Inigo Jones put me together;
Sir Hans Sloane let me alone,
Burlington brought me hither."

THE STEPS LEADING TO THE GRAND GALLERY

A VIEW OF THE GARDEN WITH A DISTANT VIEW OF THE ORANGERY AND INIGO JONES'S GATE

*R*obert Adam, the greatest architect of eighteenth-century England, spent as much care on the interiors and furnishings as on the outside walls of the buildings he designed. His sense of classical elegance was shaped in Italy by his study of ancient Roman ruins.

*S*ir John Vanbrugh, soldier, dramatist, and architect, carried stateliness to its furthest extreme in buildings like Blenheim Palace and Castle Howard. A critic wrote: *"Such noble ruins every pile would make, I wish they'd tumble for the prospect's sake."*

*W*illiam Kent was architect of both houses and landscapes. He was consulted, according to Horace Walpole, not only for furniture but "for plates, for a barge, for a cradle." Of his gardens Walpole said: "Mahomet imagined an Elysium, Kent created many."

TEXT CONTINUED FROM PAGE 56

Of what there is no doubt is that this life was wasteful, extravagant, ostentatious—an appalling contrast, as Dr. Johnson noted, to the human wretchedness of rural or urban slums; yet it was saved both by its humanity and by its taste. The houses, the pictures, the furniture, above all the landscaped gardens in which nature had been so gently subdued, are its permanent memorial and a part of the European tradition. They give style and grandeur to what might have been merely a gross and vulgar self-indulgence. These boastful, splendiferous men created enduring beauty.

There have been far richer men, before and since their time, greater connoisseurs, greater patrons of the arts, even greater eccentrics, but in the British aristocracy of the eighteenth century there met two hostile but fertilizing traditions that gave it its curious splendor. In it the feudal world was still alive in its arrogance, its fierce disregard of consequence, its personal sense of destiny, but it operated in the new world of bourgeois delights. Secure in its own greatness, the aristocracy could parade its great wealth without guilt and with a total disregard of the envy of the multitude. For these noblemen's way of life was based not on wealth alone but on a sense of caste. Their blood and

power stretched back into antiquity and looked forward to eternity. Greatness was all. Unawares, the great wave of democratic industrialization engulfed them; inexorably the end came. Yet the houses remain, and their parks that time has perfected. The paths thread through the ancient oaks and scented limes, disclosing across the calm lakes the Palladian grace of mellowing brick and stone. As one walks slowly between the trees, one is conscious of the generations of men and women who walked here. They too were full of hope. They were here and are no more; soon we shall follow them; but these houses and these parks, either in splendor or in ruin, will long outlast the life that made them, carrying their grace and beauty to stir the hearts of men for whom destiny is no longer personal.

Dr. J. H. Plumb is a Fellow of Christ's College, Cambridge, and an outstanding authority on eighteenth-century England. His books include The First Four Georges, England in the Eighteenth Century, *and* Sir Robert Walpole. *He is general editor of a 25-volume* History of Human Society, *now in preparation, and co-author of the* American Heritage Book of the Revolution.

*R*obert Adam's triumph, the most exquisite room in all England, is the Pink Room at Osterley Park in Middlesex. The tapestries were woven to Adam's order by Jacques Neilson, director of the Gobelin works in Paris. On the walls, large gold medallions frame paintings of the loves of the gods, executed from designs by Boucher; the vases and garlands in intervening spaces follow designs of the flower painter Maurice Jacques. The sofa and armchairs were all created by Adam at his peak of refined delicacy. It has been many years since anyone actually sat in them.

THE "NOTHING" PLAYS

and how they have grown on us

European dramas of grim speculation invade

our stage to match home-grown exercises in

dark groping. Needed: more light and warmth

By FRANK GIBNEY

In Munich last year I went one evening to Die Kleine Freiheit, the satirical revue theater that specializes in the pungencies of contemporary politics. Here was the salty Berlin humor of the late twenties and earliest thirties, now resurrected as if nothing had happened in between. It was still gritty, cynical, and questioning, a mode of theatrical expression that seemed the newer for its long submersion. "Of course," said a German friend, "it is not optimistic like your American plays."

Optimistic? Coming back to New York, I thought to check up on the optimism that Europeans commonly suppose to flourish in the American theater.

Next to *My Fair Lady*, I found, the most popular thing in town (including off-Broadway with on-) has been the revival, three years running, of *The Threepenny Opera*—that monument of tuneful nihilism with which Berthold Brecht and Kurt Weill had intrigued Berlin in the cynical twenties. The Weill-Brecht version of Gay's *Beggar's Opera* might have been a rare theatrical bird, if it had perched above a New York audience ten years ago. But today it is only one offering in an impressive Continental invasion of pessimism—or at least of purposeful social disengagement. The theology implied in T. S. Eliot's *The Cocktail Party* may have come as a shock to the theater public of 1950. But by this time,

after *The Living Room* and *The Potting Shed*, we are well accustomed to the far sharper religious and moral problems of Graham Greene, the Catholic whose preoccupation with sin makes Saint Augustine look like an irresponsible carnival proprietor. In plays like *Ring Around the Moon* and even *The Waltz of the Toreadors*, the light-hearted French cynic Jean Anouilh has virtually turned love into a branch of epistemology. As for classical static speculation, Broadway has had two presentations of *Waiting for Godot*, the work of James Joyce's former secretary, Samuel Beckett, who has asserted himself as the theater's foremost Irish specialist in philosophical quandaries. (The acting world was made more noble by Bert Lahr's remarking of this play's message, after giving a very fine performance in it, "What is the play about? Damned if I know.")

These cheerless writers make heavy demands on any audience's thinking powers. But even our more popular serious plays are apt to be equally despairing about human strivings and pointedly modest in their hopes of getting at any higher human—not to say divine—values. John Osborne's burnt offerings to angry young manhood, both *Look Back in Anger* and *The Entertainer*, are forceful enough to disband any Optimists Club so unwise as to visit them. The latest unveiling of the Lunts, significantly enough, marched along with

62

One advanced embodiment of the "nothing" theater is Samuel Beckett's Endgame, *a pessimistic, anarchic, seemingly purposeless debate on man's state in which two of its characters never leave their ash cans.*

the gloomy trend. Brilliantly done, *The Visit* was a moody discussion, half on the level of allegory, of a rich woman who pays a town to put to death the man who long ago had wronged her. The message of its author, the excellent Swiss dramatist Friedrich Duerrenmatt, hinged on the innate corruptibility of man, fueled by money.

But the atmosphere of gloom or uncertainty is no European monopoly in the theater. Eugene O'Neill's last great shadow cast over the spirits of his audience, *Long Day's Journey Into Night*, dominated the last season with its all too real projection of family purposelessness. The remembrance past of young Tom Wolfe in *Look Homeward, Angel* was not exactly happy-go-lucky. Even a liberal morality play like Paul Muni's long-running vehicle, *Inherit the Wind*, left its audiences feeling that the game, with all its mutual destruction, was not really worth the candle. It could almost be said that *The Diary of Anne Frank*, for all the tragedy of its outcome, was the most cheerful serious play of the last few

seasons. In this at least the devotion to life of the very young was shown as determined, direct, and immediately moving.

There are two prevailing winds in the American theater of the last few seasons, rather closely related. One of them is the European problem play about metaphysics (sometimes disguised as a play without problems that is *not* about metaphysics). This product is distinguished for its impressive, often witty language, its probing of basic problems, and its determinedly inconclusive ending—like Samuel Beckett's heads in ash cans uttering a poetic paraphrase of the old Abbott and Costello cry, "Who's on first?" If a play like this is intelligible, its author figures it as a failure. As Eugene Ionesco, the Parisian Romanian, put it in describing one of his own recent off-Broadway offerings, *The Bald Soprano:* "The people in *The Bald Soprano* have no hunger, no conscious desires; they are bored stiff." (As nearly as can be determined, audiences shared this attitude.)

Beckett's *Waiting for Godot* has become a prototype in

Beckett's Waiting for Godot *presents two tramps (one played here by Bert Lahr) in a fruitless vigil for a mysterious "Godot." It has been revived twice since 1956.*

the better plays of the day. Its plot concerns the difficulties of an adolescent couple, deeply in love, who anticipate the clergy and must settle the problem of an oncoming child by an abortion. Until the very last, both the boy and the girl feel that their parents cannot be consulted. Their plight is the story of innocents in trouble. They are unable to communicate with the very people who could help them, for the unseeing parents are almost hopelessly cut off from the cellar teen-age world of their young. The moral of the play is that people should understand, somehow.

In a similar vein, William Inge's *The Dark at the Top of the Stairs* discusses the complicated problems of the psyche that were probably bound to happen near Oklahoma City, a generation or so after the pioneers from *Oklahoma* stopped singing and forgot their Agnes de Mille dance routines. It is a very good, a moving, and, as the saying has it, an "honest" play. But another generation of dramatists might find that it stresses a highly limited sort of virtue. It tells how a family in a small Oklahoma town—husband, wife, two children—came closer together, somehow, not through courage or love or fear, but through Understanding. The key words of our psychologically oriented day are posted like sentinels through the dialogue and its stage directions: "awareness," "understanding," "unconscious guilt." It ends in the best traditions of the Family-Seeking-Understanding, with everybody needing one another.

A variant of this theme is that of the Individual-Seeking-Clarification. Of this, the extreme example was Arthur Laurents' *The Clearing in the Woods*, a provocative if not very successful play about the struggle of one young woman to recapture her real self by summoning up the shades of past stages in her life. Here was surely the triumph of psychiatry on the stage—a deadly serious culmination of what started out in 1941 with the half-comic interlude of the dream scene in *Lady in the Dark*.

Although no other play of the last few seasons was this clinical, there were many that took the same sailing directions. The quest for Understanding, as most theatergoers now know, springs out of the search for true personality and identity that psychiatry has unveiled for us. It gives us the morality play of our time. But the theatrical pilgrim on the stage seeks neither God nor goodness (except occasionally in Christopher Fry or Graham Greene). He is after clarity. If he can banish confusion by the third act (or else show how irreparably confused he and the family are), success has been achieved.

He need discover no virtue other than the fact that he thinks and feels all by himself, thus proving that he exists as a person—both theses which Descartes and Pascal each plagued to distraction quite a while ago. Thus the shade of the hero's brother in the Epilogue of *Look Homeward, Angel* calls to young Gene Gant, "The world is nowhere, no one, Gene. *You* are your world."

this field. It is actually a play of considerable artistry but minimal action, whose principal characters are two tramps sitting by a roadside. A villain enters now and then to harass them. They never stray from the roadside, but they utter a lot of cryptic talk involving the purpose of life and man's struggles in it—all reduced to the allegory of the two tramps waiting for some presence called Godot, who never comes. If acted well, strangely enough, the play can say much to an intelligent audience. (No one has ever satisfactorily explained why it had its first tryout in Miami.) But there is nothing resembling a plot or a stated message to get hold of. *Waiting for Godot*, and most of the theater pieces like it, could best be described as "nothing" plays, analogous to the "nothing" novels of Henry Green or the professionally inconclusive "nothing" stories in *The New Yorker*. "The play is about nothing," William Saroyan wrote in an explanation of *Godot*. "All is nothing. All comes to nothing. Everything is nothing . . ."

Side by side with the "nothing" play is a kindred but earthier exercise in inconclusiveness. This is a home-grown American variety, built around a theme that might be called The-Family-Seeking-Understanding. The Family-Seeking-Understanding has had its best recent representative in Herlihy and Noble's *Blue Denim*, which is by the way one of

This is surely a reaction against the socially conscious dramas of the thirties and after. In the theater of Clifford Odets' day we waited for Lefty, and he was found, after all. In fact, he came back with a whopping good contract for the UAW-CIO, and he now has a barbecue pit and a two-car garage. We worried for a while in the early fifties about McCarthyism and the Crucibles of intolerance. But many of these social and personal problems were blanketed, if not done away with, in the general Era of Good Feeling that spread over us all thereafter. While we earnestly probe our personal understandings (each to his own), we deem it poor manners to worry about social or political things excessively —if not also a mark of wanting sophistication. So now, we sit around and wait for Godot.

For there is a sure linkage between the metaphysical pessimism of the European playwrights and the successful quest for Understanding on the American stage. After you "understand" everybody, or at least yourself, where do you go? In the absence of any further directing signposts, the way is clear for the metaphysical trench-warfare of the high-brow Europeans. This dramatic struggling starts nowhere and generally leads nowhere, as the audiences may reflect. (As one Manhattan lady said of Duerrenmatt's *The Visit:* "It was a lot better to watch than it was to think about later.") It does give an audience some food for thought and considerably adds to its store of polished ideas flying around in free association.

Perhaps we are correct in looking with some amusement on the blunt, socially conscious playwrights of two decades back. They did, however, write with an idea of the good in mind, even though they sometimes confused abstract truth and beauty with the sheen from F.D.R.'s cigarette holder. In so doing, they wrote in the classic dramatic tradition. And they gave their audiences moments of inspiration. It is no small wonder that many theatergoers still prefer the less ambitious moral clarities of vintage Robert Sherwood to a Tennessee Williams heroine tossing off her pint and her Choctaw cry or a Graham Greene agonist playing three falls out of five with his soul.

There is no doubt that the interest of the Understanding plays and the speculative value of the European imports have raised the level of sophistication in the American theater. For all the noise of imported Parisian playwrights and the clangor in London's Royal Court Theatre, New York is the center of the world stage as it has never been before. Broadway could survive a mutual embargo far better than London. But it is dangerously close to the truth, also, to say that most of this important New York theater is either carefully contrived polish or laboriously discussed Understanding.

One symptom of these tendencies is the lack of precisely that political satire that flourishes in Munich, or even the relatively mild wit of *State of the Union* a decade ago. When politics does intrude in our theater it is rarely anything more

In the American Blue Denim, *Burt Brinckerhoff and Carol Lynley play a hapless pair of adolescent lovers seeking a way out of a baffling world of troubles.*

central than a few good sallies in Peter Ustinov's *Romanoff and Juliet* or the recurrent spectacle of senators falling on their faces in Ethel Merman musicals. Political ideas are either skirted completely, as in the noncontroversial family context of *Sunrise at Campobello,* or intruded grossly, like that still memorable bit of stage campaign literature, "I Like Ike," from *Call Me Madam.* It may be unwritten censorship that causes this. More probably it is the popular opinion that the nation's current leaders are either too sacred to joke about—or too boring.

But satire is not the major loss in a theater committed to the short view of life. The obsession with stock-still psyche-probing makes it very difficult for real moral and social problems to get wide dramatic hearing. They find a cool reception in an age when playwrights seem too busy playing metaphysical or psychiatric chess with themselves in lonely rooms to give much thought to the house in which they are living.

Formerly stationed abroad as a correspondent for Time, *where he acquired the background for a book on the Far East* (Five Gentlemen of Japan) *and another volume soon to be published on Poland, Frank Gibney for over a year has been editorial writer for* Life. *One of his major personal enthusiasms is the theater.*

THE BLUE MUSEUM

The skin diver and the archaeologist have joined forces

to uncover the world's greatest treasure of ancient art

Five years ago some Turkish sponge fishermen, trawling in the waters of the Aegean somewhere off the island of Kos, hauled up a great fragment of bronze, encrusted with molluscs and tangled with seaweed. When the news of their find reached Istanbul, a classical philologist, Professor G. E. Bean, at once set out for their fishing village, not far from the site of the Halicarnassus of antiquity. He came upon the bronze where it lay on the beach, propped up against some driftwood, and he leaned forward, entranced. Larger than life, sheared off at the waist, its forehead gaping with an ugly hole, the bronze was still beautiful, still charged with an unimpaired moral energy, still immutably divine. It was a statue of Demeter, the goddess of the fruits of the earth, mourning for her daughter Persephone who had been carried off to Tartarus by Hades. "A work of the full classical period of Greek art," Professor Bean decided; "almost certainly an original of the fourth century before Christ."

For the sixth time in this century, chance had led to the recovery of a priceless treasure of antiquity from the bottom of the sea. How did it get there? Scholars conjecture that the Demeter, having been commissioned by some city in Asia Minor

By C. W. CERAM *and* PETER LYON

Exploring the wreck of a Roman galley in the Mediterranean, one of Jacques-Yves Cousteau's skin divers glides over a bed of clay amphorae, in which the Romans shipped wine and grain. Below, on these pages, are some classical works of art recovered from the sea. Left to right: a panther of the first century A.D.; a dwarf and a bronze head of the first century B.C. found off Tunisia; a statue of Demeter from Turkish coastal waters; a boy jockey of Artemisium; a philosopher's head from a cargo of art works sunk off Antikythera.

FT TO RIGHT: MUSÉE DES ANTIQUITÉS NATIONALE, SAINT-
RMAIN-EN-LAYE; MUSÉE ALAOUI, LE BARDO, TUNIS (2); IZMIR
USEUM OF ARCHAEOLOGY; NATIONAL MUSEUM, ATHENS (2)

(perhaps Cnidus, perhaps Halicarnassus), was on its way from the workshop of its Greek sculptor when the ship carrying it went down. Such traffic was common enough in the days of Greece's glory, although not as great as it became in the centuries of Roman rule. When the Romans had brought the Greek world under their sway and were well on their way to making the Mediterranean a Roman lake, they helped themselves to the cultural treasures of Hellas. Westward from Greece to Italy sailed shiploads of Greek philosophers, poets, physicians, scientists—guides and tutors to the Romans in their leisure hours. And westward as well went argosies laden with artistic loot: marble and bronze statuary, and thousands of painted urns and vases.

Not all of them, however, reached their destination. In those days seafarers discreetly hugged the coast, but the small vessels—and their masters—were ill-equipped to cope with the sudden, freakish Mediterranean weather. When a pilot was guided by omen rather than by compass, sextant, and barometer, he was at the mercy of any line squall and lucky indeed to come unscathed through the rocky straits and shoaly channels that wind amongst the isles of Greece; and when he came to the Straits of Messina he had carried with him memories of ancestral fears of being beset there

TEXT CONTINUED ON PAGE 70

The legendary descent of Alexander the Great into the sea was depicted by a fifteenth-century French artist in The History of Alexander. *The text describes his adventure:*

Alexander . . . had all the glass makers of the continent come to him and he proposed that they make for him a glass barrel which would be ample enough to move around in and transparent enough to see everything through it.

When the barrel was made he had it very well attached with good iron chains to a big metal circle and to this he had strong cords attached. He took with him strong lamps. He then had the opening closed so well that no drop of water could get into it. After that he had himself brought in the high sea by boat, and lowered by the cords which held the barrel. Afterwards he could not make anybody believe what he had seen . . . because he saw fishes of such different kinds and colors that looked like beasts on the land and that walked on their feet on the bottom of the sea and ate fruit of trees that were on the bottom. . . . He said that he had seen men, women, or fishes, in that order, which were walking on their feet running after the fish to eat, as on the earth one runs after animals. When he had looked at all the marvels of the sea as long as he wanted, he signalled to those above who pulled him up onto the boat. He broke the glass barrel and went into the tent where the barons were waiting for him in a state of great worry. They were angry because he had put himself in so great a danger with no reason.

He thus answered: ". . . You must not marvel that I descended in this barrel. By it I have gained so much that I will govern my army more wisely each day of my life. I have proved that it is a great advantage to have strength in one's body, but even better to have ingenuity. I have seen in the deep sea many small fishes which by their wits baffled their pursuers, a thing which they could not have done by their strength."

TEXT CONTINUED FROM PAGE 68

by two female monsters, the Scylla of the rocks and the Charybdis of the whirlpool.

And so some of the argosies foundered, usually along the littoral, often near port; and their wondrous cargoes subsided to the sea floor, to be slowly overlaid by the centuries of silt and sea wrack. How many do the wrecks number? No one knows; but anyone can fairly conclude that the whole pantheon of antiquity lies here, awaiting only a chance summons. A half-dozen great works have been recovered already, and the resting places of another few have been guessed. This much knowledge permits the categorical statement: Along the indented coastline of the Aegean, the Tyrrhenian, and the Ligurian Seas there is the greatest museum of antiquities in the world.

If until now this rich repository has usually yielded us its exhibits by chance—to the fisherman's random net rather than to the archaeologist's informed calculation—it begins to seem that this will not always be so. One day soon, underwater archaeological "digs" may be even more accurately plotted than is presently the case on land. And this prediction is possible because of man's very recent, and very tentative, attempts to master the ocean floor. Those bold and imaginative spirits, the free divers, equipped only with mask and aqualung, have in little more than a decade pinpointed some three dozen ancient wrecks off the coast of Provence in France and of Liguria in northern Italy. Moreover, thus far, their exploits are only skirmishes in man's struggle for conquest of the submarine world.

Curiously, this age-old struggle has some salient similarities to man's efforts to conquer the air. For as long as we

In his notebook Leonardo da Vinci sketched a webbed glove and a pair of flippers that look very much like those used by skin divers today.

have been stirred by dreams, we have sought to escape from our earth-bound state, to soar or plunge into those elements that seem to belong to birds or fish alone. Men began, naïvely enough, by strapping wings or fins to their bodies and daring the alien elements naked and alone. In the air such attempts, when they were persisted in, led to death; in the sea, when pursued to any significant depth, they first crippled and then likewise killed. The realm of the air was always the stronger temptation, for it was at least visible; a sharp eye could follow the flight of the swiftest bird; the challenge and the envy were constant. But what lay beneath the green-blue water? We could only guess; this tempered the challenge, and envy was tainted by fear.

Now it is a singular fact that, whenever we are faced with such an unknown, we prefer to believe that it must be horrible. There were alternatives aplenty, but men decided that the sea was a place of maelstroms and monsters: it was a hostile and vengeful force that swallowed whole cities, like the fabled Is, whose bells can still be heard by Breton sailors, tolling in the deep; a cavernous abyss that engorged entire continents, like the fabled Atlantis. Perhaps it was not invariably unsmiling, but then its charms were treacherous like those of the Sirens who were still, late in the fifteenth century, believed to be luring handsome youths to their destruction.

Alexander the Great, king of Macedonia, never explored the sea; or, if he did, the historians of his time ignored the matter. But he was a hero, superhuman; and so in the Middle Ages the tale grew that once he had caused himself to be lowered into the sea in a barrel made of glass. When he emerged from the deep he announced, "That world is damned and lost"—and man continued to shun the depths. His supposed experience could be used to justify our timidity: if one so brave as Alexander feared the seas, who would dare them?

What fearsome serpents, what monstrously clawed lobsters, what vast and hideously tusked walruses did not lurk below? There was the leviathan, the philosophers assured us, a beast huge enough to cause the tides to ebb by swallowing and to rise by spewing forth. There was the kraken, the back of which was "about an English mile and a half in circumference"; and the brute was taken so seriously that the Swedish naturalist Linnaeus, the father of biological taxonomy, credited its existence, classifying it in the first nine editions of his *Systema Naturae* under the grandiloquent name of *Microcosmus marinus*. And who can flatly say that, like the scaly serpent of Loch Ness, such prodigies are not still cradled in the blackest abysses of the sea?

Nevertheless, there were always a few men venturesome enough to plunge into the unknown: those who earned their bread by diving for pearls, for sponges, for coral, or for sunken treasure; and those who, in wartime, found patriotism sufficient to overcome their dread. Military divers, according to Thucydides, served both Athenians and Spartans effectively in the Peloponnesian Wars; Arrian tells how divers thwarted Alexander's siege of Tyre; Livy has an account of a treasure recovered by professional divers; and Lucan, in his poem celebrating one of Caesar's naval battles, speaks of a Phocaean diver who was employed to free anchors "whose iron teeth had bitten too deeply into the sands."

Progress was slow: a first rudimentary diving bell in the sixteenth century, a first primitive underwater vessel in the seventeenth. In the eighteenth, men were still clumping along in the shallow waters, clad in prudent armor; not until early in the nineteenth century were the first reasonably efficient diving helmet and suit contrived.

And now once again the parallel between conquest of sea and conquest of air can be drawn. For while in recent times increasingly complex machines have been invented for the conquest of either element—leading to supersonic airplanes and space projectiles on one hand, and to bathyscaphes and fission-powered submarines on the other—all at once, at the height of this technological ingenuity, man is reverting to his original naked aloneness. In the air the United States Navy is developing an apparatus that will enable a man to fly by himself, like a latter-day Icarus, equipped with nothing more than a small atom-powered motor no bigger than a knapsack. And in the sea such pioneer skin divers as Jacques-Yves Cousteau, Frédéric Dumas, and Phillippe Tailliez have revealed that the silent underwater world, far from being frightful, is a realm of enchantment and delight. Thanks to the aqualung and the underwater mask, this world has been opened to us all.

Here is a drama. The stage is set: it is the Mediterranean, ideal from the point of view of the free diver, for its waters are clear, warm, and almost tideless, and great numbers of its wrecks lie less than thirty fathoms deep. To the Romans it was Mare Nostrum, "Our Sea"—at first simply because it was their constant sheath, glittering blue in the morning sunlight when they awoke and velvety black at night; later because they could claim ownership by right of rule over all its shores. But today people all over the world can call it Our Sea by right of cultural inheritance. So much that is part of our daily lives was first fashioned around its rim: our alphabet, our arithmetic, our religions; our first perceptions of what is useful and what is beautiful and what is eternal.

The unities are respected on this stage where they were, indeed, first expounded. The past, much of it yielded up by the sea, serves to show that the actors of yesterday were not very different from those of today. There is the port official, bossing an office of clerks who turn out a never-ending stream of paper work and build up voluminous files: we can recognize his hand behind a conscientiously filled-out cargo manifest from 250 B.C., with its detailed list of wines, oils, honey, vinegar, dried figs, nuts, seeds, cheese, venison,

This underwater warrior appeared in the 1532 edition of Vegetius' De Re Militari. *His equipment does not seem to include a breathing apparatus.*

wild boar meat, goat meat, and sponges. There is the greedy venture capitalist: we can deduce him from the wrecks of merchant ships that foundered because they were overloaded. There is the disdainful, purse-proud conqueror: we can trace his swaggering path through the Athenian agora as he traffics for art objects that will embellish his villa back home.

And there is the chatty journalist: "Fishermen of Methymna," he writes, "having cast their nets into the sea, drew them in and discovered a head carved from the wood of the olive tree." But this is no Associated Press stringman filing his copy from the island of Lesbos; this is Pausanias writing in the second century, and he goes on: "The head seemed to be that of a god, but it was a strange god, unknown to the Greeks. Wishing to know whether the head was that of a mortal hero or of a divinity, the citizens of Methymna consulted the Pythian oracle, which ordered them to revere Dionysus Phallen. Preserving their find, the inhabitants of Methymna made it the object of a cult and sent a replica to the temple of Delphi."

As the centuries rolled on, there must have been many other ancient gods and heroes dragged up from the blue museum; most of what was found was either tossed back again or melted down for scrap. Not until the nineteenth century did the fisherman begin to look upon such a haul in his net as potentially valuable. An excellent Apollo of the fifth century B.C., found in the Strait of Piombino off

The stateliest pleasure domes in history, without much doubt, were two barges which Caligula built on Lake Nemi near Rome. At the height of a revel, some say, the mad emperor ordered them sunk with all guests aboard. At any rate they rested on the bottom for nineteen centuries until Mussolini drained

Elba, reached the Louvre more than a century ago; a Poseidon as old, which had been lying in the shallow water of Livadhostro Bay off central Greece, was taken in 1898 to the National Museum at Athens; and there were a few other miscellaneous antiques. But since archaeology itself was not developed as a science until about 1850, it is not astonishing that the first underwater dig of any consequence did not occur until 1900.

In the spring of that year two caïques (small Mediterranean cutters), homeward bound from a sponge-diving expedition in Tunisian waters to their island of Syme, in the Dodecanese, were blown off course by a gale that drove them to seek harbor at Antikythera, a barren islet midway between Crete and the southern tip of Greece. The Symiotes have for generations been accounted the most daring and skillful of sponge divers; they were lying in strange waters; why not see if there were any sponges here? Fisherman Elias Stadiatis slipped on his helmet suit and clambered overside. Nine fathoms down he was astounded. He was amid a company of outsize bronze and marble figures lying sprawled in the sand and sea muck. An arm reached out to him; he clutched it, wrenched it free, and brought it up to prove his story.

The commander of the expedition, Demetrios Kondos, himself an old master diver, confirmed the presence of an ancient shipwreck. Salvage work at that depth was exceedingly difficult: his six divers could work no more than five minutes at a time, and that only twice a day. They were

harassed by wretched weather, the sea floor where they strained to secure cumbersome, slithery marbles with stiff ropes was steeply pitched, and their equipment was primitive. Two of the men were permanently crippled, and one died during the nine months they toiled. "Yet," said Professor George Karo of the German Archaeological Institute at Athens, "these illiterate fishermen, totally ignorant of archaeological techniques, treated the finds with quite remarkable care and delicacy. . . . Even pottery and glass vases had been brought up intact."

Among the finds were parts of a half-dozen bronzes, two fifth-century B.C. statuettes, and one superb bronze larger than life, a work of the fourth century B.C., portraying—whom? Perseus? Paris? Hermes? No one can be sure; and so it is simply called the "Ephebos of Antikythera." The marbles fared less well. There were two dozen of them, and for two millennia shellfish and sea water had been at work on them. "They look like lepers in advanced stages," wrote Karo sadly. "It is enough to make you weep," remarked the great Hellenist, Theodore Reinach, "to look at that group of statues, many of which are no doubt original Greek works, stolen by the infamous Romans." But then he added, thoughtfully, that had it not been for the "infamous Romans" and a calamitous shipwreck, the statues, leprous or not, would not be preserved today.

The find at Antikythera stirred the hopes of archaeologists and art antiquarians everywhere; but where was the money to push the search? Since there was none, the excitement

the lake and uncovered the hulls (above, left). Of the treasures recorded by contemporary writers, only a few pieces were found, like the bronze Medusa head and lion head above. The reconstruction of the barge, with its temple of the divine Caligula, is based partly on chronicles and partly on the artist's imagination.

died down, until the lightning might strike again.

It struck off Mahdia, on the northeast coast of Tunis, in 1907. This time another Greek sponge diver, prowling twenty fathoms deep three miles offshore, saw "something like cannon" half-buried in the sand. They were marble columns; and scattered about lay statuary, vases, bronze candelabra. The diver kept his discovery secret, but presently the Tunisian authorities noticed that some singularly rare items were on sale in the shops of Sousse and Sfax. When they found out what was afoot, the authorities took over and were lucky enough to land a Maecenas in the shape of an American millionaire, James Hazen Hyde, who undertook to help finance the dig. (The French and Tunisian governments also covered part of the cost.) Before long, divers brought up enough to fill six rooms of the Alaoui Museum in Tunis, but there was still enough left at the spot to interest Captain Cousteau, forty years later, and indeed amateur divers still occasionally come up with interesting trifles—a bit of statuary, a broken vase, an ornamented piece of a chair.

Then, in 1925, chance led a fisherman named Evangelos Leonidas, working from the island of Euboea, to drag his nets in the waters of the Gulf of Petali, off Marathon. He was aghast to find in them what seemed to be a bloated corpse. Indeed, "When the net was emptied," wrote R. Demangel, the director of the Ecole Française at Athens, "the women made the sign of the cross under the impression that they were looking at the black and swollen body of a

drowned man." But it was another bronze. The curators of the National Museum at Athens paid Leonidas a bounty of 300,000 drachmas (a little less than $2,000 at the time) in the hope that news of his windfall would lead other fishermen to turn such hauls over to the government. They soaked the statue in distilled water for eight months in order to resolve its scabs of molluscs; and they were at length able to exhibit a magnificent bronze (see page 74), generally called the "Marathon Boy." Some believe it to be a statue of Hermes, and attribute it to Praxiteles, who would have

TEXT CONTINUED ON PAGE 76

OVERLEAF: *The Aegean yielded these two magnificent bronze statues from the greatest age of Greek sculpture. The youth on the left-hand page, found off Marathon in 1925, dates from the fourth century B.C. His head is encircled by a narrow band, with a curving tongue at front, as worn by competitors in the Palaestra and their god, Hermes. The eyeballs are of white stone, the irises of yellow glass-flux with black rims around the missing eyeballs. Experts speculate that the figure may represent Hermes and the sculptor may have been Praxiteles. On the right-hand page is the heroic-size statue of a god recovered off Cape Artemisium in 1926. Whether it is Zeus or Poseidon, god of the sea, experts cannot decide. This is one of only two surviving examples of the great bronze divinities of the fifth century B.C. that stood in the temples of Greece.*

TEXT CONTINUED FROM PAGE 73

carved it in the third quarter of the fourth century B.C.

This find was, again, purest luck; Leonidas was unable to say where he had been when the bronze tangled in his nets. But in Athens, Professor Karo was determined to take advantage of the next such haphazard haul. In 1928 he engaged the interest of Alexander Benakis, a wealthy Greek patron of art, who provided $2,500 worth of modern diving equipment. And, the Fates intervening, some sponge divers at once brought up a larger-than-life bronze arm from the sea off Cape Artemesium, the northernmost tip of Euboea. Promptly Karo hired a team of divers and, with the assistance of the Greek Navy, set to work. The current off the Cape was strong; the divers had to work in twenty fathoms, 600 yards from the coast. Yet they did not deign to use Karo's newfangled diving equipment. One man refused even the precaution of underwater decompression: he shot up from 120 feet, laughed at his cautious teammates, and fell dead.

It was an ill omen; but fortunately the divers had already brought up the bronze body to fit the arm, and they had rescued as well a bronze race horse with his exercise boy. "The facts," Professor Karo mourned later, "simply cried out for intensified research, [but] nothing could be done." For money had run out, and so had the divers' enthusiasm; but Karo could console himself in the knowledge that he had resurrected the finest Greek bronze ever found, a work, as he said, "worthy of the great Phidias himself." (See page 75.)

Whom did the figure represent? The first experts, moved no doubt by a respect for the poetic niceties, concluded it was the god of the sea, Poseidon. Since then, however, a quorum of experts has decided it is Zeus, and a cast of it so identified stands in the lobby of the General Assembly of the United Nations in New York. But the attribute that would decisively identify it—either a trident or a thunderbolt held by the upraised arm—is still twenty fathoms deep off Artemesium; without it, who shall decide, when doctors disagree?

In the winter of 1930-31 another ancient wreck was found, this one turning up in the main basin of the harbor of Piraeus, the seaport for Athens. A dredge grated on the charred hull of a transport vessel that had apparently caught fire and sunk just as it was departing for Italy, laden with a cargo of marble reliefs. By the standards of the Periclean Age, they were inferior stuff—commercial work of the second century A.D., hacked out for the export trade—but one set of reliefs pointed a moral. In our conception of Greek art, we have had to lean heavily on Roman copies, which are often many times removed from the real thing; even a fragment of an original can, then, shatter or support a hypothesis. In this case, the marbles gave us a far clearer conception of one of Phidias' lost masterpieces, the colossal statue of Athena carved in ivory and gold for the Parthenon and unveiled in 438 B.C. The sculptor had used Athena's

Roman sea trade at about the year A.D. 2 is depicted in this bas-relief. On the stern of the ship at left, the captain offers a sacrifice upon passing the lighthouse at the entrance to the harbor of Ostia. At right,

shield to depict a battle between Greeks and Amazons, but all we know of the scene came from a tiny copy now in the British Museum. On these reliefs from Piraeus are figures thought to be copies from those Phidias put on Athena's shield in the original size. They certainly afford a more vigorous idea of the master's work.

All these discoveries, like the Demeter, were accidental. But with the development of the Cousteau-Gagnon aqualung a new period of sea-digging has been inaugurated.

From an archaeological standpoint the invention has not proved an unmixed blessing. Difficulties were bound to arise when the sea floor was all at once encumbered with hundreds of enthusiastic amateurs eagerly snatching at every artifact that came within their sight. Nor has the situation been improved by the various restrictions imposed by nations as to the disposal of artifacts found in their waters. A lively black market has sprung up, with the free diver supplying the shady dealer, and the shady dealer supplying the foreign collector. The only comfort is that a first-rate art object would be far too "hot" an item to be trafficked so; it very likely would be taken straight to the proper authorities. The black market exists for the relatively worthless item like an amphora that is one of a thousand, all alike; and it

76

partly broken away, is another ship with statues of Neptune, Bacchus, and the Emperor Augustus. From the wrecks discovered by divers, archaeologists are now tracing the trade routes of the ancient world.

has its ludicrous overtones, as when an amphora is studiously smuggled past an indifferent customs official, is thereafter triumphantly insured by its bemused owner for something like one hundred thousand times its real value, and is finally presented by him to the flabbergasted curator of an art museum, who is thoroughly aware of its worthlessness.

In the main, however, the free divers have been of inestimable value to underwater archaeology. Along the French Riviera they have banded in clubs, and the clubs' officials have imbued their members with a sense of responsibility toward the wrecks of antiquity. Their proudest discovery up to the time of writing is of an Etruscan wreck that dates from the sixth century B.C., and in the course of resurrecting their finds the free divers have afforded the scholars significant insights into the character and extent of ancient maritime trade. But if, thanks to this new, unclothed technology, we now know more about the size and seaworthiness of ancient merchant vessels, about the copper the Romans mined and the food they sent their occupation troops, about the spread of viticulture and the slowly changing shape of the jars in which the wine was carried, about the kind of anchors used by the mariners of antiquity and their apotropaic charms, still it must be admitted that the free divers

have not yet presented us with any treasures of art to be compared with those that have come our way by chance. Why is this?

In part, of course, it is a matter of the roll of the dice. As it happens, the area of the Mediterranean most thoroughly combed so far by the free divers embraces trade routes over which precious little art traveled. There was no strong motive to transport sculpture to Gaul. The ancient gods are housed in the more easterly halls of the blue museum and there await enough money to finance their discovery.

Everything else is ready: the knowledge as to where to search, the technique for searching, even the conviction that the search will be rewarded. But financing is difficult. Money is stubborn: it looks to a return. When the search is simply for more money below—bullion, negotiable treasure —no comparable difficulty exists. Thus £300,000 was raised in 1687 from a Spanish galleon; the *Thetis*, fifty feet down off Rio de Janeiro, yielded treasure worth $390,000 in 1831; in 1885 another $250,000 worth of treasure was salvaged from the *Alphonso XII*, sunk at a depth of 162 feet; $25,000,000 was taken from the *Laurentic* after the first Great War; in 1928 $6,000,000 in gold came from the *Egypt* in the Bay of Biscay; and in 1941 $5,500,000 in gold was raised from the *Niagara*, 416 feet down off New Zealand.

But an Aphrodite by Praxiteles? A Zeus from the workshop of Phidias? No price could be put upon them, and even if one could, they would not be for sale. Since the last war all the countries of the eastern Mediterranean have adopted the same ground rules: archaeological treasures, no matter by whom found or at what expense, belong to the nation in whose land or whose territorial waters they are found. They will be accepted with gracious thanks to the finder. In such circumstances, there is no clamorous scramble to search.

Public funds appear to be the solution, since only the public cares about the treasures of art that await recovery. Most modern nations—the United States is a notable exception—allot a share of their budgets for archaeological research. It is a very modest share, in most cases; Fernand Benoit, the Director of Historical Antiquities in Provence, France, has been overheard remarking tartly that his government earmarks less than $50,000 a year—"the equivalent of the government subsidy for holiday festivals"; but it is better than nothing.

In the meantime, archaeology is a patient discipline. Its scholars recognize that what rests below is quite safe in the blue museum. What has waited for two millennia can wait for another generation, or even for two.

And any day the lightning of discovery may strike again.

C. W. Ceram's place as a writer on archaeology has been established by his books Gods, Graves and Scholars *and* The Secret of the Hittites. *Peter Lyon, here collaborating with him, writes widely on historical and contemporary subjects and contributed "When Man First Left the Earth" to the first issue of* HORIZON.

AN ARKANSAS BOYHOOD

An artist comes home to rediscover the world of his youth

"Imagine a modern day artist admitting to sentiment, that he loves a certain place, or that he loves people as much as paint; imagine a poet today writing of daffodils." So writes Carroll Cloar, a forty-five-year-old painter from Arkansas, who himself does admit to these enthusiasms and who has made them the basis of his very personal art. In his unusual paintings, Cloar has set down his memories of the private world of childhood in the southern small town where he grew up. He presents images such as a prim ghost in gingham standing at the end of a brass bedstead, a tree growing bottles, or a lonely child swinging on parallel bars at the edge of a deserted playground, and gives them homely titles such as *Story Told by my Mother* (*There was a Woman, and a Panther . . . and Something*).

Cloar was born and raised on a farm in Earle, Arkansas, a whistle-stop in the cotton bottom lands along the Mississippi. His interest in art began early, and after finishing college, he left for New York in 1936 to study at the Art Students' League. Thereafter his travels took him all over the world but seldom back to Earle.

Four years ago Cloar found himself in Europe. As he tells it: "I roamed about, very lonesome most of the time, until finally I realized that I hadn't really wanted to travel any more. . . . And with this realization came another—that there was no longer any place left in the world I wanted to go but home. . . . Belonging seemed terribly important to me; I did not realize, at the time, that I had always belonged to the land, my roots too deep for breaking."

And so Cloar returned to America and settled down to painting in Memphis, Tennessee, thirty miles across the river from his home town.

"I aim to stay," he says. "I have found everything I needed here." Far removed from dominant fashions in today's painting, he has particularly found himself.

GIBSON BAYOU ANTHOLOGY: "*When I was a boy I used to wander through Gibson Bayou cemetery picking dewberries. I got acquainted with all the people buried there and had known some of them in life. Cabe Smith, whom I never saw, was a favorite because he had died violently, in a gun fight. The girl on the right, in back, is Odor Hayes, who died young. I caught smallpox from her.*"

SELF ENCOUNTER: *"This painting,"* says the artist, Carroll Cloar, *"symbolizes the rediscovery of myself, my land, and my people. Considered from another angle: Sometimes I have come face to face with someone who might almost be me—a barefoot boy in a cornfield; a seventeen-year-old, pimple on his chin, hair pasted down, going off to college with a borrowed suitcase."*

MY FATHER WAS BIG AS A TREE *(right):* *"To me my father was a giant. He was big and far beyond, and I was never quite able to reach him."*

ALIEN CHILD *(below):* *"Even as a small boy I felt that I was, somehow, different from the rest of the family. A sickly child, I had turned to books, music, and drawing, unlike my brothers, and, since a sister on either side of me had died, I was left in a lonely age bracket and grew apart from the rest of the family. I often wondered if I was really their child. Had I been adopted? Had I been stolen from gypsies? Another of my fantasies was that I had been the surviving child of a beautiful young couple who had been eaten by panthers."*

Overleaf: THE GARDEN OF LOVE *(All the Little Girls had Brown Eyes):* *"My earliest reading had been a curious mixture of the Bible and Zane Grey, and, whereas I found some pretty exciting stuff in the Bible, Zane Grey's women were always pure and lovely. As far back as I can remember, I was always secretly in love with some little girl. She always had brown eyes."*

Peter Ustinov

British? *French?* *Russian?*

Director?

Playwright? *Actor?*

Boy Wonder?

By SERRELL HILLMAN

Peter Ustinov is a British citizen of Russian, French, German, Italian, and Spanish extraction, now resident in America, who has distinguished himself as an actor, playwright, director, linguist, monologuist, cartoonist, and mimic. He has a hard time with official forms. "You will notice," he points out, "that any form asking your profession leaves you more space to write your name than what you do. They only want you to put down one thing."

He adds: "I suppose that if Leonardo da Vinci were alive today he would be told by the art critics, 'Stop messing about with trying to fly and designing siege cannons; stick to your drawing.'"

Ustinov is perhaps the most versatile personality now active in the theater. He has written thirteen plays, of which the two most successful, *The Love of Four Colonels* and *Romanoff and Juliet*, have been produced on Broadway. The first starred Rex Harrison while the second starred Ustinov himself as the befuddled, bearded, bamboozling Prime Minister. (In London Ustinov starred in both.) Movie audiences have seen him in three major roles, most notably that of the cold, malevolent Emperor Nero in *Quo Vadis*. To the television public he is familiar as a mimic and wit on many shows. One of a rare species, he invites comparison with the few other examples of theatrical versatility ("an Orson Welles under control"; "a Noel Coward who never learned to comb his hair"). Like them, in an age of specialization he encounters a widespread prejudice that a man of many talents must also be a man of lesser talents.

Since 1942, when his first play, *House of Regrets*, was produced in London, Ustinov has been cursed with the critical tag "promising." Since then, he has had both successes and failures. British reviewers argue, with some justice, that he wins his battles but loses his wars. They have been inclined to rate him a boy wonder emeritus.

It remained for Ustinov's invasion of America in *Romanoff and Juliet* in 1957 to establish him as a household word and an unqualified success. Oddly enough, Ustinov's superbly funny performance in his play was not enough to accomplish the trick. When the play began to lurch and sag at the box office, Ustinov singlehandedly turned it into a hit, simply by making one appearance after another on television. Says John Mason Brown: "Ustinov turned to a supposed enemy and converted it into a friend. He made the new medium serve his purposes. He took the plasma of TV and pumped it into the theater. He used mass communication as a means of achieving the special communication of the theater—as if he had made the ocean run upstream, into rivers."

It became virtually impossible to turn on television without finding Ustinov. He might appear as a traffic policeman —first British, then French, then Austrian. He might do his own version of a mock opera by Mozart, mimicking not only the sopranos, contraltos, and tenors but the wood winds and strings. He might impersonate a customs official in five or more languages. (Ustinov is hilarious even in languages he doesn't know, as when he enacts a Russian-speaking Japanese.)

The television audience saw Ustinov's satirical impersonations on the Steve Allen and Jack Paar shows. He was wittily erudite on the upper-middle-brow program *The Last Word*. On *The $64,000 Challenge*, he reached the $8,000 plateau before being trapped on identification of the Shalimar Gardens. He tossed off quips on Ed Murrow's *Person to Person*, ("People only get to the top because they have no qualification to detain them at the bottom"). He starred in his own satiric tragedy *Moment of Truth* (a failure on the London stage) in which he played an aged marshal reminiscent of Pétain.

But his greatest triumph came in *The Life of Samuel*

Spanish? *Italian?* *American?*

German?

Linguist? *Cartoonist?* *Mimic?*

Walter Mitty? *Genius?* *Ham?*

Johnson on *Omnibus*. For this television play studded with Dr. Johnson's best sayings, Ustinov had to spend two hours gluing down the beard he grew for *Romanoff*, stuffing himself with padding, and making fast the five-piece plastic mask fashioned after Sir Joshua Reynolds' portrait of Johnson. The production was so realistic that when actor Theodore Tenley, playing Dr. Dodd, was "hanged," he actually blacked out on camera. But Tenley so admired Ustinov's performance that he wrote him, "I'd be glad to be hanged again." Ustinov wrote back in fine Johnsonian prose: "Sir, I believe that for the crime of playing with Ustinov, the death penalty would be too severe. But I shall include in my 'Dictionary' the definition of the word 'Dodd' as 'a man who would die more than once for his friends' (rare word and rarer person). Signed: Sam Johnson."

Ustinov would rather write than act in the theater. He writes in the bathroom—"It's the one door you can lock without offending anyone." However, Ustinov says that "even if I had all the time in the world, I couldn't write 2,000 words a day, like Maugham. I'll go for long periods of silence; then there'll be a click and they can't stop me."

He finds the theater frustrating and sees little of other actors "because I find their shop talk boring and I can't get excited over backstage gossip." No actor could be less temperamental, less preoccupied with his own role. Habitually late for everything, Ustinov arrives at the theater barely in time to dress and make up for his part, and he spends the intermissions listening to the radio, reading, or writing. He insists that he never writes himself into a part ("acting in one's own play is an invitation to schizophrenia"), although many who have seen him as the Wicked Fairy in *The Love of Four Colonels* and the General in *Romanoff and Juliet*—two enormously juicy, ideally suited parts—are inclined to be skeptical of the claim.

While giving the impression on television that he is having

As the General in *Romanoff and Juliet*

As Kattah in *The Egyptian*

the time of his life, Ustinov finds TV a strain. "In some ways," he says, "it's a more difficult medium than either the films or the theater. You have to be as relaxed as you are in movies, yet sustain your relaxation as you do in the theater." On the whole, he finds that acting in movies is the most satisfying medium of all: "You get it over with, you have days off, and you have a different problem to deal with all the time."

If Ustinov's life has been relatively simple and uncomplicated for so versatile a character, his ancestry is not. On the little finger of his left hand, he wears a gold ring with family crest dating from the time of Peter the Great. On his father's side were Russian landowners with vast estates. His great-great-grandfather, who died at the age of one hundred and eight, had two wives and twenty-five children and at his death left sixteen churches that he had built, along with 6,000 serfs and 150,000 acres. Ustinov's grandfather rejected the Russian Orthodox Church and fled into exile in Württemberg, where he became a German subject. On his mother's side, Ustinov's ancestors originally were French. A Russian strain was introduced when one of these forebears became chef at the court of Czar Paul I, in 1794. Ustinov's maternal grandfather was Russian court architect; his maternal grandmother, besides bearing eight children, found time to run a huge caviar fishery.

Ustinov's journalist father, Iona (Klop) von Ustinov—the family was given a baronial title in Germany—and his mother, Nadia Benois, met in St. Petersburg during the

As the Wicked Fairy in *The Love of Four Colonels*

Bolshevik Revolution. Klop had gone there to find *his* father, who bravely but rashly had left Württemberg to assist his old friends in their time of trouble. By the time Klop arrived, the elder Ustinov had died of starvation. Klop and his bride got away on a refugee train and went to The Hague. They moved on to London when Klop received an appointment as press attaché at the German Embassy there, and Peter was born a few months later.

The realization that only by chance was he born in England made Ustinov an antinationalist from the beginning. His many racial associations have intensified his belief in international fellowship—the dominant theme of *Romanoff and Juliet*. His father's sister is married to an Egyptian; one of his father's brothers is married to a Canadian; another, to an Argentinian. Ustinov himself first married an English girl, and then a French Canadian who also has Irish and Indian blood.

Six weeks after Ustinov's birth, his deeply religious maternal grandmother, then living in Cairo, insisted that he be

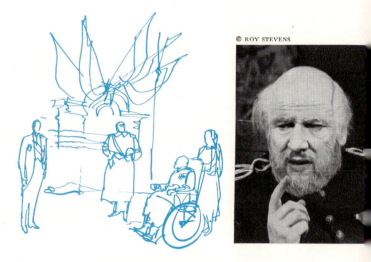

As the aged marshal in *Moment of Truth* on *Omnibus*

baptized a Lutheran in water from the River Jordan. Ustinov's agnostic father reluctantly agreed to meet her halfway, at Stuttgart, to which city he transported Peter in a basket lent by the White Heather Laundry. River Jordan water from a hot-water bottle was dripped onto Peter and he duly became a Lutheran. The ceremony had no lasting effects. Today Ustinov declares: "I believe people should be judged by their behavior rather than by what they think. I prefer an agnostic who helps an old lady across the road to a theologian too busy with his religion to notice that she wants to cross. Religion is temperamental and climatic—I can't imagine a Norwegian on a pilgrimage to Rome; he wouldn't look right or feel right."

The boy had an easy and peaceful upbringing. His mother, an amateur painter, brought home artists for dinner; his father brought journalists, diplomats, exiles—all of whom sharpened Peter's instinctive ability to catch personality, voice, and attitude. One of his earliest recollections is

that of appearing entirely nude, before his parents' friends, to impersonate Prime Minister Bonar Law. He quickly manifested the talent for drawing that today enables him to dash off lightning-fast sketches of politicians, artists, and friends. At the age of nine he outraged his mother's cook, who doubled as her model, by proposing to paint her in the nude.

As Dr. Johnson in *The Life of Samuel Johnson* on *Omnibus*

entered the London Theatre Studio and spent two years there. Among the practice parts he played was that of a golden-tressed siren attempting to seduce Ulysses as his ship passed an island. Ustinov's speaking part consisted of these words: "See, see, Ulysses, weary and wise." Ustinov, who even then was bulky, old-looking for his years, and anything but handsome, says he well understands Ulysses' refusal to linger.

"As an only child," says Ustinov, "I soon settled into a small bachelor existence. It gave me self-reliance, but at times it was lonely. I had another difficulty to contend with: I wasn't English. Oliver St. John Gogarty used to say that the only way to make the English treat you as an equal is to treat them as superiors."

Ustinov is particularly acerb about British education. "English adolescence," he says, "runs from first childhood to second childhood without a break. With Englishmen of fifty, one can see exactly what they looked like at four. With Italians, on the other hand, one can see at four what they'll look like at fifty."

His family managed to send him six years to Gibbs, an exclusive day school in London. There, Peter was subjected to the ultimate rigors of orthodoxy in education. Asked in one class to name the greatest composer, he said, "Mozart." When he was crisply informed that the correct answer was "Bach," he muttered, "Well, Beethoven was as good as Bach." For this display of independent thinking, he was given one hundred lines.

At thirteen Ustinov progressed to Westminster, where schoolmates called him "Used enough." He still flinches at the memory of parading to school in hard collar and top hat, carrying a furled umbrella. "The school prospectus," he says, "explained that the reason for the umbrella was to make a clear distinction between schoolboys and bank messengers."

At Westminster he was the traditional Sensitive Young Man of English fiction: good at English, miserable at science and mathematics, hopeless at cricket and rowing. Once he was kept in as punishment for writing a play about an American gangster. Another time, he says, he received a report stating that he showed great originality which should be curbed at all costs. He left abruptly in his third year, having decided that he couldn't possibly pass his final examinations. ("And I couldn't today.")

Ustinov's father wanted him to be a lawyer. "I said," recalls Ustinov, "that I'd become an actor instead. It was the same profession, but less dangerous." Accordingly, he

At nineteen Ustinov got a job at The Players' Theatre, doing a comic skit called *The Bishop of Limpopoland*, which dealt with an Anglican bishop who had been in Africa so long that he couldn't imagine anyone not being able to understand native dialect. It was based on a lecture given by an aged and quavering clergyman at Westminster on the true faith of Somaliland. Ustinov was an instant hit. Even then he had the unfailing ear and immediate perception of a Danny Kaye. Like a bent Coney Island mirror, he was able to take a personality or voice and, for comic purposes, throw it just slightly out of focus.

Thereupon Ustinov worked in a repertory theater, then in other London revues. By now he had added to his repertoire a Russian professor jealous of Chekhov, addled generals, decayed diplomats, and an Austrian *Lieder* singer whom he called Madame Liselotte Beethoven-Finck. Meanwhile, he wrote his first full-length play, *House of Regrets*. He waited two years for it to be accepted and produced.

In January, 1942, Ustinov became a private in the British Army. He was probably one of the most unmilitary types ever to enter the service. "I got away with it, though, by making people laugh. I looked so lost that sergeants started smiling every time I tried to fasten a button." The Army

CONTINUED ON PAGE 137

As Nero in *Quo Vadis*

MGM

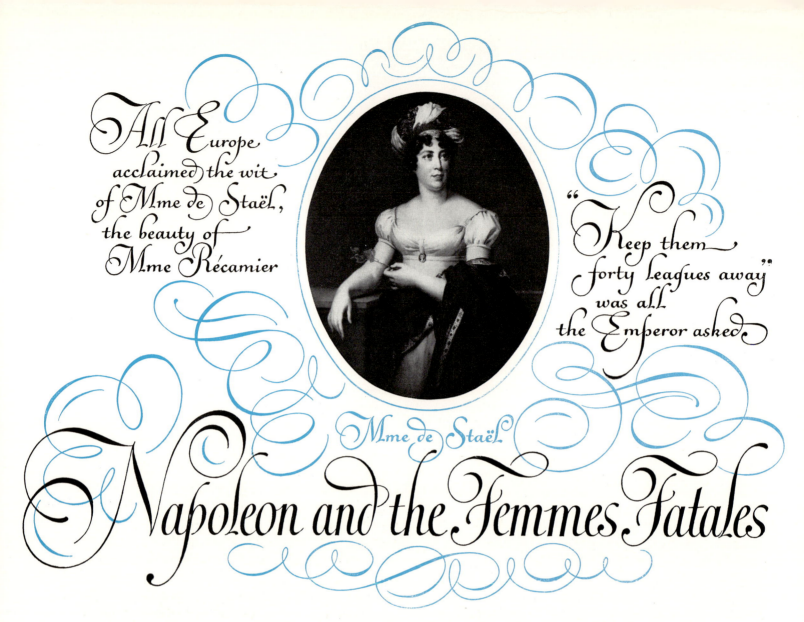

All Europe acclaimed the wit of Mme de Staël, the beauty of Mme Récamier

"Keep them forty leagues away" was all the Emperor asked

Mme de Staël

Napoleon and the Femmes Fatales

On the eve of Napoleon's *coup d'état* on November 9, 1799, a thirty-three-year-old Frenchwoman, Mme Germaine de Staël, journeyed hastily from her château at Coppet in Switzerland to Paris. The estranged wife of a minor Swedish noble and the daughter of the illustrious Jacques Necker (who had served both Louis XVI and the Revolution in its early days as minister of finance), Mme de Staël was already known in the capitals of Europe. Author of a novel and a much admired book on Rousseau, mistress of important *salons* in Paris and Coppet, active in post-Revolutionary politics and renowned for her brilliant wit and conversation, she was convinced that Bonaparte, with the wide vistas opening before him, could use some guidance from her. The fact that Napoleon disliked her heartily was something she could never appreciate; she believed to the end that a half hour's audience with him, in which she would do all the talking, would bring him around. As a true lover of liberty, an Anglophile, a proponent of constitutional government, an early advocate of free love, and one of the first to hail the

oncoming romantic movement in European letters, she stood for all that Napoleon opposed. When he disdained her, she set about expounding these ideas in print, only to find her writings banned and herself banished from Paris.

In the outside world, where Napoleon's armies inspired fear and hatred, Mme de Staël was much admired. Her château at Coppet became a mecca for the intellectual elite of Europe. Within the borders of France, however, the price of Mme de Staël's friendship was high; for her beautiful friend, Mme Juliette Récamier, it also meant proscription from Paris and the open disfavor of the Emperor.

Married at fifteen to an elderly Parisian banker, Mme Récamier had a respect and affection for her husband, but her relationship with him, as well as with all but two of her many admirers throughout her life, was no more than a close friendship. This left her free to pursue her role as the epitome of feminine charm and attraction; for the fashionable society of the Bonaparte era, she was the ideal woman of her age. In her twenties, she was doggedly pursued by

Napoleon himself; in her thirties by Prince Augustus of Prussia (who never again gave a thought to another woman); in her forties, two of Mme de Staël's chief lovers defected to her; and in her fifties, she inspired a great love in the breast of the famous essayist Chateaubriand. Only to Prince August and Chateaubriand was she moved to return any true feeling of her own; the rest of her sentimental energies were absorbed in a demanding attachment to Mme de Staël.

The emerging romanticism of the nineteenth century embraced the grand alliance of these contrasting women: the one so pure, gentle, and unattainable; the other so tempestuous, dominant, and attainable. The fortunes of both were inextricably bound up with the star of Napoleon. As long as his pervading influence was felt in Europe, the image of this persecuted pair lingered in the hearts of his enemies as a romantic ideal.

Their story is told in Maurice Levaillant's *The Passionate Exiles* (©1958 by Farrar, Straus & Cudahy, Inc.) from which the high lights that follow have been taken.

86

By MAURICE LEVAILLANT

It was full summer in 1798. Jacques-Rose Récamier, the Paris banker, had rented the Château de Clichy, a sumptuously furnished summer house that had once belonged to Louis XIV, for the hot weather. In his speedy calash he came only to dine and to sleep, but his young wife was happy there. Because of the proximity of this smiling village to Paris, her friends were easily able to visit her, and M. Récamier often brought guests to dinner. Thus it was that one summer afternoon she unexpectedly made the acquaintance of Mme de Staël, the daughter of the former French minister of finance, Jacques Necker. In one of the little-known pages of her scanty *Souvenirs*, she recalls the occasion:

One day, a day which marked a turning-point in my life, M. Récamier arrived with a lady whose name he did not mention and whom he left alone with me in the drawing-room while he went to join some people in the park. . . . Her toilet was curious; she wore a morning dress and a little hat decorated with flowers, and I took her for a foreigner. I was struck by the beauty of her eyes and of her glance; I could not account to myself for what I felt, but I was certainly thinking more of identifying her and appraising her than of making the usual conversational commonplaces, when she told me, with lively and penetrating charm, that she was truly delighted to know me, that M. Necker, her father . . . At those words I knew that she was Mme de Staël! I did not hear the rest of her words; I blushed and my confusion was very great.

I had just read her *Letters on Rousseau;* I had been much moved by reading them. I expressed what I felt more by my looks than by my words; she intimidated me and attracted me at one and the same time. One immediately felt in her a person perfectly natural in a superior nature. She fixed her great eyes upon me, with a curiosity full of benevolence, and paid me compliments upon my figure which might have seemed exaggerated and too direct, if they had not seemed to escape her, which gave her praise an irresistible attraction. . . . My confusion did me no harm; she understood it and said that she would like to see much of me on her return to Paris, for she was leaving for Coppet [in Switzerland].

FERNAND BOURGES, COURTESY *Life*

This famous portrait of Mme Récamier shows her in the classic gown which the painter Jacques Louis David derived from Roman sources and which became the model for the Empire style. The lady herself resented the rendering of her jet-black hair—of which she was very proud—as brown.

Jacques Necker, financial wizard who successfully served the regimes of both Louis XVI and the early Revolution, was the illustrious father of Mme de Staël.

Napoleon Bonaparte: portrait by David

Joseph Fouché, intriguer and head of Napoleon's secret police, was the reluctant instrument of the imperial orders that exiled Mme de Staël from Paris.

At that time she had only made an abrupt appearance in my life, but the impression was vivid, and from then on I thought only of Mme de Staël, so strongly had I felt the effect of a nature so ardent and so strong.

At the time that she met Juliette Récamier, Mme de Staël's activity was prodigious. Besides literature, she was then occupied with politics; she took the risk of making herself suspect with the Directory, which twice ordered her out of Paris. She was of small stature, eager, impetuous, energetic, sometimes virile in character and bearing, and she exercised a natural ascendancy over the 21-year-old Juliette, a graceful girl but unfinished, expansive and timid by turns, uncertain in her tastes and affections, spoiled, lacking guidance from a husband who was too mature for her and was never more to her than a brother, and fundamentally worried at not having yet found her way in the world.

During the winter that followed their first meeting, the two women saw much of one another. It became a habit to invite them together. "Mind and beauty," people murmured on seeing them together. Placed at table between them, one man maladroitly voiced the formula by which he hoped to pay a double compliment: "Here I am, seated between mind and beauty!" he said. "Monsieur," Mme de Staël responded with mock modesty, "this is the first time I have heard it said that I am beautiful."

Was she ever really beautiful? Was she at least prepossess-ing until her thirtieth year, before precocious maturity thickened her figure and made her features heavy? Not in Gérard's portrait [shown on page 86], idealized and more or less official, posthumous and painted from memory. Mme de Staël is represented there as declaiming at Cape Miseno in the symbolical attitude of the heroine of her novel *Corinne.* Inspiration shines in her face, but her pose is affected, her costume theatrical, and her attitude doubt-less far removed from what her friends of happy days used to admire. A more vital portrait by Mme Vigée-Lebrun shows also a rather stilted and premeditated character, with Mme de Staël holding a lyre in her hands.

She is younger in Isabey's painting; her hair, gathered at the crown of her head in a ribbon, curls about her cheeks and falls to her shoulders. Her eyelids, slightly lowered over her black flaming eyes, her mouth half-open upon the whiteness of her teeth, her upper lip slightly raised, all suggest that the model was surprised in the middle of an animated conversation; the eloquent words seem still to hang on her bold mouth. This is certainly Mme de Staël exercising that kind of fascination to which all her listeners have given testimony.

It was something of this enchantment that Mme Récamier experienced in the early days of their relations. Listening to the magic words, she felt her soul catch fire with ardors of which she had had only the presentiment.

François René de Chateaubriand, French essayist and novelist, had a deep influence on George Sand and Flaubert and a long-lasting attachment to Mme Récamier.

Prince Augustus William of Prussia & Mme Récamier

Charles Augustin Sainte-Beuve, headstrong French literary critic, wrote sympathetically of the friendship between the two greatest women of Napoleon's era.

In turn, Mme Récamier taught Mme de Staël graces and refinements that until then had been rather foreign to the lady of Coppet. To this strong woman she taught the power of weakness and the charm of fragility; to this passionate woman she revealed the value of tenderness, the dignity of a desire that knows how to control itself and to wait, the modesty of certain silences, and the eloquence of certain smiles. Mme de Staël must often have profited by Mme Récamier's instruction. Writing to her young friend as her "angel," she said: "You produce a supernatural impression upon my mind. You are at the forefront of my life." And she showed an extraordinary affection blended with a trace of protectiveness and a peculiar tinge of respect.

While the first threads of this friendship between the two women were being woven, French destinies were reaching fulfillment. General Bonaparte suddenly landed from Egypt. Mme de Staël was at Coppet. Realizing the importance of the General's return at a critical moment in the fortunes of the government, she hurried back to Paris. At the last stage, at Charenton, she heard only one name on every lip, from the stableman to the postilion, from the townsman to the peasant and the lackey. This was the eve of Napoleon's *coup d'état*—what came to be known by the revolutionary calendar as the 18th Brumaire.

Faced with the new master, in the early days of the Consulate, Mme de Staël was torn between anxiety and admiration. The man of destiny was going to save the country, but what would be the price? What would become of liberty? She wanted to put him on guard against himself. What ecstasy it would be if in some measure she were his counselor and inspiration! She therefore sought every opportunity to meet him, "gazing at him intently" as if fascinated; but he passed her by. She "harried" him, as the *Mémorial de Saint Hélène* shows; for he had guessed her plan, and he had no need of an Egeria.

As a result of Mme de Staël's extensive political activity on behalf of elements hostile to Bonaparte, their relations were embittered from the early weeks of 1800. To defend herself in the unequal struggle, Mme de Staël had only the power of ideas and the brilliance of her mind. Twice in this first phase of the struggle she was to hope that her writings, by forcing the master's respect, would re-establish her in his favor. But her book *On Literature*, an original and fertile work which appeared in 1800, was denounced by the critics as trying to maintain what was now considered the dangerous spirit of the eighteenth century. *Delphine*, Mme de Staël's first novel, was no more fortunate; it had some success in Paris and elsewhere, but this itself irritated the redoubtable First Consul. In its secondary characters, malicious people recognized more than one notable personage of the consular regime. Such allusions displeased the supreme judge, and

CONTINUED ON PAGE 142

An Optical
Eruption
in Downtown
New York

Some of the startling visual images Nikolais achieves in his dances are recorded in this group of photographs. At top left, the masked heads of two girls appear before the representation of a winged creature in a composition entitled "Bird." When the stage lights up for the performance of "Noumenon," illustrated at top right, the audience sees an amorphous, terra-cotta-colored cloth, which moves upward and finally glows inside with light. Within this mysterious tent move dancers wearing cloth bags with which they make weird, changing shapes. The scene above is from a dance called "Paddles," and at left, in the composition "Garden," three girls with petals or wings attached to their bodies create along with a man bearing some resemblance to Pan a fantastic theatrical garden through a combination of movement and rich lighting.

Without reaching too far for a simile, it is possible to see a parallel between the style of dance developed in recent years by a New Yorker named Alwin Nikolais and the old-fashioned kaleidoscope. Anyone who has held one of the optical instruments to his eye and, twisting it, watched the shards of colored glass constantly shift position, changing hue and relationship to one another as they fall into each new alignment, would recognize their proximity to the ingenious and sometimes shocking visual images of Nikolais' work. Even to the experienced dance fan his art may come as a startling new dimension.

Heading the Playhouse Dance Company at New York's Henry Street Settlement, Nikolais has combined an intriguing set of ingredients. First, he sets up extraordinary lighting, rich in color and far more important than stage lighting often is. Second, he employs a sound track that produces an unusual, non-Western style of music—partly excerpts from such radical composers as John Cage and Alan Hovhaness, partly percussion arrangements composed or improvised by the Playhouse dancers themselves. Finally, he sometimes dresses his group of dancers in leotards from chin to heel, their faces painted like impersonal masks, or sometimes has them move, half-concealed, within some odd-shaped cloth bag that camouflages the human body altogether.

The key word in Nikolais' approach to his medium is "relationships." For the sake of comparison, we might say that the classic ballet exploits the dancer physically—using grace, speed, lightness, strength, or agility to convey beauty or to tell a story. Modern dance, on the other hand, exploits the dancer emotionally—projecting his or her personal feelings to the onlooker. Unlike either, Nikolais exploits the relationship of objects in space—or, in effect, creates patterns in much the same fashion as our kaleidoscope. Though he stems directly from the modern school, he has turned his back on personal emotion.

Nikolais' figures move in a curious realm of the imagination, often manipulating sticks, huge draperies, ropes, nets. Although there is plenty of expert movement in evidence, there is no high kicking or rapid turning. And although a genuine theatrical atmosphere prevails, there is no storytelling, no personal clash, no emotional breast-beating.

For each work, Nikolais creates a synthetic world. Into this he injects his dancers, leading them to improvise until they have achieved some relationship to the imaginative objects, sounds, and colors that surround them. Once they have done so, Nikolais begins to construct, with them and for them, a formal choreographic composition.

It is a new idea, not only for the dance but for the theater generally. Eventually Nikolais must imbue it with deeper human values if it is to become more than a fascinating kaleidoscope of moving figures, color, light, and sound; but even now it makes for stunning watching.

The Sport of Knights

By JAY WILLIAMS

The Dukes of Brittany and Bourbon confront each other caparisoned from top to toe for a joust with blunt swords.

The spirit of fair play entered civilization when the tournament changed from a brutal, deadly combat to a mimic war ruled by the laws of chivalry

About the middle of May in the year 1357, while the Duke of Lancaster was besieging the town of Rennes during the interminable series of wars between the English and the French, a young knight bachelor named Bertrand du Guesclin asked whether any Englishman would try a passage of arms with him. Accordingly, the battle was halted while a formal joust was held between Du Guesclin and Sir Nicholas Dagworth, consisting of three courses with spears, three strokes with axes, and three stabs with daggers. The two, according to the chronicler Froissart, "behaved most valiantly, and parted without hurting each other. They were seen with pleasure by both armies." When this chivalrous exercise was over, both sides rolled up their sleeves and returned to the grim task of war, having proved indisputably the existence in the world of a new principle—that of good sportsmanship.

That principle, which today entails (at least in theory) playing a game vigorously and yet courteously and either winning or losing gallantly, was the product of the knightly caste, and above all of its greatest sport, the tournament. In the development of this mimic combat from its rudest beginnings to its cumbersome decline, the history of chivalry itself may be traced. And the mark it left upon our culture was to manifest itself ultimately in such novel concepts as fair play and an intense respect for the rules of the game.

For the tournament was a game, essentially. A rather

rowdy game, certainly, but not much rougher than football or boxing, if a little more hazardous. It was a gallant sport suited to a society based upon personal prowess in warfare. It had rigid rules and methods of scoring, and between its earliest phase, when it was considered perfectly sporting to ride one's horse over a fallen opponent, and its latest, in which jousters were surrounded with safety precautions, there was as wide a gap as there is, say, between girls' hockey and the game played by certain tribes with the heads of their enemies.

One of the most common misconceptions about the Middle Ages is that the tournament was a murderous duel. Actually, it had many forms of which the joust, or spear-running, was but one, and that only occasionally to the death. More often it was what its name implies, a "turning," a kind of slow eddying of two bodies of fighters within a fenced playing ground called the lists. No one is quite sure just when this formal game began, although in all likelihood some form of military competition must have sprung up at about the time when a noble caste of horsemen emerged in society. The English, as they commonly do with things they enjoy but are ashamed of, spoke of it as a French invention, and not a few medieval writers believed that it was the brain child of a French knight, Geoffroy de Preuilly, who died about 1063. However, most scholars consider that while De Preuilly may have codified the rules of the tourney, the game itself probably came as the logical step from the training of young warriors, a training that began for most of them at the age of seven.

Youngsters destined for knighthood were taken from the

To the shrill notes of the trumpets, the gates of the city open wide to greet the procession of the judges who will officiate at the tourney. Behind the trumpeters ride the armor bearers draped in cloaks with the insignia of the judges. Next come the four sober judges in their rich

When the lord, or baron, arrives at his lodging in the town where the tourney will take place, he mounts a long board on the front of the house displaying his coat of arms and helmet insignia, as well as those of the contestants in his party. He then unfurls their pennants and banners from the upper windows. The Duke of Brittany's signs are on the left, the Duke of Bourbon's on the opposite side.

care of women and set at the tasks of pages, running errands and making themselves generally useful. By the time they were fourteen they began their training as squires, and in addition to absorbing a curriculum that would demolish all but the most determined of eagle scouts—it included the mysteries of serving at table, carving, pouring, care and management of hawks and hounds, grooming and breaking horses, hunting, sentry duty, and the repair and cleaning of arms and armor—they began an intensive course in the use of all knightly weapons. Not unlike infantry basic training, the course embraced scaling walls, vaulting and leaping while wearing a mail coat, and the handling of the lance, sword, axe, mace, and dagger as well as a variety of lesser arms. A wooden post was used for the practice of sword cuts, and riding at the ring and at the quintain were the methods of practice for the lance. The exercise at the ring is a sport still practiced in some southern states, although in America

out of the saddle, precipitating a serious fight between English and French that ended only when the Count surrendered to the King. After this a new rule was introduced prohibiting the laying of hands on an antagonist. A little later, following a riot in which some watching English yeomen chased a group of French knights out of the lists in protest over a decision, spectators were forbidden to carry arms, and no one was permitted to raise a fallen knight except his own squire, wearing his device for identification.

Generally the tournament, either in its form of the melee or mock battle, or the joust (a hand-to-hand encounter of two opponents), was carried out, in the words of Roger of Hoveden, "not in the spirit of hostility, but solely for practise and the display of prowess." The weapons were blunted swords, clubs, or lances fitted with flattened, ridged heads called coronals. Nevertheless, upon occasion, tourneys or jousts à outrance were fought with sharpened weapons.

One of the most famous of these was the so-called Combat of the Thirty in 1351. During a truce in the long war between Blois and De Montfort, thirty Bretons met a group composed of twenty English knights and ten Flemings and Bretons of the De Montfort party. Although technically a tournament, since it was held during a truce, it was fought bitterly and on foot. At one point De Beaumanoir, the leader of the French, croaked out a request for something to drink, and one of his followers replied, "Beaumanoir, drink thy blood, and thy thirst will go off." Many of both sides were killed, and this courteous engagement ended only when one of the French knights pretended to retreat, got to his horse, and rode down the exhausted English so that the

TEXT CONTINUED ON PAGE 105

red robes, each carrying a staff of office. They ride palfrey horses covered with insignia that reach to the ground, and each is led by a footman. Following the procession come the townfolk who will cheer for their favorite contestants. The illustration is from King René's book (see page 96).

generally it is preserved only in merry-go-rounds; it consists of attempting to catch a ring on the point of a spear while on horseback. The quintain was a pivoted wooden figure; if you struck it in the center your lance broke, but if you hit it anywhere else it spun round and cracked you on the back of the head as you rode past. From these games and exercises, it was only a step to riding against an actual opponent, and then to the practice of battle in a kind of mimic war— the tournament.

In its early period, in the twelfth and thirteenth centuries, the tournament, or tourney, was hardly a sport for lightweights. Quite apart from the perils of the melee itself, tourneys often ended in free-for-alls that involved the spectators as well as the combatants. In one tourney held by the Count of Châlons, in which King Edward I took part, the Count, a powerful man, tackled the King around the neck, but Edward managed to keep his seat and throw the Count

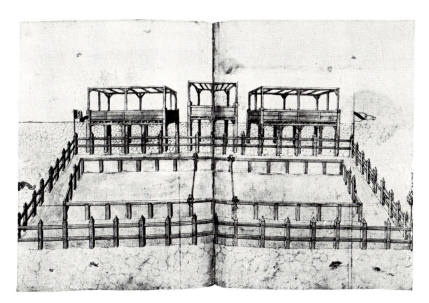

The lists are carefully described in King René's book. They should be one-quarter longer than wide, the height of a man, made of strong wood with two cross bars, the lower at knee height. An inner fence provides an alleyway to protect the manservants who are on foot and to guard the fighters from a press of spectators. For the most favored guests, boxes are built on stilts, facing the arena.

95

King René's Book

"Be my pulse calm, and my wits composed," cried an English traveler of the last century, "as I essay the description of this marvelous volume." The book upon which he had happened was *Le Livre des Tournois*, created by and for King René I of Anjou about the year 1450. Its meticulous documentation and sumptuous illustration make it not only the classic work on the medieval tourney but one of the most beautiful books in existence.

René was Duke of Anjou, Bar, and Lorraine, Count of Guise, Provence, and Piedmont, and, thanks to some vague claims of Crusader ancestors, titular king of Jerusalem, Naples, and Sicily. His joys were the tourney, with all its wonderful pomp and elaborate ritual, and the brilliant court of artists, poets, musicians, tapestry weavers, and armorers that he gathered about him. King René wrote the text of his book, detailing the maze of rules and rituals, while one or more artists—perhaps including the king himself—painted the illustrations.

The ceremonials are based on a tournament which took place in Bruges in 1392, between Jean, Lord of Gruthuyse, challenger, and the Lord of Ghistelles, defender. But the actual tournament described is imaginary, as are the coats of arms. For challenger, René chose the Duke of Brittany and for defender, his cousin, the Duke of Bourbon.

The Book of Tourneys begins with the chief herald presenting Brittany's challenge to Bourbon: "Very high and powerful prince and very revered lord, my very high and powerful prince and very revered lord, the Duke of Brittany, your cousin, sends me to you knowing fully your noble reputation for great chivalry and valor and in the spirit of love and friendship and with no ill intent, he requests and proposes to engage in a tourney and bout of arms before the ladies and maidens, in token of which he sends you his own sword."

The chief herald then sends invitations to the contestants on both sides, and the town begins to take on an air of pageantry. Shortly after the noblemen arrive at their lodgings, the blare of the trumpets announces the entry of the judges into the city. Then begin the great scenes of the tourney as depicted in the plates from King René's book, which appear on the following pages:

PLATE I—(facing page)—The chief herald displays the flags with the blazons of the judges.

PLATE II—The Review of the Helms. The ladies of the court are invited to the judges' cloister, where the helmets of contending knights are ranged for inspection. If any knight has offended a lady by word or deed, she touches his helmet. The judges review the offense, and if the knight is found guilty, he is punished.

PLATE III—The Start of the Tourney. The followers of Brittany line up on the left side of the lists, those of Bourbon on the right. In the middle, between the cords which separate the two, stands the knight of honor, the referee. His helmet has been taken by a valet to the ladies' box on the right, where it is held on a long lance for the duration of the fighting. On the left spectators' box is painted the motto: *Plus est en Vous* ("More is in you"). The four red-robed judges stand above the throng in the center; at their signal, the herald cries: "Cut the cords and start fighting at will."

PLATE IV—The Melee. Flank to flank, the horses mill around while the knights try to impress the judges and the ladies by their skill in combat. The artists' sense of humor is evidenced by the various helmets shown: an arm holding its own severed head, upturned legs shackled with chains, a bone-chewing dog, a red wheel, a flower pot. When the judges think the fighting has gone on long enough, the herald sounds retreat. The right side of the painting shows the pennant and banner carriers leaving the lists without waiting for their masters who are still busy fighting.

PLATE V—The Award to the Victor. After dinner the prize is given by a lady to the winner.

Le livre des Tournois du Roi René

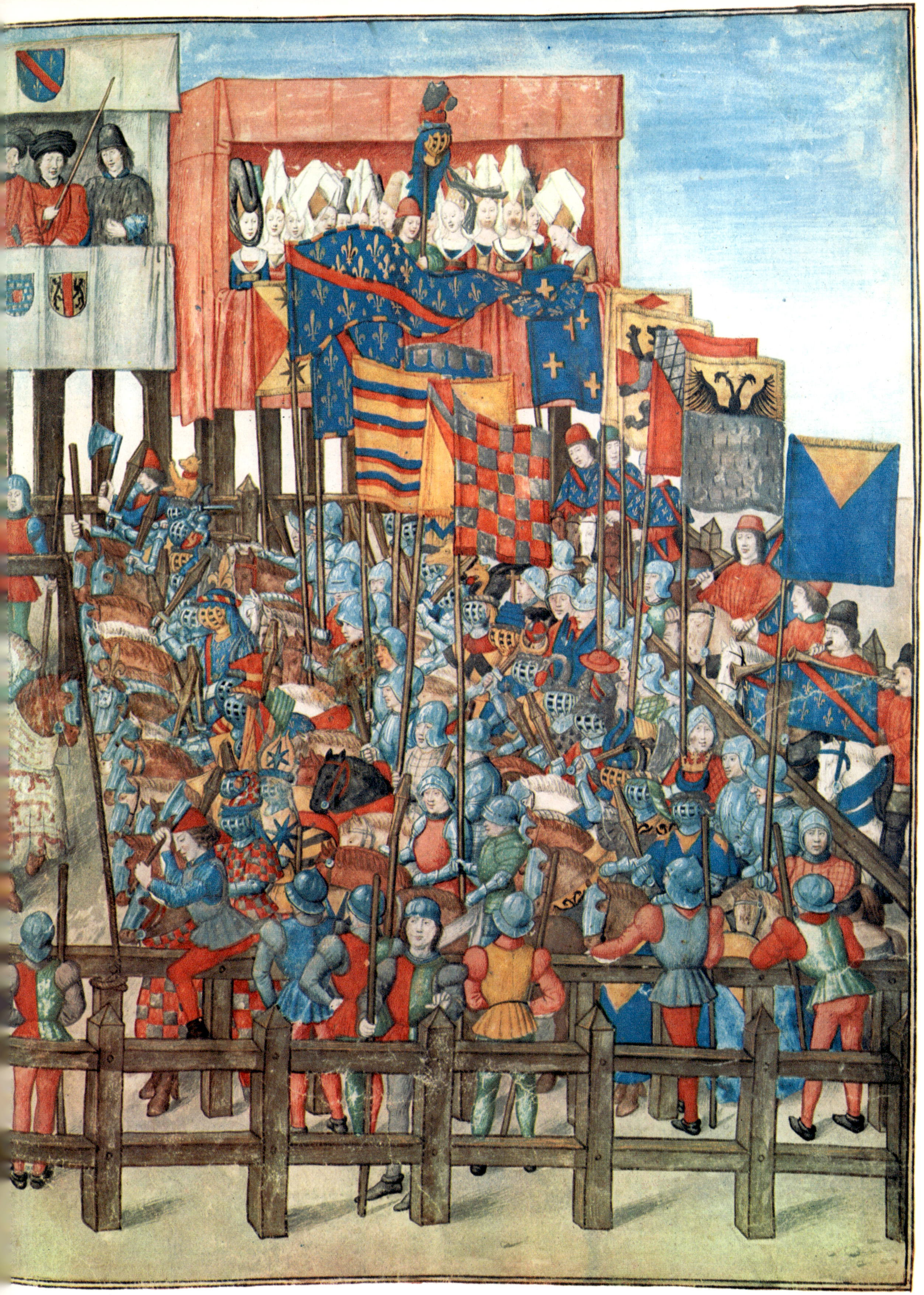

French could overpower them. The encounter was irritating to both sides, since the French counted themselves the victors and the English considered that they had lost by a cheat.

In general, however, tournaments were not combats to the death but joyous, if violent, celebrations, like the great tournament of Chauvency, a detailed account of which was set down in the form of a heroic poem by the trouvère Jacques Bretel. In it, the conduct of the game may be seen from beginning to end.

Chauvency lies on the left bank of the Chiers, in the department of the Meuse, and to this castle came many gentlemen and ladies on the feast of Saint Remy, the first of October, in the year 1285. Bretel came too, wearing new clothes and with his notebook ready. Among the nobles, he saw Louis de Looz, Count of Chiny, the giver of the tournament, with his lady and his son, Gérard; Count Henry III of Luxembourg, and a great array of knights from France, Lorraine, Luxembourg, Picardy, Hainault, and Flanders. So great was the attendance that some were lodged at Montmédy, which also belonged to the Count.

In all likelihood, the nearby villages and towns were thronged with countryfolk coming to see the sport. There were booths in the market places, jugglers and musicians (among them the renowned minstrel Henri de Laon, whom Bretel met), and the inevitable pitchmen who have been in operation with the same wares ever since the invention of crowds. Chauvency may have had permanent lists; if not, an area was marked out and enclosed within wooden fences, both to keep the combatants within bounds and to prevent interference from the onlookers.

Before the tournament began, the banners and crests of the entrants were displayed, and the judges viewed them with the lords and ladies of the court. The rules provided that if any lady complained of the conduct of a knight, he might be publicly beaten "so that his shoulders might well feel it" and barred from the game.

On Monday morning at Chauvency, when the stands and galleries had filled with ladies and knights, a series of jousts were held. Ferri de Chardogne "leaped into the saddle, his shield covering him, his helm laced, his lance in his fist," and trotted out "so hardily that all the earth trembled." He met the Lord of Bazentin and was overthrown, suffering a broken arm. The heralds, who acted somewhat as masters of ceremonies, announced each pair of contestants, and Bretel noted that they blamed the cruelty of the ladies for the fury of the combats, since men fought most bitterly under the eyes of love.

Altogether, seven spear-runnings were held on the first day, and ten on the second. Each day began with Mass and ended with a banquet (for those who had teeth left) and games and dancing. The ever busy Bretel remarked that toward midnight on the second day, Agnès de Florenville and Perrine d'Esch played the game of robardel, a kind of

medieval version of "post office."

But the great event for which everyone had been waiting, the tournament proper, began on Thursday. The guests lodging at Montmédy were designated the challenged, or "those without"; the challengers, or "those within," were the company lodging at Chauvency. Entering the lists, the two sides were drawn up facing each other across a rope— the Count of Luxembourg with Philip of Flanders at the head of his men, and on the other side the Count of Chiny with his son, Gérard, and Henri de Blâmont. All about the enclosure marshals and heralds were stationed to see that order was kept and the rules observed and to judge the conduct of the participants. At the command, "Let them go!" the rope was cut and the two sides met in a melee.

On every hand, says Bretel, war cries resounded; amid clouds of dust could be seen the colorful blazons on shields and the gleam of armor. Henri de Blâmont was surrounded by adversaries, and two of his knights rushed to his rescue; the Flemings, unable to throw him from the saddle, were driven off. Joffroi d'Aspremont, with one stroke of his sword, split the helm of the Lord of Bergues, broke its laces, and beat it from his head. Great blows were exchanged, "*Lambour!*" shouted one knight, "*Monjoie a Walerant!*" cried another; the ladies applauded, and the heralds shouted encouragement. At last, darkness fell; the chief marshal threw down his staff and ended the engagement. All then entered the castle where a feast had been prepared, and again there were games, dances, and song. Bretel himself was called upon to deliver a poetic sermon on the power of love, "and so delightful was the evening," he wrote, "that Friday came all too soon."

About 150 years later, perhaps the most celebrated account of how a tourney should be conducted was published by King René of Anjou, called The Good, who was an illustrator and writer of no mean talents. By his day, the tourney had taken on more of the air of a pageant. Special arms—helmets with wide-barred visors, blunted swords, and wooden maces—were sometimes furnished the participants by the giver of the game, and often a kind of theme was set with appropriate decorations and recitations. King René held many tourneys himself; at one held in 1449, the gallery for the ladies was a thatched cottage, the "Queen of the Tournament" was dressed as a shepherdess, and the shields of the challengers were hung on a "Tree of Honor." Somewhat earlier, King Edward III of England held a Round Table at Windsor—a tournament of great splendor in which the contestants took the names of Arthurian knights.

From the first, however, the presence of ladies was essential, so that, in the words of the chronicler Hardyng, "they might well and clearly see who jousted best for their Lady Love." Usually, a "Queen of the Tournament" was chosen, who presided along with the chief marshal and awarded prizes that might range from a chaplet to a horse, a peacock, or a lion of gold. In a famous tournament at Cambrai, where the King of France tilted with a knight of Hainault, the prize was a clasp of precious stones from the mantle of the Duchess of Burgundy; it went to the Hainaulter. Often ladies were seated in galleries constructed like miniature castles and called "The Castle of Joyous Gard" or "The Realm of Love and Beauty." In many cases, jousts were arranged for the honor of ladies, or for the performance of an act of chivalry, and some helmets had special clasps to which a "kerchief of pleasance" could be attached; this might be a scarf, a veil, or even a strip torn from a skirt.

While the melee, or tourney proper, might be fought with swords or maces, the emphasis in the joust was on the lance, the primary weapon of the mounted knight. Sometimes, however, the preliminary arrangements stipulated a certain number of passages with the spear, followed by three, five, or seven blows with several other weapons. It was not uncommon for a gentleman, in the very midst of a siege or a battle, to ask if there were someone on the other side desirous of accomplishing a feat of arms. In such a case, all action stopped, safe-conduct was given to both sides while everyone gathered to watch, and umpires as impartial as only members of the order of chivalry could be were chosen to arbitrate.

One such joust was held during the wars in Spain between an English knight, Sir John Holland, and a French challenger, Sir Renaud de Roye, who came to Spain on a safe-conduct. In this encounter three courses each were to be run with the lance, the axe, the sword, and the dagger. In both the first and second courses with the lance Sir Renaud broke his spear on the Englishman's helmet, which was counted a scoring point. Sir John also struck his opponent's helm, but the French knight had cannily tied on his head-piece with a single thong, which broke and allowed the helmet to be carried away each time it was struck. This could not be counted as a point. Sir John protested, but the umpire—in this case one of his own countrymen, the Duke of Lancaster—ruled that it was a perfectly legal trick and that Sir John might do the same if he chose, although he added, "For my part, were I in their situations, I would lace my helmet as tight as possible." The rest of the courses with all weapons were run with no harm to either of the knights. Sir Renaud received a favorable judgment on points and went home loaded with prizes and congratulations.

It was, perhaps, not so strange that even in a combat with sharp weapons neither of the contestants was seriously injured. For by this time armor had been thickened and strengthened to the point where a man might wear as much as 150 pounds of iron on his body. Extra plates were developed especially for the tourney as reinforcements for regular mail. By the middle of the fifteenth century these included hinged lance rests to hold the heavy spears, arm and elbow guards, and moulded pieces of steel called volant pieces, which were bolted on over the breastplate and the lower

part of the helm. All surfaces were carefully fluted or curved to make it as difficult as possible for a lance head to find lodgment. Armor was thickly padded inside as well, and an additional hazard arose in warm weather when men were known to faint or even die of heat inside their monstrous carapaces.

Other safety measures extended to the saddles, which were made without cantles so that a man could be unhorsed without having his thighs broken in the process. These were the ancestors of the modern English riding saddle, as the medieval war saddle was the prototype of our Western saddle. Horses were surrounded by padding and bolsters. The ground was covered with a layer of straw or tanbark to break the shock of a fall. The lance was made of light, strong but relatively brittle wood, such as fir or sycamore, which would splinter easily. At about the same time the tilting barrier was perfected. At first a cloth suspended on a rope, it later became a low fence running the length of the field to separate the two riders and prevent collisions; for in spite of the fact that horses carrying such a tremendous weight could go only at a slow trot and were in addition often blindfolded to prevent their shying, crashes sometimes occurred and might mean damage to an expensive mount.

In spite of all precautions, however, the tournament remained a sport for men who were not afraid of harm. Each year, as the craze increased, more precautions were added, attempts were made to limit the holding of tourneys, and ecclesiastical authorities inveighed against them. Very early, the monk Caesarius of Heisterbach wrote, "Those who fall in tourneys will go to hell unless they are saved by contrition." Pope Alexander III threatened those who took part in tournaments with excommunication, a threat that was renewed by both Innocent III and Innocent IV. In addition to spiritual dangers there were physical ones: when William the Marshal, a renowned English knight, was sought after one tourney so that he could be proclaimed victor, he was found in a smithy with his head on the anvil and the smith busy with a hammer and pincers trying to remove his battered helmet. Sir William Montagu was killed in a joust by his own father, whose father had also died in a tourney. Since one of the highest points that could be scored was the breaking of a lance fairly on an opponent's helmet, flying splinters were a serious menace. King Henry II of France was killed in this way by the shattered end of a lance striking his visor and a splinter piercing his brain. A rule was consequently introduced, making it mandatory for a knight to drop the stump of his lance the instant it broke.

Ordinarily, scoring in a tournament was done by the marshals who kept count of the number of points on a tally sheet. Beside each knight's coat of arms, a system of checks was made showing the number of "attaynts," or courses, run and the number of well or badly broken spears. A spear broken on an antagonist's helmet was counted as one point; a man thrown from the saddle or disarmed so that he could not run the next course was counted as three spears broken. The higher the lance was placed, the better the point, and to strike an opponent on the thigh—that is, "below the belt"—was counted a foul. To shiver a lance to bits on a foe was better than to break it in one place. A lance broken a foot from the coronal was considered no point but a good try. Broken spears might be disallowed under certain circumstances; for instance, if broken against a saddle (one point off), by hitting the barrier (two off), or if broken twice against the barrier (three off).

"Next to death," say the rules of a tournament held in Naples, "to fall from the horse is most reproachful." A man who fell could not take part in any further events of the day unless he fell standing on his feet and was also a challenger, in which case he was bound to return to horse and answer all comers. To hurt a horse was almost as shameful as getting oneself killed, since this was above all a horseman's game. To strike an opponent crosswise with the lance was a foul; while to drop one's weapon, to sit loosely in the saddle, or to govern one's horse badly was an almost certain way not to be invited to any more tourneys.

By degrees, as chiavlry became outmoded and the knightly caste slipped from its eminence, tourneys became the occasions for elaborate costume parties, and the joust, hedged with safeguards, almost totally displaced the old melee. More and more rules were introduced, as well as devices to keep the contestants from injuring themselves. By the end of the sixteenth century, men were so heavily padded and encased—a helmet alone might weigh twenty pounds—that they had to be lifted into the saddle with a winch; once in place, their vision limited to a tiny slit at the front and their huge gauntlets literally locked around their spears, they were started off at an amble on either side of the barrier and could do little more than keep going in the same general direction.

Now and then the artful Germans came up with novelties. One such was a contest in which each man wore an elaborate crest made of parchment. Armed with a baston, or wooden club, each tried to knock his opponent's crest off. Another was called, in language as unwieldy as the armor of the time, *Geschifttartscherennen*. For this, a special shield was used that, when hit squarely in the center, released a spring that flung the metal surface of the shield high in the air in wedge-shaped pieces. This turned out to be unexpectedly dangerous: "It is certainly amusing to look upon," says a contemporary, "though with often sorrowful results to one or other of the combatants by reason of the wedges flying into the eye or nose."

By the seventeenth century the once proud and valiant game was as old-fashioned as the oath of chivalry itself. Its place was taken by the duel of honor, which in another hundred years became first illegal and finally slightly comic.

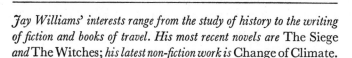

From time to time, however, attempts were made to revive the spectacle and pageantry of the tournament. In 1868, for example, a tourney was held in Turin to celebrate the wedding of Prince Humbert and Princess Margherita of Savoy. Another was held in London in 1912, which was well stage-managed. In 1905, a joust modeled after the great tourney of 1452 was presented in Brussels; it was carefully rehearsed and beautifully costumed, but like the others was no more a true game or sport than a Hollywood version might be.

The most famous, if not the best managed, of such reconstructions was held at Eglinton Castle in Ayrshire, Scotland, in 1839, at the peak of Sir Walter Scott's popularity as a novelist. The young Earl of Eglinton, then twenty-seven and an ardent reader of *Ivanhoe*, was the patron and one of the participants; others included Prince Louis Napoleon, Charles Lamb, the Marquess of Waterford, the Earls of Craven and Cassilis, and any number of other gentlemen. The event made all the front pages as well as a couple of chapters in a novel titled *Endymion*, by a young literary chap named Disraeli.

For three or four days before the tournament the whole thing was rehearsed, for it was found to be exceedingly difficult to train the horses to run toward each other. Armor was borrowed from a number of private collections, which made for some odd combinations of suits. A great banquet hall was built, lists were marked out and fenced, and for days beforehand the prices in local taverns and hotels soared as crowds pressed in to see the revival of a fine old English tradition. Unfortunately, the Earl had not counted on another fine old English tradition: shortly before the start of the event it began to rain, and it kept raining all day long. By the second day the armor had begun to rust and the lovely fourteenth- and fifteenth-century costumes of the ladies were sodden wrecks. Luckily, the third day was clear and fine, and the tourney was then run to its conclusion.

The over-all showing, by medieval standards, was pretty poor, partly because of a general lack of proficiency and partly because of a mistaken notion that courses ought to be run at a gallop instead of a slow trot. Most of the contestants missed each other completely, while others dropped their shields or lost their lances. But the violence and danger of earlier times were recaptured in the melee on the third day, during which two men were severely bruised by falls and a third had his wrist scratched by a sword stroke. Ivanhoe might have chuckled, but the Eglinton Tournament remains the last noble occasion on which blood was actually shed in this chivalrous game of war.

Jay Williams' interests range from the study of history to the writing of fiction and books of travel. His most recent novels are The Siege *and* The Witches; *his latest non-fiction work is* Change of Climate.

LOVE AMONG THE ROMANS

By GILBERT HIGHET

The Romans wrote a great deal about passionate love between man and woman, but it was usually illicit or unhappy or stolen love. In all their thousands of verses of love poetry there are very few lines about the love of a wife for her husband or a husband for his wife. Some social historians have concluded, therefore, that there was very little real love between married couples in old Rome; that there was, at best, the companionship of two dumb working animals which happened to pull at the same plow or share the same stall—a feeling too inarticulate and too crude ever to be worthy of the noble name of love.

However, there is plenty of evidence on the other side, although it is more difficult to assemble. Pick up a volume of Ovid's love poems (for instance, his *Art of Love*, translated by Rolfe Humphries), and there you have a mass of documentation about sexual escapades, enough to make you believe that they were the chief occupation of every Roman lady and gentleman below the age of sixty. To find a rebuttal, you have to go not to poetry but to history, to memoirs, to biography, and even to inscriptions carved on stone.

One of the most moving of those old Roman inscriptions was put up by a husband as a memorial to his dead wife, three or four years before the birth of Jesus of Nazareth. It tells almost the entire story of their lives together—an unusually exciting story involving exile, murder, and other adventures, once at least approaching divorce, and ending, if not in happiness (because of the bereavement of one partner), at least in peace.

The adventures of the inscription itself are almost as strange as those of the couple whom it commemorates. It was put up some time between 8 B.C. and 2 B.C.; there is no date, but we can judge by the content and by the style of the letters. It was carved in fine big letters on two marble slabs about seven feet high. It had a title running along the top, in very large capitals; when new, the whole thing must have looked like two gigantic pages from a marble book. Perhaps it was attached to the front of the dead woman's tomb. Where the tomb was, no one now can tell. Doubtless it was beside one of the highroads that ran out of the city of Rome; as you walk or drive along the Appian Way today, you still see many relics of such buildings, the final homes of the Roman dead.

As Roman civilization began to decline into the Dark Ages of ignorance and barbarism, the Italians and their half-savage invaders began to break up and pillage earlier sanctuaries. The marble slabs carrying this inscription were torn off the tomb and sawn into a dozen pieces or more. Seven of these pieces survived for many centuries, and four of them are still in Rome. The two largest sections were cut down by a few inches and made into part of a coffin for one of the early Christians. In modern times, they were discovered in the catacombs; and they are now in the Villa Torlonia, where it is almost impossible to see them. Another part was carried off into a saloon and used as a gambling table; so we can tell from the lines that have been scratched on its back. This piece was found a few miles outside the city by workmen who were digging the passageway for a new sewer; it is now in the museum that was constructed out of the baths of the Emperor Diocletian.

One smaller piece was built into the wall of a Cistercian abbey in Rome; there it was seen and copied several times by antiquarians during and after the Renaissance. A good thing, too, for now the abbey is gone, the wall is gone, and the inscription is gone; the copies remain, in the Vatican library. Two other pieces also survive only in copies made by equally devoted scholars. The last piece of all was discovered by Professor Arthur E. Gordon of the University of California (Berkeley campus) just a few years ago. He has an exceptionally good memory and a fine eye for Roman lettering. He and his wife were going through a Roman museum, looking at inscriptions that no one had yet managed to place (it was the big collection in the Baths of Diocletian), when he spotted a fragment which had some words that seemed unusual to him: not the regular list of official dignities, but far more personal phrasing with touches of genuine emotion. Also, the style of the carving belonged to the "best period." So he copied it down, and when he put the words in it together with the words remaining on other fragments and copies, the sense was almost perfect.

This was no longer ago than January, 1949. It is entirely possible that Dr. Gordon, or some other alert scholar, may turn up another fragment of the inscription. What matters is that with the existing fragments and the copies

This is a copy of one fragment of the inscription discussed by Gilbert Highet.
Below, to the right of the center space, is a translation of the Latin; on the left,
in italics, Dr. Highet suggests what the missing parts of each line may have been.

XORIS

DIA·FVGAE·MEAE·PRAESTITISTI·ORNAMENTIS
VM·OMNE·AVRVM·MARGARITAQVE·CORPORI
DISTI·MIHI·ET·SVBINDE·FAMILIA·NVMMIS·FRVCTIBVS
DVERSARIORVM·CVSTODIBVS·APSENTIAM·MEAM·LOCVPLETASTI
ITIS·QVOD·VT·CONARERE·VIRTVS·TVA·TE·HORTABATVR
VNIBAT·CLEMENTIA·EORVM·CONTRA·QVOS·EA·PARABAS
OX·TVA·EST·FIRMITATE·ANIMI·EMISSA
TIS·HOMINIBVS·A·MILONE·QVOIVS·DOMVS·EMPTIONE
EXVL·BELLI·CIVILIS·OCCASIONIBVS·INRVPTVRVM
NDISTI·DOMVM·NOSTRAM

IN PRAISE OF MY W IFE

You provided me most generously with re	sources in my exile; your jewels
you sacrificed on my behalf; you took off	all your golden and pearl ornaments
and sent them	to me; and constantly, with servants, cash, and produce,
skillfully evading the	spies set by my enemies, you enriched my absence.
In my peril you saved my life,	an endeavor in which your virtue encouraged you.
Your loyalty pro	tected me by appealing to the mercy of those whom you opposed;
nevertheless your v	oice was always uttered with resolution of spirit.
When a gang of desperadoes was col	lected by Milo (whose house, through purchase,
I had acquired during his	exile), and in the disorders of civil war tried to break in
and loot, you successfully repelled them and defe	nded our home.

of others, we have rather more than two-thirds of the original inscription, including many of the most interesting and moving passages. What we do not have, strangely enough, is the name of the man who put it up and that of his wife. On the face of one fragment (the piece with the gambling table scratches on it) there is carved, in extra large letters, *XORIS*—which, if we add the initial *V*, means "of my wife"; but that is all.

The inscription is a curious thing—unique, I am tempted to say. Memorials usually say "Here lies X, the beloved wife of Y, who for twenty-seven years . . ." and then go on to describe the deceased and her virtues. This one does not. Instead, it is in the form of a speech—a farewell speech addressed by the husband to his wife just after her death.

Some Roman monuments actually call on the public to read them; they say *siste viator*, "stop, passer-by," and then go on to explain whom they are commemorating. There is a very amusing scene in the satiric novel by Petronius, where the vulgar millionaire Trimalchio tells his executor exactly what kind of tomb he wants to have—very pompous and showy, with sculptures showing his wealth and generosity, a statue of himself pouring out money as gifts to the public, and "a clock in the middle, so that anybody who wants to tell the time will have to read my name, whether he wants to or not." But in this particular inscription no attention is paid to the public. They may read it if they wish. Indeed they are invited to, if it was expensively carved and put up in a public place, but they are not explicitly asked to read it; at best they can, as it were, over-hear the husband saying good-bye to the wife he loved.

In doing so he retells the whole story of their mutual trust and co-operation. They became engaged and were married in times as troublous as any that we have so far lived through; in fact, more grievous, inasmuch as civil war with its treachery and unnatural hate is worse than any foreign war. They were threatened before their marriage with separation and impoverishment; after it, with the banishment or death of the husband. The girl was born about 70 B.C., the man perhaps in 75. They became engaged about the year 51 or 50.

In those years Julius Caesar was just finishing the conquest of Gaul, which he had undertaken partly in order to extend the Roman Empire, but more emphatically to enrich himself and his unscrupulous supporters and to train a private army utterly loyal to himself personally, which he could use to dominate—and if necessary to invade and conquer—his native country, the hitherto free Republic of Rome. Caesar kept making demands that his opponents found impossible, because they would, if granted, have built him swiftly into an irresistible dictator. The demands were refused; they were renewed with greater vehemence; the people of Rome began to split into passionate supporters and passionate opponents of Caesar, and a civil war was evidently ready to break out.

In the first months of 49 B.C., civil war did break out. Julius invaded Italy at the head of his army. There was no force in the country capable of opposing him; so his opponents left to raise other armies in the provinces. With them went the young fiancé, to fight with the supporters of the Republic. He left the girl living quietly in the country with her parents. Their house was attacked, and both her father and her mother were murdered. We are not told by whom—the inscription says simply "by a gang of criminals" —but obviously the murder must have taken place during the early disorders of Caesar's invasion, when governmental authority had, for the time being, broken down. How the girl escaped we cannot tell; but she did escape, and what she did thereafter was noteworthy. As soon as order was restored, she set up an investigation of the murder of her parents; she found witnesses and collected evidence and instigated a prosecution of the criminals, and (says the inscription) she "took full vengeance on the guilty." The man who later became her husband adds that while the case was proceeding she could not live alone in the home of her dead parents because her life was not safe; she went to the house of her married sister, who had slaves and freedmen to protect her. She was a courageous and strong-willed young woman.

After this, she moved in with her fiancé's mother to wait for the outcome of the civil war. Two more dangers now appeared.

The first was that several years earlier her fiancé had bought a house from the estate of an extremist politician, Milo, who had been convicted of murder and had his goods confiscated and sold by auction when he went into exile. Now, in the disorder of the civil war, Milo returned to Italy; a gang of his armed supporters tried to break in, take over the house, and drive the women out onto the road. The girl enlisted her servants and, perhaps with help from the neighbors, drove off the gang in complete defeat.

The second danger was that her fiancé chose the losing side in the war. He was against Julius Caesar; and Julius—although he was never so brutal as Hitler or Stalin—issued an order prohibiting his opponents (for a time at least) from returning to Italy. During the time of this order, the young man was in effect an outlaw and of course had no money. The girl sold all her jewelry, turned it into cash, and sent him the proceeds for his support. Even that had to be done through clandestine routes. There always has been an underground working against totalitarian governments, and there always will be.

Now there was a pause, while Caesar consolidated his victory. At this moment, the girl was involved in a further problem. It was a lawsuit so complicated that modern experts in Roman law can scarcely understand it. In outline, the case turned on the fact that Roman women were not considered capable of managing their own affairs. A girl who had any male blood relatives living was assumed to be the ward of the nearest of them. If she had no close male relatives, she was treated as the ward of any distant relative of the same name. For instance, if a girl called Arria were left an orphan with no uncles or cousins, anyone called Arrius could come in and take over her property and administer it for her, provided he was a distant member of the same family or clan.

This girl had been through several trials already. She faced the new one with confidence. Her murdered father had left all his property to her, to her fiancé, to her sister, and to her sister's husband. Some men bearing the name of the family now turned up and claimed that her father's will was invalid because he had made a second marriage after signing it; therefore he had died intestate; therefore the girl held all his property; and since they were members of the same family or clan, they could take it over. The girl went to court. She proved that the people who claimed to be her guardians because they bore the same name as she did, were in fact not related to her at all. She won the case.

By the time this crisis was over, Julius Caesar had conquered the forces of the Republic and had virtually become monarch of Rome. In the short interval of peace, he allowed his opponents to return home. Our young friend came back with the rest, married his girl, and settled down. But quite soon Julius was killed by lovers of the Republic and of liberty. Another civil war broke out. The husband joined the army of Brutus and Cassius; with them he was beaten; with their supporters he was outlawed and condemned to death without trial.

By now, we know the character of the woman who was his wife. She at once set out to have her husband's sentence annulled. The Empire at this time was being run by three men: Mark Antony, who was out in the East; a stupid, selfish little fellow called Lepidus, who held Italy for the moment; and Octavian, who was to become the Emperor Augustus. The young wife sent her brother-in-law to intercede with Octavian for her husband's life, while she herself appealed to Lepidus. So low had the Romans sunk then that she had to lie prostrate, begging for mercy; and so harsh had the heirs of Caesar become that she was brutally pulled away, kicked, and bruised. But her brother-in-law was more successful; he got a free pardon from Octavian (who was technically equal to Lepidus, but, in prestige, and therefore in fact, stronger), so that the husband was saved and could return to Italy as a free citizen or (if he had been in hiding) emerge into the free air. At this point in the inscription there is a little note that reminds us of the young woman's behavior after the murder of her parents. "Through your patient endurance, the man responsible for my danger was detected and revealed; and therefore your determination proved to be his undoing."

There the story ends—or almost. The husband had been through two civil wars. Now, when he was about 33 and she about 28, they settled down like hundreds of thousands of other ordinary people, to accept the rule of Octavian and to enjoy the peace he spread over the Western world.

One more problem confronted them. This was a family problem: they were unable to have children. (It looks as though she had suffered a miscarriage, for in the inscription he says, "We prayed for children, and our hopes expected them, but fortune turned away and ended our hopes.") She now offered to give him a divorce, so that he could marry a young and fertile wife; she promised that she would not only share her property with the new family (the pair had always held their property in common), but treat the children of the new marriage as though they had been her own. At this point we can almost hear the husband's voice from the stone slab. "I must confess," he cries, "that I was so distressed by your proposal that I almost lost my mind. To think that you could plan to leave me, when you, at a time when I myself was almost banished from life, remained wholeheartedly faithful!"

So the proposal was dropped, and the couple remained together, childless and aging, until the last. After forty-one years of marriage he buried her. Almost the final words on the inscription are these: "I know that you deserved everything, and yet I did not manage to give you all you deserved." He is not very eloquent, but his simple frankness is more convincing than richer periods and more complex paragraphs. We do not know his name, or hers; we do not know if any portrait of them is extant—although they may well be looking at us from one of those Roman funeral monuments which show a husband and wife, sober and thoughtful, gazing out as though from a window at the passer-by. What we do know of them is the essential: that they risked their lives and fortunes for each other; that they lived together for over forty years; and that neither found those forty years long enough to express and enjoy their love. In such men and women was the true strength of ancient Rome.

Tombs along the Appian Way

THE GODS IN ART

CONTINUED FROM PAGE 16

the churches, and art becomes the common property of all the faithful. It is the great age of Romanesque sculpture, when Christ, "for so long the prisoner of the apse," finally "abandons His kingdom of shadows and appears on the church portals. . . . Rome decides that the Last Judgments shall be lit by the setting sun. With the bas-relief—for the first time in how many centuries!—the figure of Christ rises outside the church."

This Christ is not Jesus—or not yet. His message is love—but of a certain kind. Later ages, looking upon the figures of medieval faith, tend to ignore the distinction. "What our time understands best about the Romanesque and Gothic faith are the things that are not, properly speaking, faith: exaltation and brotherly love, those imperceptibly rationalized images of Saint Bernard and Saint Francis, everything that permits us to confuse the charity of a saint with the devotion of a physician, the construction of a cathedral with that of a giant dam, the Crusades with the Revolutions. . . .

"Before bringing the promise of heaven, salvation demands the rebirth according to the spirit, the knowledge of God. . . . The martyrs did not throw themselves to the beasts to win a kind of permanent holiday in the country. . . . The fundamental emphasis of Christianity is not paradise, which Christian art scarcely represents. Nor the moral preaching of Jesus. Nor even the Crucifixion. It is the secret of God, as revealed by Christ. This revelation is contained in three lightning words: God is love. However, it is not human love, but sacred love; it is part of the very mystery of the Eternal. Revelation does not bring the elucidation of that mystery, but communion with it."

The same is true of Romanesque art. To begin with, at least, its Christ is still a majestic, Biblical, even Byzantine Christ. The figure that dominates the great tympani of Moissac, Beaulieu, and Autun is Christ in His aspect of the Eternal, the Pantocrator (see pages 12-13). But gradually, a major metamorphosis takes place. Perceptibly, the features soften, the severe and austere masks give way to increasingly human traits, the love that is at the heart of the eternal mystery gives way to the love that is in the heart of man. "As Christ turns increasingly into Jesus, God recedes. . . . In art, as in faith, Christ detaches Himself from the God of Abraham, in tympanum after tympanum, from Moissac via Chartres until the last cathedrals."

The change begins when artists introduce men into the world of God. These human figures may be more symbolic than real—"no Romanesque sculptor ever created a *shepherd*, but all created Christmas shepherds; without Christmas, no shepherd." But they are human figures nonetheless, and "Christ Himself is also of the earth, invisibly present in the seasons and streams, in the actions of every day, in the works of hand and spirit. Here is the bishop, but also the pilgrim and crusader; the shepherd, the thresher of wheat, the vintner in his vat. . . . Their patron saints have led them to Him, trade by trade, and He has told them: 'I have shed such and such a drop of blood for the vintners.' . . . The Christ of Byzantium ignored the vintners. So did Byzantine art: it knew only Biblical figures, manifestations of God."

But so far, the metamorphosis has taken place within a symbolic world. The figures of Romanesque sculpture are not yet subject to external appearance. This, too, begins to change—with Chartres. The Romanesque Christs dominated the surrounding human figures; not so the Christ of the Royal Portal of Chartres (see page 13), who seems to mingle with them—"a figure which is at the same time inspired and abandoned by the Sacred." What has happened is that "the relation of the Son to the Father, of the Incarnation to the basic mystery, is inverted. Hitherto, the Father had been the God of Job, the Unfathomable. [But] for the initial credo, God is love, the secular piety of the Gothic period substitutes: *God is Jesus*." The Teaching Christ of Chartres evokes Saint Francis, the saint without theology. "Everywhere, the mystery fades before love, the otherness of God before the nearness of Jesus, worship before communion, the fall of man before the *feeling* of Christ's victory." Original sin has not disappeared, and neither has the figure of the Judge. But the Judge who now lifts His pierced hand above the Last Judgments exhibits a kind of compassionate majesty. As for the deep world of Satan, the cathedrals represent it only satirically, and little remains of it beyond a sort of infernal police force.

Throughout Christendom spreads a triumphant sense of Redemption accomplished, of Christ victorious in His kingdom. Christ the Eternal is replaced by Christ the King, the realm of the Sacred replaced by the City of God. "Gothic sculpture, properly speaking, begins with the Coronation at Notre Dame de Paris (see page 16), where the royalty of the Virgin blends with the royalty of Christ above the City of God, and which symbolizes the genius of the cathedrals as the giant Saviors symbolized the Romanesque genius, as the nude will later symbolize the genius of the Renaissance."

Yet the Gothic glories do not endure. The continuous curve in civilization and art that some historians like to draw from the eleventh to the fifteenth century does not stand up under examination. "In 1050, Western Christendom is nothing; in 1099, it takes Jerusalem. In 1090, what is sculpture? Fifty years later, it is Chartres. In 1250, sixty quarries are at work for cathedrals or churches, and labor proceeds in great hopes, nourished by more than a century of conquests.

Twenty years later, Saint Louis is dead, the Latin Kingdom of Jerusalem is lost, the Crusades are abandoned." Thomas Aquinas writes his *Summa* when conquering Christianity is about to disappear. The work reveres the divine mystery, but classifies it—and in a sense banishes it. In the second half of the thirteenth century, the great Gothic drive disappears. "The cathedrals, symbols of the Gothic *élan*, also symbolize its failure. None of them was completed. . . . At Reims, seven steeples had been planned; at Chartres, nine." And so, "what once was the torrent of Christianity loses itself in the sands."

THE HUMANIZATION OF ART

In the waning Age of Faith, beauty moves from the saint to the statue—Mary, Queen of Heaven, becomes the suffering mother of Christ

The Gothic revelation of the City of God, the art of the Coronation period, was the work of a Christian imagination still concerned with Truth. Now, that imagination becomes increasingly concerned with mere figments. For nine hundred years, the great image-makers were artists only in the sense that the prophets of Israel were poets. But now, as happened in Greece, the self-abnegation of the artist ceases. As the gods did before, the saints become statues. The Beau Dieu of Amiens was beautiful only in the sense that beauty was considered a divine attribute. And when the people of Liège called their Virgin (see page 16) the most beautiful in Christendom, they referred to the Virgin and not to the statue; without her crown, she would not have been the most beautiful young mother in Europe. But now, the word "beautiful" refers to the work of art itself. "It expresses an admiration quite distinct from religious sentiment. . . . The aesthetic sense is born in Christendom."

The artist clearly leaves his mark on his work; statues of prophets or apostles now typically display ostentatious curls, coil-shaped or pinpointed beards, fluted robes. Realistic touches are mixed with the bizarre. The Prophet of Strasbourg "lifts a hand whose veins are minutely copied from life toward an archaically Chinese bronze beard." The religious, no longer expressed naturally or easily, becomes stylized. "Without realism, no human figure; without stylization, no saint."

The very nature of worship changes. The cathedral was, among other things, a community. But in the fourteenth century, as society becomes increasingly secular, "the collective and liturgical faith of which the cathedral was a shining expression is replaced by a new relation between man and the divine: Christ does not address Himself to *all* but to *each*." The chief object of devotion becomes that "secret intimacy" with the divine of which Cardinal Newman would later say that it made the church a solitary

place. "Communal faith is dismembered like an empire." Private devotion brings with it pathos on one level, mysticism on another. Neither "the piety of women who own an ivory Virgin" nor "the fervent murmer of the great mystics" has much in common with the faith that once rose before the great stone assemblies of the cathedrals. While the Gothic period was aglow with the triumph of Christ—while even Calvary was transfigured to the point where, in the Annunciation of Reims, a laughing angel announced to Mary the mystery of the Incarnation—religious art now emphasizes suffering. On the mystical level, there is a "communion with pain, perhaps conceived as the essence of the secret of the world," and expressed in sorrowful, thorn-crowned crucifixes like the Devout Christ of Perpignan. On the pathetic level, the cross becomes less a reminder of suffering than a source of compassion, which finds expression in the cult of Mary. She is no longer the majestic Mary of the Coronation. "The world in which the Eternal appeared, and the world in which Christ crowned the Virgin, fade before the world of man in which the Mother gazes at her dead son."

Increasingly, the realm of sentiment replaces the realm of the soul, and pathos is accompanied by tenderness. Mary fondles the infant, then plays with him, finally suckles him. The Amiens Annunciation took place in the world of the Angel, but private piety suppresses that world to the point of contradicting Biblical texts. "In its Crucifixion scenes, this piety invents the swooning of the Virgin; *stabat*, said the text, 'she stood upright.' . . . But she now becomes the swooning mother—and the little girl whom Saint Anne holds by the hand." The Annunciation also belonged inseparably to the cathedral; but "the Pietà has no other cathedral but the hearts of men."

Where does the world of the Angel, of the Coronation, live on? Not in sculpture, which is increasingly occupied with the living—with kings and princesses, figures that are "strangers to God because they do not pray, strangers even to the church because they reign in palace halls." The world of the Angel lives on in painting—first and unforgettably in the painting of Giotto.

ART OF PICTORIAL FICTION

The dawning Renaissance bids farewell to Eternity, dragons, and sacred art—Venus descends from Olympus to become a naked woman

Later ages, particularly the Renaissance, praised Giotto for his illusionism, his still relatively primitive (so it was thought) but nonetheless revolutionary faithfulness to nature. Giotto does indeed break with the rigidly formalized Byzantine tradition of painting, but not in the cause of realism. He does not, for example, invent the sky, as is sometimes said; he uses a deep-blue background which is sometimes mistaken for being realistic, although it completely ignores the horizon; in fact, it is not the sky of man but the sky of Christ. Similarly, Giotto's towns are anything but realistic; "when photography isolates their details, they make us think of a religious Cézannism." Giotto relates events, as does the narrative imagery proliferating on the elaborate altar screens—the narratives which Christendom henceforth expects of art. His medium is akin to the Christian imagination of the great Gothic period, but where that was linked to the cathedral, Giotto's is linked to the new world of pictorial fiction. He invents an imaginary theater whose plays are still sacred events, and whose human characters bear the same accent of majesty that Romanesque and early Gothic sculpture gave to Christ. Giotto's great achievement is that "he discovers a *power of painting* hitherto unknown to Christian art; the power, without sacrilege, to place a sacred scene in a world that resembles the world of man."

Flemish art develops that power further. Here the figures of saints dressed like petty lords or shoemakers, appear not above imaginary cities, but above familiar Gothic towns. God for the first time is apt to look like a debonair or majestic old man, like emperor or pope. "The kingdom of Archangels, Thrones and Dominations is increasingly confused with the Garden of Eden, and Eden with an earthly paradise." This art still expresses faith. Van Eyck's "Mystic Lamb" is a deeply religious work; nevertheless, it marks the invasion of Eternity by time. "No religious art before ever fixed the passing of the hour. . . . The mosaics knew only one kind of light, that of the sanctuary itself; the stained glass windows were illuminated by the living light of God, as were the statues, for sculpture knows no light except that which is shed by any given time of day." But in the fifteenth century, "the source of light passes from God to the painter." It is the artist who paints whatever light he wants into his picture, and hence fixes its hour. "This hour, while still religious, nevertheless tolls the defeat of Eternity."

It is still not a question of complete realism. "Like the movie makers, these artists use only certain selected, isolated, *controlled* parts of a reality [which] is not yet the despotic model it will later become. . . . The Flemish primitives are realists like Kafka." Painters of Van Eyck's time and after do paint pictures that resemble actual scenes, but it is not that likeness we admire most, but the difference from the scenes they resemble. "The painters show their skill by the resemblance, their genius by the difference."

In Van Eyck's "The Virgin and Chancellor Rolin" (see page 17), the artist does not add the Virgin to a picture of the chancellor at home; he introduces the chancellor into a picture of the Virgin. "Our familiarity with fifteenth-century painting hides from us how really extraordinary is the world in which a contemporary of the painter kneels, in his own house or in a church that could be his own house, before a Virgin being crowned by angels, while peacocks walk in the lanes, and while two careless subsidiary characters watch the afternoon draw to a close over the town. . . . But while this world is not Giotto's, it is not the chancellor's either: it is a *world of painting*. It is the heir of Italian pictorial fiction—become independent of the place of worship. . . . The chancellor and the Virgin meet in the world of painting, just as Macbeth and the witches meet in the world of poetry."

In a sense this produces a crisis of the imagination. The Middle Ages knew the supernatural only as reality. Angels were no more surprising than elephants; if anything, medieval people knew angels better and saw them more often. Angels and demons were not part of the earth, but they were part of Creation by the same token as elephants—and men. The medieval imagination was never concerned with things that could not exist, but with things that could exist only through God, or that existed in the lands where knights killed giants and dragons—the dragon, after all, might be only an elephant one had not yet seen. From Byzantium to the fourteenth century, fable and myth had never quite disappeared from the manuscripts. Mercury in the guise of a bishop, Apollo in the guise of a physician, turbaned Diana and Saturn with a sickle, mingled with Mars in a cart and Vulcan in a smith's apron. Venus was painted in medieval books as planet or as chatelaine, in the zodiac or in the garden. But when she ceases to be planet, demon, or allegorical figure, she becomes merely a character in an anecdote. In *Les Echecs Amoureux* at the end of the fourteenth century, Venus appears in the "Gardens of Nature" (see page 14), which strongly resemble a kitchen garden. Although the painter sees his goddesses as symbolizing the Modes of Life, he tries to represent Venus merely by painting a naked woman—and does not manage to identify his kitchen goddess except by hanging a label above her. Artistically speaking, she is the sister of Proserpine and Pluto who hold court in another scene of the same work; they are figures of strained, satirical allegory, suggesting that the painters of the period are no longer at ease in realms of fantasy.

It is impossible for a painter to introduce Venus into the plastic universe of Van Eyck, "just as it would have been impossible for a sculptor to introduce her into the assembly of saints on the portals of Chartres. . . . The world of Flemish painting can accept her only as a woman, because it knows only what *exists*. . . . Van Eyck paints his lost 'Hunters,' like the 'Arnolfini Wedding,' because they exist; he paints Eve, the Virgin, and the saints because they exist even more so. But Italy is about to paint Venus because she does not exist." The famous Botticelli Venus "brings with her a quality that Christian art had never known: the unreal." It is no longer the subdued babbling of the fairy tale, but "the domain in which the Christian for the first time dares to set up the images of his dream in rivalry to the images of the world of God." Italy has discovered the pictorial domain in which "Venus could become the rival of the Virgin, the nymph rival of the angel, and the unreal the rival of the City of God."

ACHIEVEMENT AND FAILURE

Malraux arrays all art beneath a soaring arch of philosophical vision . . . but the philosopher is left seeking salvation in the aesthetic "World Beyond"

Thus Malraux. At this point, he abruptly concludes *La Métamorphose des Dieux*. He plans to continue the work in a future volume, but even as far as it goes, his account of the "immemorial pageant in which the gods march side by side with creative man" is a first-rate achievement. It is not a book to be read so much as to be experienced, and it often has the air of something talked rather than something written—reflecting Malraux's overpowering conversational abilities, which are legendary among his friends. The work seems designed not only to persuade the reader, but to take him by the shoulder and push him against the very special window through which Malraux sees the world.

The illustrative technique of the Imaginary Museum helps to accomplish this. It is a technique that has been bitterly attacked by art critics and other professional aesthetes, on the ground that no work of art can really be judged on the basis of reproductions and photographs, no matter how excellent—particularly when, as is often the case in Malraux's books, only details are shown. Charging that Malraux's technique mutilates the originals, one French critic has accused him of causing a "Buchenwald of the plastic arts." Malraux admits that in the world of the Imaginary Museum, "the fragment is king." He even happily approves of lighting sculpture in certain ways, photographing it from certain angles, to make his points. It is in fact sometimes disturbing to compare the complete work of art with the face or hand that Malraux has excised from it; almost invariably the total effect is utterly different. But as long as the Imaginary Museum is not taken as the only place in which to experience art, the technique remains valid and fascinating in that it offers, almost literally, a new sense of sight.

What makes *La Métamorphose* an especially haunting work is not originality in the usual sense. Some of Malraux's seemingly solitary positions are quite artificial; he sets up straw men—particularly straw critics—and knocks them down. A case in point is his repeated assertion that naturalistic representation is not art, and that changes in the development of style cannot be explained by changes in technique. Who really disagrees? Despite a great deal of nonsense that is still being written on these subjects by those who reduce art—and life—to material terms, this is basically a nineteenth-century battle. Furthermore, a great many of Malraux's observations can be found in standard art histories. Other writers have noted the slide from Egypt's gods to Greece's godlike men, the humanization of Christ, the pathetization of Mary; in short, Malraux did not discover the metamorphosis either of the gods or of the arts. Clive Bell, to quote that very rewarding critic once again, knows as well as Malraux that "with Gothic architecture, the descent began" (and adds in an irreverant aside: "A Gothic cathedral is a tour de force; it is also a melodrama. . . . You may groan 'Aah' and collapse: you will not be stung to austere ecstasy"). From Nietzsche to the present, the concept of an organic rise and fall in art, paralleling the rise and fall of civilization, has been familiar. But it matters relatively little whether outline or detail of Malraux's work can be found elsewhere. No one else has ever looked at art in quite his way.

What stamps Malraux's work as extraordinary is his intensity; when he writes about a statue, one has a vision of Malraux standing before it with a burning determination that this piece of stone *must* yield its secrets to him. He admits that it is not the same statue for him as it was for a distant and long-dead spectator who saw the work in its own time. But Malraux is determined—this is one aspect of the metamorphosis he sees at work in all art—to extract the meaning that is valid for his own day. And in this he succeeds, especially because he never treats any work of art in isolation. His exhibits are not arranged along a museum-like corridor of mere chronology. They are displayed, as in a huge tympanum, under the single arch of his vision. This means that sometimes they are cramped, even confused; occasionally figures (and theories) are made to fit that simply will not fit. But the whole produces a stunning effect. And this effect comes chiefly from the immense tension of the covering arch, a tension almost physically felt in a work that insists on spanning the distance from pyramid to cross, from cross to cubism.

It is in the second segment of the arch that Malraux strains too hard. And it is here that his view of art as determined by the otherworldly breaks down.

The view itself is not easily fitted into the filing cabinet of established aesthetic systems, and that is perhaps one reason why, up to a point, it is so convincing. It has obviously nothing to do with art for art's sake. On the other hand, it has little or nothing to do with art for morality's sake, as advocated by thinkers from Plato to Tolstoi. It is neither hedonistic nor really utilitarian. It has very little in common with Benedetto Croce's ideas on "intuition" and nothing with Santayana's notions of art as pleasure and beauty "objectified." It is linked with religious emotion, but scarcely to the more hardheaded religious theories about art. Etienne Gilson, for example, expresses the widespread view that Christian art is a kind of "visual aid" in teaching Christian doctrine and for that reason necessarily representational and therefore in many instances not art at all. Man, says Gilson, may in his own humble way try to imitate the Creator by creating art, but "God does not seem interested in creating paintings."

There is in Malraux's view a romantic mysticism which

seems echoed, but not duplicated, by Carlyle's view that in art "the infinite is made to blend with the finite . . . eternity looking through time"; and also by Bernard Bonsaquet's assertion that the " 'idealizations' characteristic of art are not so much products of an imagination that departs from reality as they are revelations of the life and divinity that is alone ultimately real." But whatever the amalgam of ideas, the precise mixture is Malraux's own; and it is sweepingly, exhilaratingly persuasive when the "world beyond" of Malraux's theory is in some measure a religious world. The view that art is determined by faith—by man's picture of himself and his gods—makes at least as much sense as the more familiar idea that it is determined by society, or economics, or history; because ultimately, all these are in their turn determined by faith. The theory also works negatively, when it is applied to pictures in no obvious way connected with religion; a Renaissance canvas glorifying man also says something about faith, or its absence. The break in Malraux's great arch occurs when he tries to equate the "world beyond" with the world of art itself.

In his preface to *La Métamorphose*, which actually reaches beyond the time span of the book itself, Malraux writes: 'The Milkmaid' by Vermeer, 'The Housekeeper' by Chardin certainly do not belong in a world of Truth in the sense of the Egyptian statues [or] the kings of Chartres. . . . Nor do they belong to the exalted world of the unreal which, in the cases of Michelangelo and Rembrandt, succeeded to the eternal. The sculptor of Zoser undertook to 'eternalize' a Pharaoh; Vermeer did not undertake to do so with a milkmaid. And yet the word 'eternalize' stops us. Did Vermeer not also try to lift *something* out of time?" Vermeer painted his picture *that way* because he wanted it to "enter the world in which the surviving works of the past are united. . . . The Egyptian sculptor believed that he could release his model from time. Vermeer wanted to release *his picture* from time." Again, Malraux writes of Cézanne: "His genius rejects appearance as much as the sacred arts did; and faced with so many centuries which rejected it in the name of Truth, we ask ourselves if Cézanne does not reject it in the name of a Truth he does not know—but to which he spectacularly devotes his life. He saw the death of works which Michelangelo believed immortal. He knew they were forgotten for over a thousand years, and that during five hundred the cathedrals were thought barbaric. Nevertheless, if God had told him that his paintings would not live, Cézanne would not have believed Him and would have led Him to the Louvre." Cézanne paints "to attain that world in which Poussin is united with Tintoretto . . . in which The Architect with the Plan will be united for us with the Kore of Euthydykos and the kings of Chartres, the Pietà of Avignon with the Ajanta frescoes, and Vermeer with Rembrandt—the world which renders present, in our lives, that which ought to belong to death."

In short, Malraux invents a kind of Great Beyond of art.

As noted above, he describes at one point in his book how Eden was replaced by the vision of an earthly paradise; he himself replaces it by a paradise of paint. What does it mean to say that Cézanne paints so that his works might enter this paradise? If anything, it means that he paints because he wants to be "immortal." Does such a desire ever shape a picture? Only in the event that the painter copies other "immortals"—obviously not the case with Cézanne or any good artist. But simply feeling a sense of exalted empathy with masterpieces, and wishing to join their company, cannot possibly account for major artistic creation.

It must be that Malraux is misled by his basic notion of art as an antidestiny, a comfort against the thought of death, a defense against nothingness. He sensed that here his ground was shaky when he wrote in *The Voices of Silence*: "Feeble indeed may seem that brief survival of [an artist's] work which does not last long enough to see the light die out from stars already dead." Yet in the next breath he insisted on the beauty of "the thought that this animal who knows that he must die can wrest from the disdainful splendor of the nebulae the music of the spheres and broadcast it across the years to come"; insisted again that in the "house of shadows where Rembrandt still plies his brush," the artist can find survival and a kind of eternity. It is, however, not eternity at all, only "immortality." Malraux himself in another context has pointed out the difference. Stripped of Malraux's special and compelling eloquence, the statement reduces itself to the thundering cliché that man can leave behind him "footprints on the sands of time."

Judged in the light of the Eternal, which Malraux himself constantly evokes, these footprints are the puniest sort of survival—indeed, no survival at all. From the human point of view, the difference in the shapes of the footprints matters. It matters not at all in the light of Eternity ("God does not seem interested in creating paintings"). From the human point of view, there is a meaningful and fascinating difference between a pyramid and a skyscraper, between the Christ image of Moissac, the Christ image of Rouault, and a saccharine picture-postcard Jesus. In the light of Eternity, the difference is negligible.

The trouble is that Malraux appears to find himself in that unhappiest position of a man who wants to believe but cannot. However, a substitute faith—in art or anything else —offers no real way out of the dilemma. One cannot have it both ways. Either man is the master of his fate—a fate limited to his little globe, spinning through a godless universe, or he is a handful of dust in God's universe. If man is the first, then his art—the works of his flesh-and-blood greatness—will not give him life beyond the grave (but Malraux is not enough of a humanist to be satisfied with that). If man is the second, his art is immortal only in the sense that his soul is immortal, through God's law and grace; and all the works from the Pyramids to Chartres to Vermeer cannot increase or diminish the soul's survival through God

116

(but Malraux is too much of a humanist to accept *that*).

The matter is summed up in an exchange between Malraux and Jean Ominus, the French critic previously quoted. Malraux: "Since art no longer assists religion in creating a world in which man is not a stranger, it is attempting to do it singlehandedly. And the alcove of Vermeer, a flower painting of Chardin, give us a view of a world where man is less ant-like than in his own." Ominus: "What anguish in these few lines! And, in fact, perhaps what misgivings! Does Malraux seriously believe that Vermeer's alcove, Chardin's bouquet, however beautiful they are, contain within them the power of salvation . . . ?"

Having said this, however, it is necessary to add that while Malraux may vainly search for salvation in art, in the course of that search he is nevertheless seeing the art he passes on the way with sharp and luminous eyes—and describing what he sees in a manner not equaled in the field. The Imaginary Museum, he has written, "is the song of history, not its newsreel." Either as newsreel of considerable fascination, or as a song to art of considerable beauty, Malraux's work is a unique experience.

Born in Vienna and long resident in France, Henry Anatole Grunwald is now a senior editor of Time, *in charge of the Book and Religion sections. He has been a student of literature and religion in general and of Malraux's writings in particular for many years.*

Out of the Old Met, the New

CONTINUED FROM PAGE 28

whom, Gluck and Beethoven, have been heard only on rare occasions from under the old arch that enshrines them.

This is only one of the many contrasts between the genesis of New York's first opera house, inexpertly designed as a fashionable resort for the age of gilt and diamond tiaras, and the second—a steel and glass center designed to serve the needs of today's entire diverse opera-going community in the world's greatest city.

Even when the old Met was opened in 1883, criticism of the structure was heard. Architect Cady, who numbered among his attainments the designing of St. Andrew's Church, the Hudson Street Hospital, and the fortress-like 77th Street façade of the American Museum of Natural History, answered his critics by declaring in the *New York Herald Tribune* that "probably no other building in the country has been given so much care and thought." He stated that he had given much attention to sight lines, using London's Covent Garden in particular as a model. He did not mention the building's acoustics, although he might well have done so, since this was his most notable achievement— opera can be heard almost perfectly in all of the Met's 3,616 seats. But its sight lines are the worst in any major opera house anywhere, there being nearly 1,000 seats from which only a portion of the stage is visible. Moreover, such was Cady's ignorance of theatrical requirements that its backstage area was wholly inadequate from the start. Although his building covered a whole city block, no space was set aside to store scenery. As Irving Kolodin remarks in his history of the opera, "Cady imagined that an area below the stage could serve this purpose. This was not only inadequate, but a hazard that contributed so much to the fire of 1892 [which burned out the interior of the structure] that its use was thereafter forbidden."

All these lessons—along with many others learned in seventy-five years of working at the crowded old stand at 39th and 40th streets—are to be applied to the new house to go up on the vast area of west-side urban wasteland now being razed and converted into the Lincoln Center for the Performing Arts. The building will face a plaza as large as the Piazza San Marco in Venice. This part of the plan is not new to Harrison, who thirty years ago (when there was already talk of moving the Met uptown) helped draw up a design for Rockefeller Center calling for an opera house where the RCA Building now stands, overlooking Manhattan's most popular plaza. But nothing in that earlier plan was as dramatic as Harrison's new concept of a façade of five soaring arches, each more than eight stories high. The vaulted ceiling, 228 feet wide and 225 feet long and hung on the cantilever principle, is to extend back over the lobby and auditorium space to meet a fourteen-story stage loft. "The columns in front," Harrison explains, "are not so much for its support; rather they should be thought of as holding the ceiling down." Three sides of the house will consist of walls of glass 80 feet high to give an air of openness and lightness akin to the glass-walled United Nations Headquarters for which Wallace Harrison was one of the architects.

Behind the curtain there will be *six* stage areas, the main one equipped with trap elevators and measuring 108 feet by 80 feet. A second stage of equal size and equipped with a turntable will extend behind it—a sharp contrast to the present Met, which long lived without the revolving stages that are a commonplace in Europe and only got around to installing one in time for a 1954 production of *Don Pasquale*. The Metropolitan opera company owns the scenery and props for about eighty productions, but there is so little storage space in the present house that even those needed for a single week's repertory must be trucked at immense expense from a warehouse at 129th Street before each performance. Even on arrival, they are often stacked on the pavement of Seventh Avenue behind the stage, subject to winter weather and the indifference of garment-area workers. The new house will not eliminate the 129th Street warehouse altogether, but the opera will for the first time be able to store about half of a season's repertory on its own premises.

In designing a home for a great opera company, innumerable vested interests of varying degrees of expertness have to be taken care of—from the general manager and his professional cohorts to boards of directors, finance committees, and influential box holders. Almost inevitably, the final design turns out to be a compromise or at least a balancing of forces. Harrison has received advice from possibly 10 per cent of the Met's over 600 employees, has weathered innumerable committees, and evidently is in accord with the Opera's president, Anthony A. Bliss, who this year wrote in the company's *Opera News* that "on one point of architectural style there has never been any question; the warmth and excitement that make any performance at the Metropolitan a major experience must be retained. . . . We doubt that an ultramodern building would be acceptable to the opera audience, or suitable for the repertory it will support. We must build, we feel, for the repertory we have—classic and romantic operas—not for whatever the next century may bring; that's why an auditorium of arena style was considered but rejected. . . . The auditorium will not be cold or austere. We've been very careful about this. Originally we wanted no side seats of the sort that run to the ends of the present horseshoe, right up to the stage. Now we are convinced that empty walls are chilling, that contact between the audience and the stage is imperative. . . . At Lincoln Center, when an aria is over, you'll still find those currents of excitement carried back and forth along the walls between singers and audience. That's opera."

Harrison's plans for the interior are traditional in feeling although not necessarily so in style. General Manager Rudolf Bing wants to see a "modified horseshoe" with improved sight lines; but the traditional Diamond Horseshoe will be carried over, with thirty-five or so Grand Tier boxes. Meanwhile the upper tiers are to be made more comfortable than the ones before, although again there will be a "peanut gallery." The new Met is to have 3,800 seats, an increase in capacity of nearly 200, which should come in handy when Maria Callas or Renata Tebaldi is packing them in. In fact, there is no worry at the Met on the score of sheer size, since during the last season in particular the company operated at 96 per cent of capacity—a record surmounted only by a few Broadway smash hits.

In order to gather further ideas for the new house, Harrison in 1956 made a whirlwind tour of European opera and theater centers in company with President Bliss and John D. Rockefeller III, head of the Lincoln Center. Covering fifteen cities in fourteen days, they ranged from new German houses in Cologne, Düsseldorf, and Duisburg to the rebuilt opera houses of Vienna, Hamburg, and Milan. At La Scala, most glamorous of all, Harrison observed with displeasure that the space per seat in the top balcony (be-

loved by generations of music students of every nationality) was far smaller than that permitted by law in Manhattan. The same objection was voiced concerning London's new Royal Festival Hall (whose staggered boxes have also brought down the criticism that they look "like bureau drawers left hanging open"); but Harrison had only praise for the space allotted there for coats, restrooms, and bars. Side views of the new opera house in New York lead one to suppose that the new Met will most resemble the Festival Hall in outside appearance; but the stage structure itself has, at the insistence of General Manager Bing and his staff, been adapted from those at ultramodern Cologne.

Cologne's arrangements, General Manager Bing told *The New York Times* some time ago, "are as ideal as one can hope to have today. . . . There are a main stage, two side stages and a stage in the rear, and each subsidiary stage is as big as the main one. Any of those subsidiary stages can, in whole or in part, replace the center stage within a few seconds. If we had those facilities we would have an entire four-act opera set up and ready to go, hours before the performance. In Cologne, they have eight elevators on the stages, and what an immense amount of work this eliminates! All the backstage shops, for carpenters and painters and so forth, are beautifully planned."

Rudolf Bing's most distinguished predecessor as general manager was the late Giulio Gatti-Casazza, who held the job for a record-breaking twenty-seven seasons. Arriving in 1908 to convert the Met into the American counterpart of La Scala, he tactfully told the press: "It is a noble house." He soon learned better. Nine years later the late Cornelius N. Bliss, father of the present Anthony and also in his time a president of the company, began putting documents in a file labeled "New Opera House Project." One of the most interesting of these was Joseph Urban's 1927 plan for an opera house to be built between 56th and 57th streets and Eighth and Ninth avenues, where the Parc Vendome apartment-hotel now stands; this was to have been financed by the banker Otto H. Kahn. Another banker-philanthropist, Felix Warburg, planned a music center at Columbus Circle. Still another scheme located the house on 57th at Sixth Avenue. None ever got beyond the discussion stage.

Many of these trials and tribulations over the decades might have been avoided if anyone connected with the original building had actually cared anything about music. The villain of that piece is not really architect Cady, but the man who hired him—William H. Vanderbilt, son of the "public-be-damned" Commodore and heir to $90,000,000. From 1854 to 1883 the citadel of New York society was the horseshoe of opera boxes at the old Academy of Music on 14th Street. These were occupied by a glittering battery of old Knickerbocker names whose prosperity dated from Revolutionary times or earlier. The Vanderbilts conspicuously did not belong to this elite, and all their latter-day millions could not buy them a box there. Vanderbilt there-

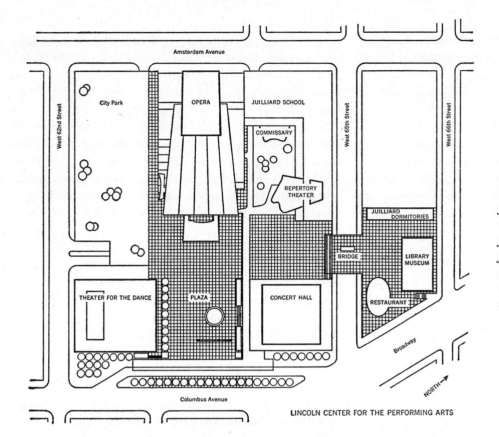

LINCOLN CENTER FOR THE PERFORMING ARTS

This plan shows the tentative arrangement of the various buildings that will surround the new Metropolitan Opera House and its plaza. The Lincoln Center for the Performing Arts is the most ambitious cultural center ever planned. It will include theaters for repertory and the dance, a concert hall for the New York Philharmonic Orchestra, a library museum of all the performing arts, and the Juilliard School of Music. It may be 1963 before the Center is completed.

upon decided to build his own opera house; his associates included other *nouveaux riches* such as Ogden Goelet, J. P. Morgan, Cyrus Field, Jay Gould, and William Rockefeller.

With what was regarded in some quarters as exquisite appropriateness, the new Metropolitan Opera opened its doors with the story of a man who sold his soul to the devil: *Faust*. One Old Guard reporter sniffed: "The Goulds and the Vanderbilts and people of that ilk perfumed the air with the odor of crisp greenbacks. The tiers of the house looked like cages in a menagerie of monopolists." But the odor of new money took on another savor at the first season's end, when the box holders in the first two tiers picked up the tab for an initial deficit totaling $600,000. Within three years after the opening of the Metropolitan, the rival Academy of Music was done for. Retiring as its manager, the same Colonel James H. Mapleson who had described Cady's new building as that "yellow brewery on Broadway," tossed in the towel with the weary statement: "I cannot fight Wall Street."

Opera in Europe, born in the courts of Italy and France, was long the playground of princes and the privileged. It is no surprise to learn that the money barons of the late nineteenth and early twentieth centuries made the existence of opera in America possible. As Eugene Bonner said in *The Club in the Opera House:* "With the establishment of what was, in effect, a sort of Republican Court at the new opera house, the parterre boxes gradually took on the semblance of individual drawing rooms where the hostesses—during the intermissions, when they were not distracted by the

music—could receive visitors. The majority of these consisted of unattached and eligible males who either had seats in less exalted parts of the house or who (after the good old European custom) simply bought General Admission and cruised the boxes until vacancies presented themselves. As these gentlemen, mostly of the younger set, were frequently going on afterwards to the same parties as were the occupants of the boxes they visited, they were generally welcomed as escorts for the unattached ladies usually present on such occasions." Monday night became society night at the opera because Monday was dancing night at Delmonico's, where the Patriarchs Club, the Assembly, and the Family Circle Dancing Class held forth. People in society would appear in their boxes at the Metropolitan around 9 P.M., after dinner regardless of curtain time, and move on later to other functions on or around Madison Square. (The only hangover of this gaudy era is the fact that the Met is the world's only major opera house in which late-comers are seated during the acts, to the intense annoyance of all others already in place when the curtain goes up.)

And festivities in the house were by no means confined to the on-stage drinking scenes that are part of many operas. In early days, champagne was served from the bar to the boxes. If the popping of corks and the clinking of glasses was appropriate for the ball scene in *La Traviata*, one can only surmise what it must have sounded like during *Parsifal*. Once during a performance of *Tannhäuser* the jolly, gregarious noise got so out of hand that the conductor Anton Seidl—probably the best of the Metropolitan maestros before Toscanini—daringly halted the performance until it subsided. As a result of his brave defiance of his bosses, eating and drinking were thereafter confined to the bar and restaurant of the Opera Club, where high jinks on one occasion even precipitated a raid by the New York police department.

In these years the opera being performed was incidental to those who paid, and paid handsomely, to support it. One reporter noted: "Tiaras flourished among the boxes and conversation interrupted the music except when some favorite reached a popular aria." Works were sung in languages that almost nobody understood and in competition with the most elaborate social pageantry a gilded age could produce. In a day when singers sent secretaries or understudies to rehearsals when it did not suit them to attend in person, it would be easy to conclude that the standards on the stage were low. But, surprisingly, they were not. Metropolitan productions were lavish, and the foremost singers and conductors of Europe were on the payroll at salaries far in excess of those they could command at home. The American millionaires who paid for the opera probably knew no more about opera than Andrew Mellon and Henry Clay Frick knew about old masters, but they all operated on the same principle: only the best would do. They got it.

Three people were chiefly responsible for converting the Metropolitan Opera from a social circus to one of the world's top opera houses, and none of them was ever listed in the New York Social Register. They were General Manager Gatti-Casazza, the then unknown conductor Arturo Toscanini from La Scala, and the thirty-year-old tenor Enrico Caruso. The Toscanini legend seems unlikely to die so long as great music is greatly performed. One of the most typical of the innumerable stories concerns the complaints of the men in the opera orchestra about the foul language young Toscanini used at them when he was displeased. "But gentlemen," remonstrated Gatti-Casazza, "you should hear what he calls *me!*"

If one could pick a night to go back to the old Met in its golden age, everybody might have a different choice. One might be the 1910 world *première* of *The Girl of the Golden West*, when curtain calls were shared by David Belasco, who wrote the book; Giacomo Puccini, who wrote the music and came over from Italy for the occasion; Arturo Toscanini, who conducted; and Enrico Caruso, who starred. Another might be the season's opening night in 1918, when the great golden curtains swept up on the massed flags of the Allies. The exact date was November 11—Armistice Day. Still another might be Geraldine Farrar's farewell after sixteen triumphant seasons in the house, an occasion which precipitated the biggest demonstration in the Met's history. Or one could come down to our time and to the November night in 1956 when Maria Callas made her Met debut in the title role of *Norma*—followed by the party at the Ambassador Hotel in her honor, at which the beautiful star swept

in after midnight in ruby-red velvet and ablaze with $1,500,-000 of Harry Winston's diamonds, as 200 of New York's musical artistic and social elite were on their feet to toast her with champagne. No entrance in any opera was ever more dazzling.

Since 1950, the key man in the entire Met operation has been Rudolf Bing, a lanky Vienna-born Englishman who made his reputation at Glyndebourne and afterward at the Edinburgh Festival. In 1903 the first American production of Richard Strauss's *Salome* was withdrawn as indecent at the personal insistence of board member J. P. Morgan. One index as to how times have changed in forty years is the fact that it is now inconceivable that any member of the board would for any reason demand that Mr. Bing withdraw a production.

In one respect, it is possible to say that Mr. Bing has simply been lucky: the current rivalry between adherents of Mesdames Callas and Tebaldi has been the biggest box-office bonanza since the days of Caruso and Farrar. Yet in other ways Mr. Bing has left the imprint of his own intense personality on every phase of Metropolitan activities. It was he, for example, who imported to the Met a long list of show-wise people like Margaret Webster, Alfred Lunt, Cyril Ritchard, and Garson Kanin to stage new productions of old war horses like *Die Fledermaus*, one of the biggest successes in the Metropolitan's history, and *Cosi Fan Tutte*. In the field of design, the Met has benefited handsomely from the contributions of a distinguished easel painter like Eugene Berman, whose *Don Giovanni* is surely his masterpiece, and of an experienced stage designer like Rolf Gerard. Even the once-moribund ballet has taken a new lease on life. When Bing in his first season rehired the foremost Wagnerian soprano of the day, Kirsten Flagstad, over complaints that her late husband had been a notorious Nazi collaborator, Bing faced the storm with a characteristic statement: "Quality alone . . . is the test. . . . If there is to be any shooting, let it be at me."

There will, of course, be plenty of shooting when the new house is opened in the fall of 1961. Between now and then literally thousands of questions must be settled. Which composers, if any, should be honored with an inscription on the proscenium arch? Which opera would be the most suitable for the opening? Who should sing in it on that historic occasion? Should the new house be inaugurated with an American work—Samuel Barber's highly successful *Vanessa*, for example—and should the repertory under Wallace Harrison's airy, modern roof lean more to the new and challenging than it has? "Once the curtain is up," says General Manager Bing, the architect's chief professional client, "there can be no excuses."

A former art and music editor of Newsweek, *Nelson Lansdale is a free-lance writer who has published in* Town and Country, House and Garden, This Week, Promenade, *and many others.*

FAMILY

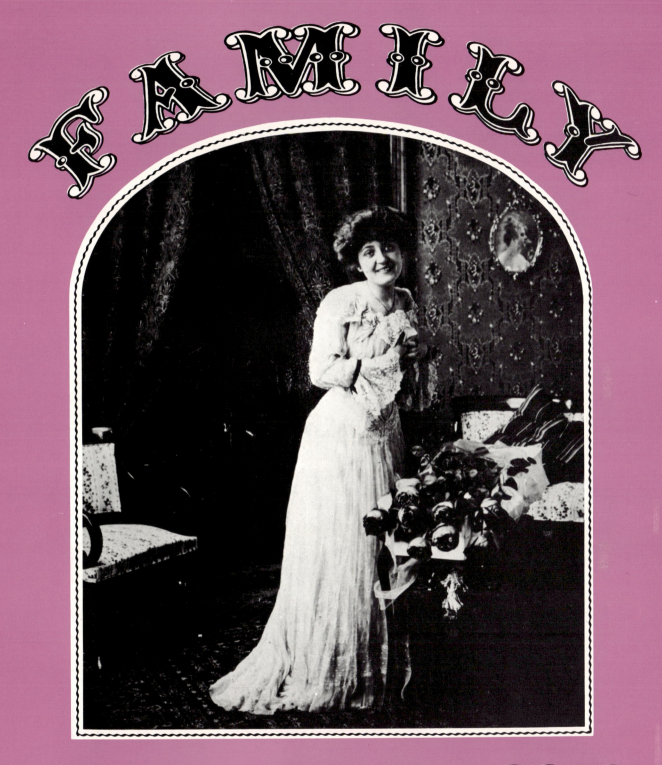

ALBUM

BERTHA F. BEASELY

"Little Me"

Not long after the untimely death, at one hundred and two, of the late Bertha F. Beasely, this album of her photographs was found in her attic, hidden from prying eyes behind the pianola boxes and underneath the lantern slides of "A Trip to the Holy Land." Small wonder that she kept it secret! Here are private thoughts, personal opinions, family secrets. Here, to coin a phrase, is the innermost Bertha F. Beasely.

Bertha Footly—to use the name by which she is best-known, since her romance with Horace Beasely, a rubber-cement manufacturer, was an autumnal flowering—was the historian and poet laureate of Footly Falls, the historic New England town which lies east of West Footly, west of East Footly, and a short distance—southeast by east and a half east—from Footly Center. She was descended from the Reverend Cotton Footly, a founder of the community, and from Jedediah Footly, the only patriot wounded in the Battle of Footly Falls. Although fickle fame has bestowed more attention on the ensuing engagements at West Footly and Footlyville, it was Bertha Footly's tireless research that has amply proved the fact that the ancestral shoulder abrasions were not shed, that is, suffered, in vain.

But enough of encomiums! Let Bertha F. Beasely speak for herself, for the comments beneath the photographs are in her original words. She would, I feel, have liked it that way.

OLIVER JENSEN

By the Same Author

SCENIC WALKS IN HISTORIC FOOTLY FALLS✻
WITH FIRE AND SWORD IN FOOTLY FALLS✻
THE FLOWERING OF FOOTLY FALLS✝
SOLDIER, STATESMAN & INVENTOR:
    A BIOGRAPHY OF JEDEDIAH FOOTLY✝
MORE WALKS IN HISTORIC FOOTLY FALLS✻
THE BOY OF THE LIMBERLOST✤

✻ Privately printed
✝ Unpublished
✤ Withdrawn, by agreement with attorneys
    for Gene Stratton Porter

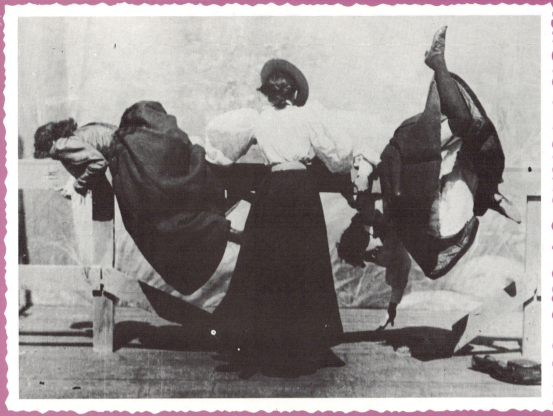

"Coming home from Chautauqua: that naughty photographer!"

"I suppose it was my body that Horace really wanted."

"After Father's forehead got so badly scratched, Mother never wore sharp buttons again."

"I don't really belong in your world, Horace Beasely."

"... more memories"

"I am clay in your hands, Mr. Beasely.
Mould me as you will."

"I knew that dreadful story about where children came from was all a lie."

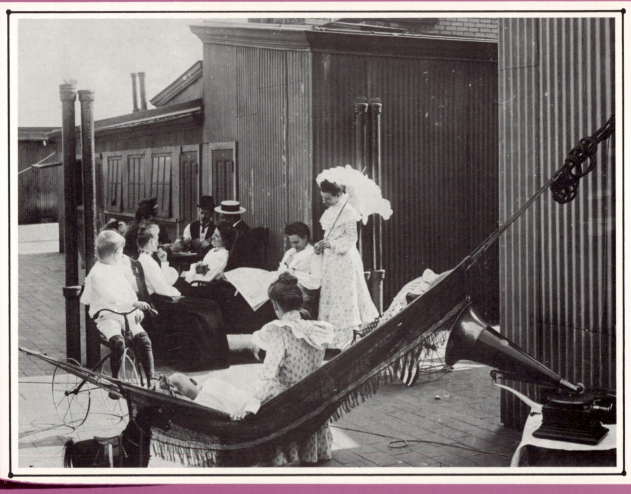

"Lunch chez Al Fresco! That's Mr. Fresco in the plug hat."

"Come along, Horace, they're not really looking for four-leaf clovers."

"Clifton Van Doren Beasely: He grew up to be a book reviewer."

*"Off to Gomorrah Falls in the Stearns-Knight —
what a radiator cap Elsie made!"*

*"Aunt Esther and 'Queen Victoria';
she never tired of 'Just before
the Battle, Mother.'"*

*"I liked Baba-au-Rhum but
Baba-au-Rhum didn't like me."*

"Men were fun...

But what...

"'I play for keeps,' I told
that Mr. Fothergill."

Were they really after?"

"I was a wild free creature until Mr. Footly tamed me."

"The sea always brought out the nymph in me. (Arbor Day – 1901)

Even as a child......

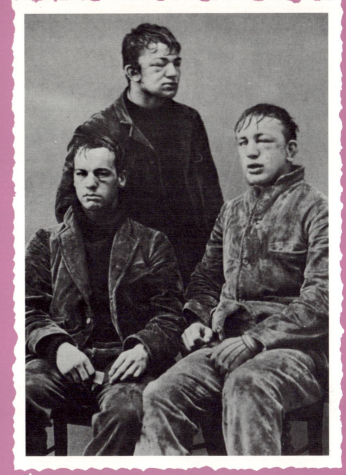

" The Ketchum Boys, constant 'chums' and always ready for a lark."

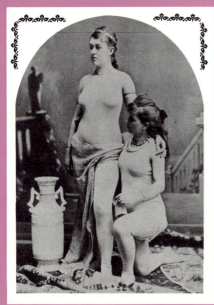

I knew my body.....

Was a temple. (I'm sure I heard something snap!)

" There are some things a girl would rather walk home from than!" (After the Blaine 'Victory Ball').

"Before the dreadful accident with the electric fan."

Behind the Golden Curtain

CONTINUED FROM PAGE 27

the Opéra. Conductors, musicians, singers, stage directors, and all others go through their routine with a nonchalance that would not be tolerated in a large Montmartre night club or in the kitchen of La Tour d'Argent. The scenic and choreographic possibilities of the house are enormous, and the ballet is very good, but that is about all. The company has some very good singers, but no effort is made to forge them into an ensemble. The Opéra (and also the smaller but more interesting Opéra-Comique) are run by bureaucrats. Crises are frequent, strikes occasional, feuds and recriminations perpetual, and the Opéra is often closed down.

The repertory is conventional: Gounod's *Faust* is the most popular work and could be performed twice a week to capacity audiences. Perhaps because Richard Wagner was so badly treated in Paris (where he spent several weeks in a debtors' prison) and because of the scandal after the unhappy performance of the revised *Tannhäuser* on March 13, 1861 (after 163 rehearsals, with Adolphe Sax called in with his saxophone to supplement the stage horns), there is now a small, dedicated Wagerian community in Paris for whom the Opéra puts on *Der Ring des Nibelungen* every year, with a German company conducted by Knappertsbusch, the greatest contemporary Wagner conductor.

The Opéra has derived fame from Lon Chaney's film, *The Phantom of the Opera*, from occasional gala balls and elegant charity affairs, and from being one of the most photographed buildings in the world. Everybody wants to go to Paris, but did you ever meet anyone who wants to go there because of the Opéra?

East Berlin State Opera

The old German Staatsoper in the eastern sector of divided Berlin is the show place of East Germany and possibly the most important opera house behind the Iron Curtain. Opened in 1742, during the reign of Frederick the Great, it was a fine example of the "Berlin Forum" style with its austerely classical façade and baroque and rococo touches. (An official East German publication explains that the opera house then was "the salon of a feudal regime, with no inner meaning for the people.") During the Seven Years' War the house was closed; during Napoleon's occupation it became a storage house for bread. In 1843 the opera burned out but was quickly rebuilt. After the turn of the century the Hofoper, as it was then called, became one of the world's leading houses; Muck, Strauss, Kleiber, Blech, Furtwängler were its conductors. During the Nazi era Goering was the Staatsoper's protector. When it was bombed by the Royal Air Force in 1941, Goering gave orders that it must be rebuilt and reopened a year later, and it was. In 1945 it was bombed again, to be rebuilt again—this time with Soviet aid.

The old building has been faithfully reconstructed, with new emphasis on marble, like the Moscow subway. It stands on Unter den Linden—once an elegant avenue, now a desolate ghost street—between the ruins of the former Crown Prince's palace and the old Royal Library. After all the rubble and ruins outside, one is not prepared for its profusion of crystal mirrors, chandeliers, carpets, and marble. Its luxurious basement buffet is the only place in East Germany where anybody can buy food without a ration card.

The famous Staatskapelle, the State Opera's orchestra, has a precise quality and excellent wood winds and brass, but its sound is sharp rather than luscious. The staging is often dull and provincial, with old-fashioned papier-mâché props; yet sometimes it is revolutionary and stunning, with lights and shadows and nothing else. The Staatsoper has a large roster of artists from both the East and the West, and the average quality of the productions is good, though rarely up to that of the leading houses in the West. The performances are well rehearsed and the artists tightly disciplined. They are well paid and the costumes are often expensive. The tickets are low-priced and distributed mostly among workers' groups and Party bureaucrats, but there are no budget problems. Although no figures are published, it is known that the government provides whatever is needed to make this the country's operatic show place. The repertory is large and interesting. Russian, Czech, and Polish works are given along with two dozen works by Mozart, Verdi, Puccini, Wagner, and Strauss.

Inevitably, the question is asked whether there is a difference between opera houses on opposite sides of the Iron Curtain. There is. Not on the stage; the days of revolutionary sets and party-line staging are gone, and a production of *Aïda* or *La Traviata* is not a question of *Weltanschauung*. But the listener from the West becomes aware of the difference when the curtain falls and the lights go on. He notices that the warmth and intimacy of the East Berlin auditorium itself are in contrast with the audience's restraint and self-consciousness. The people are not relaxed as are opera audiences in the Western world; instead of a festive spirit there is always an undercurrent of tension. And the gold leaf and pompous marble stand out in contrast with people's bad shoes and rough shirts. One leaves with the impression that even more than under the Prussian kings the beautiful East Berlin Opera House has become "the salon of the regime."

Once a music student at the Vienna Conservatory in the 1920's, Joseph Wechsberg is now one of America's leading commentators on the cultural scene in many countries, writing for The New Yorker *and publishing numerous books, the latest of which is* Avalanche.

My Uninvited Collaborator: G. B. S.

CONTINUED FROM PAGE 20

content and betterment, tempered by the fear, not of artificially manufactured punishments, but of genuine natural consequences, to be faced or funked, as the case may be, in the light of kindness, humour and common sense." One would have liked to watch the cynical smile on the face of a commissar as he read that, just after committing a few thousand discontented liberty-lovers to a concentration camp. Here is a further saying of Shaw's: "No nation can prosper or even continue to exist without heretics and advocates of shockingly immoral doctrines." He also asserted that no civilization could progress without declaring impunity for criticism, and "for propositions that shock the uncritical as obscene, seditious, blasphemous, heretical and revolutionary." He even admitted that "no single criminal can be as powerful for evil, or as unrestrained in its exercise, as an organized nation . . . not only does Society commit more frightful crimes than any individual, king or commoner: it legalizes its crimes, and forges certificates of righteousness for them, besides torturing anyone who dares to expose their true character." I followed these quotations with the perfectly truthful statement that Shaw's influence on the world of his time had been a quickening and liberating one, and that he had done everything in his power to make people critical of institutions, antagonistic to persecution, sceptical of authority, and healthily rebellious. In spite of which, I said, he had praised and supported the Russian dictatorship, which suppressed free speech, murdered its political opponents, starved its recalcitrant peasants to death, enslaved everyone else, and, generally speaking, made the Robespierres and Marats of the French Revolution seem like a bunch of mealymouthed meliorists by comparison.

When Shaw arrived at this section of my book he showed irritation. "You must cut all this out," he said. "The quotations you've given don't contradict my present attitude toward Russia. What do you know of the Soviet Government? Nothing whatever. You've simply picked up a lot of hearsay nonsense from the English press which you believe religiously. Have you ever read a newspaper account of something you happen to know a great deal about?"

"Yes," I replied.

"How true was it?"

"Scarcely a word."

"And yet you dare to believe the twaddle any journalist cares to invent about Russia because he knows it will please his proprietor, his editor and his readers. Really, Hesketh, I'm surprised at you!"

"But is there no suppression of free speech or shooting of opponents or slave labour in Russia?"

"No more than there is at a time of crisis in England. Just try to tell the truth about this confounded conflict or impede

the war effort and see what happens—"

"Ah, well, in wartime things are different."

"Russia is perpetually at war. She is ringed round with enemies. She can trust no one. Therefore, if she were guilty of the things you say, she couldn't help herself."

"You'll be telling me next that England's attitude to Communism is the cause of all the horrors that take place in Russia."

"Prove your horrors before you talk of them."

"How can I?"

"Exactly."

I had to think of something else.

"Suppose it could be proved that what I have written there is true, would you still support the Soviet?"

"Yes, because worse things have happened in other countries, especially Germany, and the Russians are trying to create a new and classless society. But don't run away with the idea that my critical sense is suspended where they are concerned. I have criticised freely and openly, and will continue to criticise, their mistakes; but I don't depend upon a hostile press to tell me what they are. I would as soon expect a completely objective view of a mongoose by a cobra."

He then handed me what he had written about his attitude toward Communism and his trip to Russia, and I gave his version roughly in my biography, though I couldn't help leading up to it with some of those anti-institutional quotations which he thought had nothing to do with the subject, together with his own reply to a question he put after his return from Moscow: "Had we not better teach our children to be better citizens than ourselves? We are not doing that at present. The Russians *are*."

One afternoon at Ayot St Lawrence, when we were discussing certain passages in my book, he dealt lightly with several points I raised, at the same time warning me not to burden my biography with the details, which I am giving now for the first time. I happened to ask him whether he had been hissed or hooted at any of his first nights since the memorable Sunday performance of *Widowers' Houses*.

"I once experienced something far worse than a hissing or a hooting," he replied, "and that was polite indifference expressed by half-hearted applause from a few well-wishers and dead silence from the large majority. But I had a companion in my misfortune, no other than Sir Arthur Pinero. It was during Charles Frohman's attempt to establish a repertory at the Duke of York's Theatre a year or two before the First World War. Everyone thought it would be a wonderful thing if the playbill could announce three one-act plays by the three leading dramatists of the hour: Pinero, Barrie and myself. Accordingly we set to work. Pinero did a neat bit of craftsmanship called *The Widow of Wasdale Head*. I did what I thought an entertaining thing called *Overruled*. Barrie did a charming piece of barriefication called *Rosalind*. Pinero's playlet fell flat, mine fell flatter, and by contrast Barrie's magic worked as it never had before and never has since. The relief to the audience after the Pinero-Shaw mystifications was stupendous. They simply howled for Barrie, whose pleasant little comedy made them realize how much they hated us. If we had dared to take a call after the show, one author would have been carried shoulder-high round Trafalgar Square, the other two would have been torn limb from limb. Next morning Frohman's producer, Dion Boucicault, rang me up to suggest a few cuts. I replied that there were only two possible cuts—Pinero's piece and my own—and I advised him to advertise a WARNING in capital letters in the press and over the box-office window, with the following simple statement beneath: 'Mr. Barrie's piece commences at 10, before which the theatre bars are open.'

"But," concluded Shaw, "keep all this triviality out of your biography."

Another topic that afternoon was Shaw's vegetarianism, which was due partly to his disgust at eating dead bodies and his repugnance at the thought of the world as a vast slaughter-house, but also to considerations of health. I wanted to know whether his diet has made him immune to the ills that the flesh of meat-eaters is heir to. "How do I know?" he said. "How do I know what health I might have enjoyed if I had been carnivorous? But I remember one occasion very vividly when I suffered all the tortures that should have been reserved for corpse-devourers and whisky-swillers. It was about thirty years ago, and I was in the middle of a rehearsal when I became acutely conscious that all was not well in my interior. I handed over the production to someone else and managed to get out of the stalls without giving the game away. But I collapsed with pain in the corridor, where one of the theatre staff, assuming I was dead drunk, passed me without a word. Somehow I got into a taxi, becoming delirious after giving my address. The taxi-driver was most solicitous, and helped me indoors with soothing words—'There, there! Go to bed. You'll soon be better,' and so on. A doctor was summoned and stone in the kidney was diagnosed. I couldn't believe it. Stone in the kidney after a manhood nourished on the diet of Pythagoras! Out of the question! Preposterous! Another doctor was sent for, and he agreed with the first. For hours I lay in bed writhing in agony and being hideously sick at regular intervals. The stone eventually left my kidney for my bladder, after which the pain changed in kind but not intensity. Three hours of my raving and groaning and cursing and bawling got on the doctor's nerves and he administered morphia. When I returned to consciousness the pain of the stone's unhurried journey racked me again, and the damned thing didn't emerge until about 8 in the morning, after I had sped its de-

parture with a series of unparalleled paroxysms that broke the bedsprings. Having been X-rayed I dashed up to Southsea for a Labour Conference, where I made the speech of a man who has fought with wild beasts and then fed on them. However the reading public won't be interested in my inside, so you'd better content yourself with the announcement that I am an unrepentant vegetarian on health grounds. The stone in my kidney was probably inherited from my alcoholic ancestors."

On the same afternoon Shaw told me about Erica Cotterill, one of the many young women who had been strongly attracted to him. I had seen a letter from Shaw's wife, Charlotte, to Erica, and was curious to have his version of the affair. It began, he told me, when his plays were being performed at the Court Theatre. "Erica opened fire with an impassioned plea that we should meet. I warned her that nothing could come of it. But her correspondence became longer and warmer; so I started giving her a little advice. Instead of putting her off this incited her to more eloquent appeals, and at length I met her, hoping that a rational interview would abate her enthusiasm. It had precisely the opposite effect, and she did a monstrous thing: she took a cottage in this village in order to see me and be near me. I at once explained the whole position to my wife, so as to prepare her for possible incidents and intrusions. Though I had strongly advised Erica to remain invisible, she stupidly called at our house. Charlotte of course was furious and showed by her manner that the girl's behaviour was highly improper. Then, as you know, Charlotte wrote forbidding her to call again. This did not prevent Erica from maintaining a barrage of letters to me, several of which would have led an ignorant reader to believe that we had been sexually intimate. One phrase I recall ran something like this: 'At night, when I have you alone to myself.' Now that can only bear one interpretation except the true one, which was that Erica lived in a fanciful world of her own. However, as the whole affair was extremely distasteful to Charlotte, who accused me of encouraging the girl, you must keep this to yourself until no one's feelings can be hurt by reference to it."

Charlotte's letter, which had been shown me by a friend of Erica's, was firmly expressed. It informed Erica that when a woman made a declaration of her feelings to a married man they were bound in honor to see no more of one another. The present case was a specially dangerous one, said Charlotte, because her husband was not a common man, and if Erica and he became at all intimate he would be a necessity of life to her and their ultimate unavoidable parting would cause unnecessary pain. "I could not trust him to keep you at a distance," Charlotte confessed; "he is quite friendly and sympathetic with everybody, from dogs and cats to dukes and duchesses, and none of them can imagine that his universal friendliness is not a special regard for them. He has already allowed you to become far more attached to him than he should, and I do not intend to let you drift any further into an impossible position." Charlotte ended by saying that her letter admitted of no argument or reply, that she would enter into no correspondence on the subject, and that her decision was quite irrevocable.

These three episodes which I have reported here were not the only omissions from my biography of Shaw. When the whole work was in type its length was more than the publisher and I had bargained for, and by the spring of 1941 the war had caused a shortage of paper. I informed Shaw that the book ran to about 210,000 words, and he called this outrageous. "Your original estimate of 150,000 was if anything excessive. Even if your publisher were prepared to foot such a printing bill and such a price as it would impose, I should advise you for the sake of your own reputation for readability to cut down ruthlessly." But he must have ruminated on the pruning of so many words, because the next time we met he showed me Denis Mackail's *Story of J. M. Barrie*, telling me that it contained 346,320 words in 722½ quite legibly leaded pages of thin but opaque paper, plus twelve pages of index, the book being quite handy enough. However, the publisher having asked me to reduce the length of my work by 35,000 words, I journeyed to Ayot St. Lawrence with the typescript for a session with Shaw, which lasted two hours in the morning and another hour after lunch. Our excisions consisted chiefly of quotations from his letters and criticisms, but he also blue-penciled two of my reports of his talk. The first dealt with the attitude of dramatic critics to the seasons at the Court Theatre from 1904 to 1907, when Shaw's plays first met with success in London and his position as a dramatist was finally secured. This was what he said to me:

"My first new play to be done at the Court was *John Bull's Other Island*. The critics denounced it as no play at all and said that the actors did their best with impossible parts. Then came *Man and Superman*. This was voted dull and uninspired compared with its predecessor. *Major Barbara* followed, and the critics promptly burst into raptures over *Man and Superman*. But *Major Barbara* was duly described as a masterpiece when its successor *The Doctor's Dilemma* was dismissed as a feeble joke in bad taste. So I seized the first opportunity to make a speech at a public dinner at which all the leading dramatic critics were present. 'I want to make a suggestion to the press,' I said. 'I don't ask you to stop abusing me. It gives you so much pleasure to say that my plays are no plays and that my characters are not human beings that I would not deprive you of it for worlds. But for the sake of the management, Vedrenne and Barker, not to mention the actors, may I beg you to reverse the order of your curses and caresses? Instead of saying that my latest play is piffle, the one before it brilliant, why not acclaim the latest as a masterpiece compared with the disgusting drivel I had the impertinence to serve up last time? That will satisfy you and assist us. In short, don't heave bricks at us while we are struggling in the water and then load us with lifebelts when we have reached dry land.' "

Shaw canceled these passages, saying: "Why waste words on the critics? I have already wasted too many."

The other episode he removed from the book was the description of what he had told me a few years after the production of *The Apple Cart*. At an accidental meeting between two of his sea voyages I asked him whether there was any truth in the general belief that King Magnus in his comedy was a veiled portrait of the then reigning monarch, George V. He replied cautiously that if people liked to think so, he had no objection. I pressed him to be more precise. "Well, there is a king on the throne, and there is a king in my play, and if the king on the throne happened to behave like the king in my play you could say they resembled one another." I remarked that there was not the slightest resemblance between them. "The real King Magnus is sitting within a few feet of you," he announced. "Never having been offered a throne, I have had to seize one and crown myself. But I have a lot in common with the present monarch: we are both human beings and we were both christened George, and I dare say he dislikes the name as much as I do."

On the same occasion Shaw assured me that the part of Orinthia was a lifelike portrait of Stella Patrick Campbell, and that the wrestling match between Orinthia and Magnus had actually occurred between himself and Stella. "Sometimes, when I got up to leave her, she would pin me down and do her utmost to make me late for meals at home. It used to be a real tussle between us until I learnt how to grip her wrists: then I became master of the situation. One of our bouts did actually end with both of us on the floor fighting like mad." Stella heard that Shaw had portrayed her in *The Apple Cart*, and insisted that he read the play to her before it was produced. He was nervous and did his best to get out of it. But after several evasions he surrendered, called at her house in Kensington Square, and went through the performance which he described to me:

"The first act nearly sent her to sleep. She yawned through it. 'Now for us!' I said when we arrived at the Interlude. She instantly became attentive, and I was keenly conscious of her interest throughout the scene. The atmosphere was like that of a law-court just before the jury's verdict is pronounced. I expected a few laughs, but she didn't oblige me with so much as a chuckle. It would have been heart-rending if my heart had been rendable. At its conclusion there was a long pause. I was determined not to speak first. Then she said: 'The whole thing is invented; it's not a bit like you or me.' I jumped into the opening she gave me: 'Of course it's invented. This is fiction, not history.' She couldn't think of an immediate reply, and to gain time told me to go on. I read the last act, but she wasn't listening: she was thinking of what to say about the Interlude. The job finished, she asked to look at the play. I handed it over, saying, 'Chuck it in the fire if that will relieve your feelings; I have plenty of copies.' She went through the Interlude, objected to several passages, which I promised to alter, and told me that, if true, the scene was libelous; if invented, it was rubbish; and in both cases it was vulgar. Having expressed my disagreement at some length, and said that, whether fact or fiction, the scene would immortalize her, I made a dignified exit just before, as I fancied, she was about to hurl a cushion at my head.''

Shaw's reason for the omission of all this was simply that quite enough had already been said about Stella Campbell in the earlier part of the book, and that his comments on King Magnus were not biographically important.

Just before the book was sent to the printer I had what I thought a brain wave, and when Shaw referred to the "unique private history" which he had contributed to my pages, I made the suggestion that everything he had written should be shown in the text either between square brackets or by indentation. His reply was vigorous and decisive:

"Not on your life, Hesketh! What I have written I have written in your character, not in my own. As an auto-biographer I should have written quite differently. There are things that you may quite properly say which would come less gracefully from me. I have carefully avoided altering your opinions except where you had not known the facts. For the rest I have either retained or paraphrased, leaving you to reparaphrase if I had misinterpreted. You can of course in a foreword say that as you know me personally your authority for much hitherto unpublished information is G. B. S. himself at first hand. But if a word is said to connect me with the authorship of the book or its first proposal or its commercial profits, I shall be driven to the most desperate steps to disclaim it. It must appear as

Frank Harris' book did, to which I contributed a good deal to save his widow from destitution.''

I wrote my note of acknowledgments on the lines he suggested, showed it to him, and said that I would tone down some of his more Shavian phrases. Handing me his last batch of emendations, he said: "Let nothing tempt you to tone any of this down. Tone it up as much as you like. Don't run away with the notion that your readers—least of all the critics—will spot any difference between your stuff and mine. They won't. In the Harris book they didn't. If the story carries them along they won't start detective work; and, anyhow, my style won't disgrace you. Since you must consider the copyright question as between your executors and mine, I strongly advise you to do what I did in the Harris case. When the book is safely in print, take the copy and burn every scrap of it. It will then be forever impossible for either of us to lay a finger on any page or passage and say 'This is Pearson's copyright, and this is Shaw's.' It will be all yours without any possible question; and let nothing tempt you to part with it. I have no duplicates. Your prefatory note is all right. If you are unbearably ashamed of some of my sallies you can add 'In reporting what he has told me I have endeavoured when possible to use what I can remember of his own vivid phrases.' There! Will that satisfy you?"

His final sally, which gave me a good laugh, occurred nearly a year after the book's publication. Seeing my own copy of it, he took up his pen and wrote on the flyleaf under my signature: "Also his humble collaborator G. Bernard Shaw."

Starting out in 1911 as an actor who appeared in many prominent London stage productions, Hesketh Pearson later turned to criticism and biography and numbers among his books, apart from that on Shaw, studies of Charles Dickens, Oscar Wilde, Sir Arthur Conan Doyle, James Whistler, Beerbohm Tree, and Sir Walter Scott.

Peter Ustinov

CONTINUED FROM PAGE 85

was as conscious of Ustinov's talents—and limitations—as he, and assigned him most of the time to documentary movies. With the novelist Eric Ambler, he wrote one of the best to come out of the war, *The Way Ahead*, starring David Niven. During production, for purposes of military protocol, the disheveled Ustinov was given the unlikely assignment of batman to Colonel Niven.

Ustinov's first three plays were produced while he was in the service. *House of Regrets*, a story of Russian exiles, reached the stage largely because James Agate, the waspish but influential critic of the *Sunday Times*, had seen it in manuscript and warmly praised it. The second play was a Chekhovian effort, *Blow Your Own Trumpet*, written in three days.

(Ustinov now says that Chekhov plays "are very selfish— everybody talks and nobody listens.") Agate turned mercilessly on Ustinov when this drama opened and wrote that the author had "every quality of a first-class playwright except one: he cannot think of a story." But Ustinov's third play, *The Banbury Nose*, a third-generation play in reverse (starting in the present and working backward in time), brought about yet another Agate reversal. Agate wrote: "He is the greatest master of stagecraft now writing in this country." Ustinov was then twenty-three.

In the years since, Ustinov has written such disparate plays as *The Tragedy of Good Intentions* (about the Crusades), *The Empty Chair* (about the French Revolution), *The Indiffer-*

ent Shepherd (about a pastor), and one about the South American liberator Simon Bolivar, which never reached London. He has remained equally unruffled by failure and unswayed by success. In 1953, when his play *No Sign of the Dove*, an allegory about Noah and the Ark, was blasted by critics and booed by audiences, Ustinov replied: "The sound of booing, when directed against you personally, is particularly unmusical, but it does clear the mind as no amount of adulation can.... I shall write as I think ... even if I have to boo the gallery from the stage." The play tottered through eleven performances.

Ustinov's first major success was *The Love of Four Colonels*. It ran two years in London, had the longest run (1,300 performances) of any postwar play in France, and has traveled to thirty countries. In this play, four colonels—an Englishman, a Frenchman, an American, and a Russian—have joint jurisdiction over a castle in which, it develops, lies the Sleeping Princess. The Wicked Fairy offers each colonel a chance to win the Princess by acting out a playlet. The Englishman, an Elizabethan at heart, does his wooing in Shakespearean form and verse. The Frenchman's style is pure Molière. The American is a romantic puritan; in his play-within-a-play, the Princess is a floozie whom he tries to rescue from a fate worse than death. The Russian is a Chekhovian procrastinator. Ustinov appeared in each playlet as the Wicked Fairy; in the British, as a Fool; in the French, as a cuckolded husband; in the American, as a gangster; and in the Russian, as an old uncle in gray whiskers and Panama hat.

Some of Ustinov's lines were finely tooled. In the Molière-ish sketch, the woman says: "Without a husband to deceive, a lover's an empty pleasure." Later, when the wives of the four colonels are talking together, the British woman says: "Even if a woman has nothing to hide, she should be at great pains to hide it." But as usual, Ustinov won better notices for his acting than for his writing. The British critic T. C. Worsley complained: "The only difficulty is that as an actor he steals the scene from himself as playwright. ... Mr. Ustinov's ideas are always better than his technique."

As an actor, Ustinov appeared on the London stage as the inspector in *Crime and Punishment*, with John Gielgud. He made several movies in Hollywood, including *Quo Vadis*, *The Egyptian*, and *We're No Angels*. Ustinov likes Hollywood because it has provided wonderful new satiric material for him. "Initials stood out on the shirts of producers like Gothic cathedrals above the infinite horizons of their trouser tops," he says; "Of course, all this was before cholesterol."

In Hollywood, Ustinov fell into the movie colony's obsessive habit of violent exercise. With Gene Kelly he used to sneak away from Hollywood parties at night to play tennis ("we'd serve a moth and volley bats across the court") and return without anyone's having discovered their absence. He argues that "Hollywood people are always doing things that are good for them, like sports. The result is that the place is full of people aged fifty who look like a healthy sixty."

Ustinov lives a sober and respectable married life with his second wife, Suzanne Cloutier, a charming French-Canadian actress whom he met in 1951 when acting in *The Love of Four Colonels*. Like Ustinov, she has suffered for being non-British. As the daughter of the Queen's Printer in Ottawa, Suzanne was presented at sixteen at Government House. "I can remember as I was curtsying," Suzanne recalls, "hearing one woman say: 'Isn't she pretty?' and the woman with her saying: 'Yes, but she's French, you know.' I just went poop; I didn't care any more. I knew how Alexander Korda felt when Peter and I were married in London. He warned me what to expect. He said: 'I've lived in London most of my life, I've done a lot for England, but they still think of me as 'Korda the Hungarian.' "

At seventeen, Suzanne, whose family hoped she would become a nun, ran away from home with $63 in her purse and bought a ticket to New York. She could barely speak English, and in terror of the big city she spent three days in Grand Central Station until a model named Bijou Barrington spotted her as she was combing job advertisements with the aid of a French-English dictionary. Suzanne became a successful model and then a not so successful movie actress, chiefly in French movies, before marrying Ustinov. They now have two young children, and Suzanne is too busy running a somewhat chaotic household to act, except very rarely. Only once has she been in a Ustinov play. In *No Sign of the Dove* she had one word to say: "Boccaccio." Says Ustinov: "She said the word very effectively."

The Ustinovs lead a cheerfully nomadic existence, blithely picking up and discarding maids, cooks, and secretaries as they come and go. Any Ustinov ménage, in any part of the world, is a wild jumble of shrieking children, fluttering servants, tumbles of papers, cacophonies of telephone calls. At the moment the head of the family spends much of his time shrinking from its latest acquisition, a cat named Minou, which Suzanne bought for one dollar. "I hate the texture of cats," Ustinov explains as he makes desperate and futile attempts to shoo Minou from the room by throwing a coat in front of it, bullfighter-style.

The Ustinovs serve admirable food and wine and enter-

"The Watchdogs of the West": a cartoon by Peter Ustinov.

tain often. Still more often, being a singularly engaging couple, they are asked out. Few people in the theater are so genuinely popular. "I've never met anyone so easy and cosy as Peter," remarks Henry Fonda. At any party Ustinov is apt to spill his talent profusely, to imitate cab drivers or United Nations diplomats he has heard on the radio, or to sit on the floor and draw quick, brilliant sketches of political figures.

Ustinov is intensely interested in politics but generally keeps his basically liberal opinions to himself. He spoke out both wittily and eloquently, however, in a broadcast to the BBC from the United States on the McCarthy hearings. He characterized Senator Joseph McCarthy: "Words come to him more easily than sentences, which is normal; but even words fall grudgingly from his lips—his eyes, meanwhile, having all the dispassionate intensity of a lion who is having his private troubles gnawing a juiceless knuckle."

In the theater, mimicry remains Ustinov's great forte. "I wonder," he says, "how acting can be learned indoors. When you're outside you see more people. The whole business of it is imitation. If you have a quirk recognized by the audience as something they do—or something a friend does—you can touch nerves gently that usually aren't touched at all. As for the audience itself, he remarks, "It is a mysterious thing; everyone of them is different. It's like putting a frontier in water. In the theater, one has to cultivate and train one's instincts, just as a driver at the Indianapolis Speedway doesn't *drive;* he controls his car."

In his work as mime, Ustinov's ear is constantly tuned to subtleties of accent and word usage. "The American language," he says, "is still in the process of formation. It's being added to every year by the influx of minorities. Certain Jewish expressions, for instance, begin to get general acceptance—such as 'You went out and bought a hat, yet!' or 'You bought a hat, already!' As a consequence of the changes in language, I find there is less respect for language in America—it's such a fluid thing. To actors who practice the Method, emotions are more sacrosanct than words. They'll even change a playwright's words to get at the emotions.

"The French have greater respect for language—and theirs is much more demanding than the looser-linked, richer English language. The English predilection for stuttering doesn't come so much from a national affliction as from a hesitancy over choosing the right word. Englishmen, notably the politicians, will even search for the wrong word with extreme care. In France, however, there's always a correct and an incorrect word; there's no debating it. Since the theater reflects the way people talk, Chekhov and some of the modern Americans are hard to play in French; the French, you see, never have any doubt how a sentence will end, once it starts. In French, you can even have a lucid discussion between two cab drivers.

"When in England recently, Arthur Miller complained that over there we were writing about frivolous subjects. That's not entirely true. Here again, language is a factor. The English are less communicative, less emotional than Americans. Their heart is inside their sleeve, not on it. In my own plays, I try to blend the comic with an undertone of seriousness. I don't think a play which even comically deals with politics or the behavior of men on a large scale is less sociological than one dealing with the sorry lot of stevedores."

Today, Ustinov is almost frantically in demand. Like other television performers, he is gnawingly aware of how fast comic material can be used up, and he has a horror of repeating himself too often. He has been toying with a skit based on a highly successful program he performed in London for the BBC. It would add sentences before and after famous quotes. "Thus," explains Ustinov, "to Queen Victoria's 'We are not amused,' I would reply: 'Actually, Your Majesty, it wasn't meant to be funny.' Then I'd have an elaborate African safari, with men groaning and slogging through the forest. Finally, one of them would say: 'Dr. Livingstone, I presume?' And the answer would come back: No, as a matter of fact, my name is Thompson.' To John Paul Jones' 'We have not yet begun to fight,' there can be only one reply: 'You'd better start soon; the ship is sinking.' To Drake's 'There is time to finish the game of bowls, and then beat the Spaniards,' I would say: 'Well, not really. You see, it takes three minutes to get to the ship and five more to cast off, and by that time the Spaniards will be round the corner.' And Drake will say petulantly: 'Oh, very well, then.'"

Ustinov is now taking *Romanoff and Juliet* on an extended coast-to-coast tour of the United States. Then he will make a movie version of *Romanoff* in Italy and appear in a film about Spartacus and the gladiators with Kirk Douglas. He plans to produce, direct, and star in his play *Paris Not So Gay.* This play, an ironic treatment of the Trojan War, was written in 1946 but not produced then and has since been drastically revised. Some time ago, Ustinov received from Hollywood the highest compliment it could pay any actor from Britain: he was offered the lead as the Brooklyn doctor in the movie version of the best seller *Last Angry Man.* Ustinov felt honored that his Brooklyn accent was considered so proficient, but declined the role.

Of himself he remarks: "I've never had enough money for it to embarrass me. I'm glad I started without a bean. It made me fend for myself. If I leave anything, I won't make it easy for my children to get hold of it. As far as I'm concerned, the best thing I've ever done in the theater is what comes next. I'm a Walter Mitty at heart. I constantly dream of winning at Wimbledon."

Serrell Hillman is presently the New York correspondent for Time, *with a special interest in the field of entertainment along Broadway.*

A Thoughtful Remembrance

for your favorite Egyptologist. Why not send him this handsomely designed, modern portable Hieroglyphityper? Helps him take down inscriptions in a jiffy and saves long tedious hours at the "dig." Writes over 80,000 different characters, or "glyphs," with less than 40,000 keys. In several gay colors, with trailer, this discerning gift is only 88,000,000 drachma at the Little Archaeology Shoppe, Athens. Free two-week guarantee. Camels for hauling extra. Budget givers will be interested in smaller models in Phoenician and Hittite.

AMUSING Oil Well GAME,

for that Texas friend, is easily set up in back yard or patio. Ideal for large parties. Concealed wire to well permits host to set off detonator which cleverly simulates gusher coming in, showers guests with washable black sludge. Extra containers of sludge, $10 each. Sophisticates, Inc., Ft. Worth.

HELP A DRINKING FRIEND

in that long struggle, with a year's membership in "The Pop-of-The-Month Club." Imagine how his eyes will brighten as each month's shipment brings a fresh surprise in the form of four weeks' supply of some new, stimulating nonalcoholic, nonhabit-forming drink. Pop-of-The-Month delivers one large case each month of such tangy thirst-quenchers as Sarsaparilla, Saratoga Water, Slippery Elm Tonic, sauerkraut-ade, etc. P-O-T-M "extra dividends" like the bottle of Denatured Cooking Sherry, sent gratis every July 30, will only serve to keep the giver's memory warm all the year long. Mail orders only.

KNOW A "V. I. P."?

For that friend in the Administration no present will be more appreciated than this can of Dr. Adams' Hound's Tooth Powder. Harmless sulphuric-acid scouring action keeps any surface clean, no matter with what it comes in contact. At all drugstores, $1.

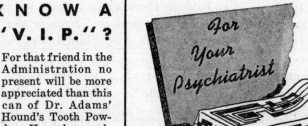

Aunt Jane Embroideries, Inc., of Brooklyn has a tasteful gift so appropriate for One To Whom You Owe So Much. Brand new this year is the "Psycho Couch Cover," a handsomely embroidered coverlet for his working area offered in a number of contemporary and Olde New Englande designs to suit Doctor's personality. The pair: $8.95; half dozen: $23.50. Please indicate whether Willow Pattern, Currier & Ives, Mondrian, or Jackson Pollock design preferred. An early order will assure a happy analyst at Yuletide!

MERRY CHRISTMAS FOR ART LOVERS!

Show your discernment and make your art-loving friend happy by giving an "Old Master Coffee Table." A limited number of these beautiful heirloom pieces are available, since each has a genuine Italian oil painting from the fifteenth century or earlier cunningly embedded in its surface. Beautifully cropped to retain all the sacred qualities lovingly painted long ago by bonded craftsmen, these "hard-to-get" canvases are treated with transparent plastic which neither water nor alcohol will stain. A limited number of Botticellis and Michelangelos will be included *for those who order early.* All tables certified by leading museum directors. Help your friends live with real art! If religious painting preferred, state faith, giving two alternates. Box 18.

FOR THE IVY LEAGUER

you simply can't give another regimental tie to, this 9-button cobra-hunting jacket in orange-and-blue plaid is years ahead of famous Brooks Brothers of New York. Eye-catching button-down Prime Minister's robe, as modeled by Rt. Hon. Kwame Nkrumah of Ghana, is another Xmas bull's-eye. Both only £3 10s. at Brooks of Accra, Ltd.

FOR "MOM-IN-LAW"!

Home witchcraft set is a "different" present sure to hit the mark. Black-peaked hat, wand, folding broomstick, attractive matched bottles containing mildly poisonous potions for practical jokes at teas, pie-baking contests, church suppers, etc. Paper of hex pins and small rag doll in image of giver included, provided recent photograph is furnished. Mather Novelty Co., Salem, Mass.

By Oliver Jensen

GIFT SUGGESTIONS

ILLUSTRATED FOR HORIZON BY CARL ROSE

DO THEY HAVE A FOREIGN CAR?

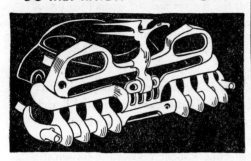

Here's a gift for the whole family! Get them a "Detroiter" Americanizing Kit. Every kit contains handsome 40 lb. false front-end of chrome-dipped plastic easily fitted to all foreign makes from Rolls Royce to Volkswagen, plus easily applied decals in two Day-Glo colors which give two-tone and "side-lick" look to plain European finish. Amber-tipped tail fins; sequined upholstery in interesting zebra pattern; ranch-mink tail for radio antenna and bronzed booties for hanging in rear window—all these will help some lucky family give their car that 100% American look. Xenophobe, Inc., Detroit, Mich.

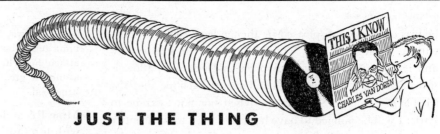

JUST THE THING

for that bright child is this record set, *Everything Charles Van Doren Knows*, recited by himself in 3,126 twelve-inch long-playing records. Handsome album bindings blend with playroom walls. Ballroom-length cabinet in curly maple or fireproof bakelite, only $800 extra. A gift that lasts a lifetime at least. From Mecca Records, Inc.

DOES HE LIKE YACHTING?

Then the new "Romanette" pre-fab trireme, complete with owner's cabin, oars, leg-irons, neck-chains, whips and mohair couches for eight concubines, will give him an unforgettable Christmas! Imagine the merry scenes as male friends take to the rowing benches, and are locked in place while the ladies relax on the beauty-rest couches! There's your friend, striding along the overseer's gangway, enjoying every moment of this wholesome outdoor fun! Also ideal for club outings, Y.M.C.A., and religious groups.

NIKITA DOLL!

Amusing "stocking present." Lifelike figure in washable rubberoid smiles, lolls tongue, says "Peace" when tilted. Exclusive, patented mechanism makes teeth snap unexpectedly when doll is approached too closely, inflicting small, painful wound. (Disinfectant and first-aid kit included.) This hilarious party-giver's helper only $5.95 at all better toy shops.

NO LITTLE DELINQUENT

will fail to respond to "Educational Candy." Wide assortment of figures in pure cane sugar includes two gangs of 24 members each, all with ducktail cuts and leather jackets, plus one set of 24 Debs. Your teen-ager will appreciate these lifelike chocolate figures, easily arranged for "rumbles," fights with cops, etc. Jumbo box (5 lbs.) also contains standing and recumbent figures for "mugging" scene, as well as hard candy ammunition to fit any size zip-gun. Whole-Sum Candy Corp.

DO-IT-YOURSELF BUGS

will welcome something new, and here is a surprise indeed. Architects Unlimited, Inc., has full-scale models, with plans, elevations, etc., for the Colossus of Rhodes. Its twenty-eight million parts, each carefully marked in ancient Greek, will keep that handy, lucky friend of yours busy for years, or longer. Natural colors. A gift to be remembered!

CIVIL WAR BUFF on your list?

This Hallowed Ground, Inc., Gettysburg, Pa., has just the thing for you. An actual section of the Gettysburg battlefield, 12 feet by 12 feet by 6 feet deep, will be shipped directly to your happy recipient on orders received before Dec. 10. Clever chemical compound holds earth together and preserves vegetation while permitting all the fun of digging for old Minié balls, belt buckles, bones, etc. Endorsed by leading historians, educators. Only $1,200 postpaid. Prices for larger sections and portions of Cemetery Ridge furnished on application.

JUST FOR "𝓗𝓔𝓡"

A polished-bone alimony calculator will be a welcome present. Mastered with only a few moments' study, this precision instrument quickly arrives at daily, weekly, monthly, and lifetime alimony payments, together with deductions, tax figures, and other data so important to That One Girl, provided only that ex-husband's income is known. No ugly batteries. Will not stain clothing. Simulated leatherette case.

Napoleon and the Femmes Fatales

COTNINUED FROM PAGE 89

he was even more displeased by the tendencies of the book, with its apologia of love, which it set above all social rules, and its excessive eulogy of divorce. In December, 1802, it provoked the following harsh judgment: "I hope that the friends of Mme de Staël have advised her not to come to Paris: I will be obliged to have her taken back to the frontier by the *gendarmerie*." Thus she remained interned on the shores of the Lake of Geneva. She had left Paris early in May, taking with her a sick and ruined husband, who died of an apoplectic fit at an inn on their way through the Jura. For sixteen long months she made no further move.

In that same spring Mme Récamier, too, was exiled from the capital, but for a shorter period. Had she received, as seems to be the case, discreet advice to make herself scarce? Or did she move from a spontaneous desire to escape the interest which the First Consul had shown in her on several occasions?

The earliest of these had been in 1801, when she had been obliged to approach Napoleon obliquely as a supplicant. Her father, M. Bernard, recently appointed post office administrator, had been so imprudent as to permit a letter to enter France from royalist agents to the insurgent Bretons. Discovered and arrested, he was in danger of death. Jean Bernadotte (later to become one of Napoleon's marshals and then King of Sweden) to please Juliette whose acquaintance he had just made, hurried in the night to the Tuileries and extorted mercy for the culprit. It was to Bernadotte alone that Mme Récamier was indebted. The Consul, however, had greater hopes, as the evidence of his old comrade and private secretary, Bourrienne, makes quite clear: "Bonaparte expected feelings quite other than those of gratitude. . . . and I have not forgotten on what conditions the reinstatement [of M. Bernard] was to have been granted."

Years later, as the Imperial Court was being established, the minister of police, Joseph Fouché, went to Clichy charged with a very strange mission. In a private conversation he declared to Mme Récamier that the Emperor was "deeply wounded" to see "the slight trace of opposition growing" in Mme Récamier's salon. The messenger further said: "Since the day when he met you, the Emperor has neither forgotten you nor lost sight of you. Be careful and don't offend him further." These were first overtures with implied threats, aimed less at Mme Récamier herself than at her husband's business. In another interview, Fouché enjoined his hostess to ask for a place as lady of honor at court, assuring her that this place would be granted in advance. When Mme Récamier objected that her tastes were too simple, the tempter, according to Mme Récamier's memoirs, went to the limits of insinuation:

The Emperor, he added, has not yet met the woman worthy of him; and nobody knows the extent of Napoleon's love should he attach himself to a pure woman; assuredly, he would let her assume a great power over his spirit, which would be wholly beneficial.

Mme Récamier testifies that she listened to this crude offer with less indignation than "disgust," and extricated herself with a few jocular retorts. But she remained anxious.

Shortly before Napoleon left Paris to undertake the campaign of Ulm and Austerlitz, Fouché resolved to hasten the climax of these delicate negotiations. Sure of success, he arrived at Clichy, drew the mistress of the house aside, and said, "You must give no more refusals. It is no longer I, it is the Emperor himself who proposes a place for you as lady of the palace; and I have been ordered to offer it in his name." Mme Récamier informed her husband of the situation. Told of his wife's "invincible repugnance" to the offer, he left her free to draft her refusal.

After this indisputable act of defiance, Mme Récamier found herself listed with her husband in the Great Book of Suspects. Worse: her features and her name remained engraved in the implacable memory of the Emperor. She had preserved her good name; she was soon to learn the cost.

In that same autumn of 1805 when Mme Récamier was imprudently defying the master of France, Mme de Staël had fled from him across the Alps. From Milan, where Napoleon had just assumed the Iron Crown as King of Italy, she brought back to Coppet in June nothing but vague and indirect assurances of good will. In the "court" of friends that quickly re-formed around her, she felt herself at a loss. She had wanted to spend the winter in a town some twenty leagues from Paris, whence she might easily reappear in the capital. But on August 29, from the camp at Boulogne where he was preparing the crushing renewal of his offensive against Austria, the Emperor sent his minister of police these orders: "Make known to [Mme de Staël's] friends that she must remain forty leagues away. We must put all the elements of discord at a distance from Paris." Forty leagues instead of twenty! The circle of proscription was enlarging.

Mme de Staël resolved to go at any rate to the limit of her forty leagues; at that distance she could communicate with her friends more easily and watch more closely over her children's studies in Paris. She made arrangements to occupy a house at Vincelles, some forty-two leagues from Paris. The Emperor, when informed, merely growled, "She must not pass the forty leagues!" This master of strategy had guessed his obstinate enemy's plan: to nibble, league by league, at the prohibited terrain, and by successive leaps to push forward to the gates of the capital.

During this period the printing of Mme de Stael's new novel, *Corinne*, had been completed and the work was to appear at the end of April, 1807. Forced to return to Switzerland as a result of an indiscreet appearance in Paris, she left *Corinne* behind her, thinking that this great book would assure both revenge and salvation. This was an illusion which events were to destroy pitilessly.

What did the Emperor think of the work that was intended to soften his heart? It is said that he received it late at night in his East Prussian camp, ordered an aide-de-camp to be roused, and for two or three hours made him read many pages. Then he interrupted sharply to say, "This is rubbish." When he reread it coolly, the politician and ruler in him were equally injured: "I cannot forgive Mme de Stael for having in her novel disparaged the French people."

In fact, with unintentional maladroitness she had chosen a Scotsman for her hero, and had lost no opportunity of praising Anglo-Saxon ways. The heroine, Corinne, went so far as to bewail the abasement of character in a social system from which liberty had been banished, which might be regarded as an open attack on the Emperor, his government, and his glory. Far from soothing the anger of Napoleon and his henchmen, *Corinne* sealed it.

Politically, it was a dangerous setback. This "novel-poem," as Sainte-Beuve called it, both established her fame and made her exile certain. It had scarcely appeared before it achieved a "universal and instantaneous success." Not that the press of the time had helped this triumph. Periodicals and reviews were by no means free, and the reasons why the book displeased the master were well known. But the book became the rage, and official displeasure may have increased public curiosity. In a few weeks not one of the great capitals was ignorant of her masterpiece.

It is not surprising. The adventures of a high-minded woman who, "seeking glory," had tried "only to make herself beloved"; who had not succeeded, who had died of it after having "exercised her capacity to suffer in its entirety," perfidiously rejected by society but admired— these adventures came close to the romantic sensibilities of all countries. For a quarter of a century, until the coming of George Sand, *Corinne* symbolized for women all the emotions of the romantic muse. Its author was everywhere given the name of her heroine.

Sainte-Beuve wrote that "with *Corinne* Mme de Stael definitely entered into glory and empire." This empire, the château at Coppet on Lake Leman, so often forsaken, underrated, and spurned by its chatelaine, was to become, during the summers of 1807 and 1809, the glittering capital. On two occasions Mme Récamier went there to reign beside her friend. Thanks to the "genius" of one, the beauty of the other, and the misfortunes of both, Coppet was soon wrapped in a sort of legend. Its light began to radiate gently, as Sainte-Beuve says, like "the intellectual Elysium of a whole generation."

Having reached Coppet in deep despondency, it was not long before Mme de Stael lifted her head again. She heard the growing clamor of her fame. Soon Goethe had read *Corinne* and had told her of his enthusiasm. A brilliant season was developing for her, and it began in the second half of July. Geneva was the crossroads of Europe, and peace swelled the influx of travelers that summer. All those who mattered in the intellectual world of any country had themselves presented to the illustrious "Corinne." The majority were only passers-by; a few were kept at the château for several days, but others were invited in advance for a lengthy stay. For some six or seven weeks, Mme de Stael gathered around her about thirty people.

Among the elite minds of her court, Mme de Stael reveled in the pleasure which was for her the best of all, the pleasure of talking. A biographer wrote that:

At Coppet they began to talk at breakfast at eleven o'clock; they began again at dinner at about six; then in the garden or while driving in the carriage; then between dinner and supper in the twilight; then at supper at eleven, and they continued far into the night.

In addition to conversation, the theater held a prominent place in the diversions at Coppet. The stage was set up at the end of the vast library. Coming from Geneva, Rolle, and Lausanne, the spectators crowded in, overflowing onto the terrace through the French doors. Rehearsals filled the fine evenings agreeably.

Mme Récamier arrived at Coppet in a state of mind that made her particularly susceptible to emotion and enthusiasm. Unhappy and tired, she was in great need of rest; yet she found nothing there but agitation. She had courageously borne two blows: her mother's death and her husband's financial ruin. She had also experienced another deep sorrow: Prince Alphonse Pignatelli, who had loved her and of whom she had been genuinely fond, had died of a long complaint. All her sorrows, it seemed to her, had come upon her in one year, the year of her thirtieth birthday. She was moved to draw up a balance sheet of her life. She had been guilty of innumerable flirtations; but had she ever tasted any profound emotion? Was she forever to stand at the gates of love? Mme de Stael was not unaware of this state of mind; doubtless persuaded that a "Royal Highness" might make her forget the Italian prince, she had invited Prince Augustus of Prussia to join them.

He came. In a week a guest described him as being already "very much in love" with Mme Récamier. Under the constant pressure of his admiration, Mme Récamier felt her heart soften. She wrote to M. Récamier, asking him to recall her to Paris. Poor Jacques-Rose saw and guessed nothing. He ponderously replied "that his still insecure credit required the government's support; that the presence of Mme Récamier who, because of her association with Mme de Stael, was like her in disgrace, might be prejudicial to his business." It was better that she remain at Coppet.

It was at this point that the Prince deliberately told her that if she broke her union with M. Récamier, he would ask her to become his wife, a remarkable proof of esteem as well as of passion from a prince of a royal house, profoundly imbued with the prejudices of rank. The Church, he pointed out, would not refuse to annul a marriage that had remained unconsummated in deference to what M. Récamier later termed his wife's "susceptibilities and aversions." Juliette, who until then had repulsed any proposal that was too precise, felt all strength leave her; she argued no longer. Henceforth the two lovers considered themselves affianced; they lived amid the tumult of Coppet, always close together and cradled in their dreams.

Time, meanwhile, was pressing. A letter from Berlin demanded the Prince's return, so he got Juliette to write the decisive letter to M. Récamier in which she was to make clear her determinations. Rashly they plighted their futures, though they did not even know if the first and apparently the least of obstacles would ever be removed. They exchanged oaths to marry and rings to serve as tokens. The Prince fastened a gold bracelet to Juliette's wrist, hung a gold chain about her neck with a pendant heart of rubies, and left the next day before dawn. He had scarcely departed when the post from Paris brought her husband's reply.

M. Récamier would agree to divorce "if his wife requested it"; but that she might not do so, he appealed to "all the feelings of a noble heart," expressing regret at "having respected the susceptibilities and aversions without which a closer relationship would not have permitted this idea of separation." Thus the thunderbolt fell upon Juliette's dreams. The obstacle which she thought would collapse at a breath had become even more difficult. To achieve her freedom, she had to do violence to M. Récamier's wishes. With the letter in her hand, "she remained for a while motionless and dismayed; then her heart hardened and duty took control."

When it was all over, she felt that her sentimental experiences were ended; and so they were for about ten years, until Chateaubriand came on the scene. She was thrown back on her cult of friendship. It was now her opinion that Nature had not made her for any other feeling. It is true that for her, friendship assumed many of the colors borrowed from love. Later, Sainte-Beuve prettily said that her heart willingly halted "in early spring when the orchards are covered with white flowers and have yet no leaves." Henceforth, the sentiment which Mme Récamier preferred and which she imposed on her most persistent admirers was a friendship both cruelly and voluptuously loving.

This kind of friendship ended in uniting her destiny to that of Mme de Staël, who wrote her one day: "I love you with a love surpassing that of friendship. I go down on my knees to embrace you with all my heart." But only to Mme de Staël did Juliette permit this delirium of affection.

In absence, the Prince persisted in the mystical worship of his idol. His letters became fewer after 1819 and came at longer intervals, but he wrote thirty more, filled with chivalrous affection and devotion. The ring which Juliette had given him at Coppet and which he had long hoped to turn into a wedding ring went with him into the grave, as he had sworn, as token and proof of their eternal betrothal.

The final summer of 1809 at the symbolical château passed amid the upheavals of war and passion. The season was less carefree than the one that had preceded it; no one could forget that the all-powerful Emperor had set a watch on the chatelaine and her group. Mme de Staël found parting from Mme Récamier more painful this year:

Since your going, I have fallen into an incredible languor; you were my link with hope, I believed in the future because your charming looks proclaimed one, but without you I fall back upon the past which is a living death. . . . You have made me know all that is really sweet about love for a woman; it is the alliance of two weak creatures who face their oppressors together. If we were living together in Paris, we could spend a lifetime to ourselves, watching the lives of others flow by . . .

Yet she was at work; her sorrows found their consolation

Mme de Staël's château at Coppet

LILLI RÉTHI

in pleasures of the mind. The writing of the book on Germany was sufficiently far advanced to envisage its publication the next year. In spring the censors granted their "visa" to the first two volumes. This bred a false confidence for the third, which Mme de Staël's friends felt would certainly receive official authorization. But suddenly, from behind the smiling features of the censor, an incautious step brought forth the disquieting face of the new chief of police, Savary, and beside it the terrible shadow of the Emperor. As if she had the intuition that other eyes were now bent on her book, it occurred to Mme de Staël to take this opportunity of bringing herself into the memory of her imperial enemy. If she could only obtain a half-hour's interview with Napoleon, she could tear down the veil of misunderstanding that hung between them, and even perhaps get him to revoke the orders which condemned her to exile. She drafted a letter to the Emperor.

Savary, however, was only his master's tool; the Emperor took the matter into his own hands. He had not yet been able to read Mme de Staël's long letter, but having the two volumes of sheets that had been submitted to the censorship brought before him, he perused the work of his old enemy with angry curiosity and ordered the printing to be stopped. He wished, he said, to proceed to a rigorous examination of the text himself. Mme de Staël judged the situation carefully. She laid out her strategic plan: while protecting herself from Savary's hostility, she had to get to work on the Emperor without delay. Mme Récamier exerted her influence on many people in high places, and what a friend called "a campaign of friendship" was organized in defense of the work and its author. Finally, Mme de Staël prepared to make a further appeal to the Emperor in another letter that would be given into the proper hands without delay.

In October, 1810, after two days' activity, the coalition of friends almost succeeded. Savary had softened to the extent of authorizing later publication of the book, with revisions. One cannot believe that he made such a decision without the Emperor's agreement, since he had been with him at Fontainebleau that Sunday. Would it not have been wise to have left things there for the moment? But Mme de Staël wanted to secure more and she clung to the idea of her letter, perhaps the more obstinately because the first, carried by Mme Récamier on September 25, had brought no reply. Then suddenly, two days later, Savary addressed a letter to Mme de Staël which condemned her and her book without appeal.

The reason for such a sudden change was nowhere but in the thoughts and feelings of the Emperor. On October 1 or 2, intercessors had spoken to him about Mme de Staël and mentioned her request for an audience. So many representations and so much insistence overtaxed his patience. In order to give a definite answer to the petitioners, he took the book up again and lost his temper with the passages

that had already worried him. The negotiations of September 29 and 30 had almost saved the book; but by her direct solicitations, Mme de Staël had lost it. She had reawakened an almost dormant anger.

Not only were actual politics involved between Mme de Staël and the Emperor; there was more than a hostility of circumstances. There was more even than a temperamental incompatibility; there was an essential opposition of characters, ideas, and minds.

He was cold and crafty even in his angers, secretly ardent, busy from a distance with his most far-reaching plans, and dependent upon the future. She, on the other hand, preferred friendship and love, burned eagerly for systems and men, concealed nothing: an improviser, changeable and entirely given up to the present. He unjustly despised humanity, while she imprudently trusted it. She was generous and he was implacable; she was a utopian and he a calculator. She wanted to draw the Revolution back to its principles, to steep it again in its sources; he wanted to fulfill it in its consequences, to drown it in its own overflow. She wanted to moderate it; he wanted to transcend it. He was descended through Robespierre from Louis XIV and Caesar; she was the daughter, through Mirabeau, of Rousseau and Montesquieu. She believed in ideas, which he distrusted; in enthusiasm, at which he smiled; in the intellect, which he feared. He sought to establish order by strength; she sought to establish happiness by justice. He was intoxicated with grandeur; she, with liberty.

Decidedly, there was no place for her in the imperial edifice. Their conflict resulted from the nature of things. Through the voice of imperial wrath, destiny had spoken.

Banished once more, Mme de Staël dawdled and loitered along the way home to Switzerland. She pathetically compared herself to La Fontaine's pigeon, regaining its loft "lamed, trailing its wing and dragging its foot . . ." In Geneva she learned that both she and her son Auguste were henceforth forbidden to enter France without police permission. There was no longer any question of the "forty leagues rule"; it was proscription. Thus Coppet was likely in the end to become Mme de Staël's prison. Should she resign herself to living alone, or nearly alone, in that vast château once so full of friends, to writing no more, or at least to publishing nothing? Mme de Staël felt the noose tightening, and desired the comfort of her dearest friends about her. Mathieu de Montmorency, Mme Récamier, if only she could see them, even for a few weeks!

Mathieu de Montmorency, ever faithful, did not hesitate to respond to the appeals from Coppet. In the middle of August, after joining Mme de Staël at Orbe, he returned with her to Coppet. He knew that Mme Récamier would not be long in joining her there. His arrival at the château became known in Geneva and was reported to Paris the same day. By return post, Mme de Staël relates, Mathieu "received his letter of exile"—a letter that inflicted upon him, too, the penalty of a forty-league limit from the capital. To this grief a cruel anxiety was added. What would happen to Mme Récamier?

Juliette set out for Coppet on August 23, accompanied by her adopted daughter, Amélie. Deeply grieved by her friend's letters, she did not believe she was taking a great risk by going to console her. Arrived at Coppet, she had been there only a day when she was torn away by her nephew, Paul David, who had hurried there to remove her from the danger to which she was exposing herself. Nevertheless, it was soon learned at Coppet that Mme Récamier, too, had been struck by "the forty-league penalty." Auguste de Staël left on horseback, asking at every stage on the road to Paris for the Récamier carriage. "He caught up with us," Amélie records, "at our last sleeping-place before Paris." But Mme Récamier already knew her fate; M. Récamier had hurried to meet his wife at Dijon and it was there he had told her of the decision which made her an outlaw.

It was in vain, however, that Mme Récamier was confined outside of Paris. Through Mme de Staël's letters she lived in thought at Leman. In her replies she became the consoler of suffering more bitter than her own. Throughout her stay in exile she listened to the long lamentation from Coppet, rising, strophe by strophe, regularly and sadly.

But the wall suddenly collapsed. Two weeks in the spring of 1814 were enough, at the end of which the Emperor was an outlaw himself. Exiles flowed back to Paris en masse. In May Mme de Staël hastened to Paris; Mme Récamier returned unhurriedly from Rome. When their first ecstasies died down, did each woman find the other really the person she had left? Until now they had been accustomed to love one another only in the midst of anxiety or misfortune. How would their relations stand up in prosperity?

In her own home Mme Récamier luxuriated in fashionable success. Quickly wearied by these mundanities and reproaching Juliette for her immoderate appetite for them, Mme de Staël left for Coppet on July 15. Mme Récamier vainly urged her to return to Paris for the autumn, but she did not reappear until more than a year later, and then only to make a final stir—and to die.

In this last year of her illness, it first occurred to her to invite Chateaubriand and Mme Récamier together. Seated side by side at dinner, they seemed overcome by reciprocal awareness: "I did not look at her," he relates, "she did not look at me; we did not exchange a word." Only toward the end of dinner did she "timidly address to him a few words about the illness of their mutual friend." In a miraculous exchange of glances, their hearts were revealed to one another. By the gleam of this wonderful moment, they understood that Mme de Staël "left them, at a sad meal, the memory of her and the example of an eternal affection." Had she guessed in fact that for about two years her beautiful friend had been secretly disturbed by this tempestuous author? Was it her desire that he should take the place in Juliette's heart that she herself was soon to vacate?

What did Mme Récamier do during the days of mourning which followed two weeks after? She wept, certainly, for the vanished friend, but she dreamed, too, of the man this friend had bequeathed her. Did she already know that at this moment Chateaubriand, disgraced and exiled in a château in Perche, was evoking for her, in a volume of his memoirs, the eager reveries of his youth and tracing the outlines of the charmer he was later to call his Sylphide?

In Revolt Against Togetherness

CONTINUED FROM PAGE 33

still other instruments of unanimity in the form of batteries of IBM machines run the records of tens of thousands of students through their electronic fingers. To enable the records to fit the machines, all students have to be given questions in their various subjects that call only for "Yes-No, Right-Wrong, Check One" answers, and that permit of no "Maybe" or otherwise divergent responses. Any hesitation or further thought, any reluctance to apply the proper check mark that the machine can record, downgrades the student as departing from the norm. It is by these means that the fate is being determined of all applicants for higher education under the College Entrance Examination Board, as well as of candidates for places in innumerable businesses and professions and the Foreign Service of the United States.

In salesmanship, also, there are "motivational research" and, as of last year, "subliminal advertising"—both involving the assumption that practically all customers are alike in that they are basically irrational animals who can be made to respond like Pavlov's dogs to given stimuli. This makes them fair game even in the recesses of their private souls—that is, if they still have any. Television, not to be left out, has its own particular brand of Togetherness, perhaps best exemplified by the habit of announcers and masters of ceremonies of treating guests on whom they have never laid eyes before like old cronies, grabbing them by the shoulder, calling them by their first names, and asking them to make public property of their private lives by airing them across the nation's air waves. And in religion, the Reverend Norman Vincent Peale preaches to millions that so long as we all think positive thoughts about each other and suspend criticism, all will be well. A few unreconstructed individual worshipers have, however, taken to thinking negative thoughts about Dr. Peale.

146

Americans, we have been told time and again, are joiners from way back, and learned critics have explained that this may arise in part from our diverse cultural and racial origins, which leave citizens impelled to band together for solidarity and assimilation. Many European nations harbor freemasons, but none so fantastic a proliferation of them as our own, where a member may be simultaneously a Grand Generalissimo of the Knights Templar, a Supreme Alchemist of the Ancient Arabic Order of Nobles of the Mystic Shrine, a Sovereign Grand Commander of the Scottish Rite, and a Chief Seneschal of the Order of DeMolay. We are unique in our Elks, Moose, Lions, Odd Fellows, Mazzini, and Liederkranz societies, and so on down to the National Women's Barber Shop Choral Groups of Sweet Adelines, Inc., with some sixty local singing chapters. Yet grouping for a purpose—and assimilation is certainly a meaningful one—is different from simply grouping for grouping's sake, of rushing out together in motivation-researched family in-groups to buy the same brand of split-level, hard-top, or matching pajamas.

This year, of course, we haven't been rushing out to buy those cars—which may become recorded as a harbinger of the American individual's revolt. Psychologists who had advised Detroit to build them as "status symbols" for a status-hungry America have since discovered suddenly that the car's own status as a symbol of status has been lost. As one General Motors salesman complained, "It has now become fashionable not to buy a car"—which of course may be a form of Togetherness in reverse.

Another hint of incipient rebellion was given when a Women's Congress on Housing, convoked in Washington by the Administrator of the United States Housing and Home Finance Agency, produced the response that what women wanted in their houses was not communal living inside identical picture windows at all, but individuality—and maybe a little privacy. And a further women's conference called by "The Magazine of Togetherness" itself led to precisely the same response, which must have been somewhat unsettling to the idealogues of *McCall's*. "I just don't want my house to look like everyone else's," remarked one housewife. "Emphasis on Privacy Marks New Construction," ran a headline in the real-estate section of *The New York Times* last summer. It doesn't yet, to any considerable degree. But even to state that privacy is desirable is a challenging step.

Motivation research, also, has been assailed by non-conformists and anti-Pavlov-dog individualists, even to the point where in some quarters it has taken the self-protective measure of going underground. All Madison Avenue advertising agencies have their MR teams, one executive admitted some time ago to *Business Week*, "but generally they keep them well out of sight in the back room—wary of invoking the 'hidden persuader' label." And subliminal advertising on TV, another effort at total psychic engineering, has come under the suspicious gaze of the Federal Communications Commission as well as under the temporary ban of most broadcasters themselves, while the Methodist Temperance Board—not hitherto thought of as a crusader for personal liberties—has added its own bit to the cause of privacy by issuing warnings against the danger of collective subconscious lures to liquor.

Such critics of unanimity as William H. Whyte, Jr., (*The Organization Man*), and of the manipulation of it as Vance Packard (*The Hidden Persuaders*), have done pioneer work in trying to break us from our thralldom. So, paradoxically, have the Soviets, who in sending up their sputniks well in advance of ours achieved the fall-out effect of arousing us to examine the caliber of our own collective education. Yet the Thinkometers, the groupthink sessions, the cultists of total agreement among young and old, rich and unrich, the bright and the not-so-bright, still flourish at their stands. To be sure, one home-furnishings company now advertises "Separateness," while Viceroy cigarettes have taken to plugging their product as designed for "The man who thinks for himself"; but the individual worm—if that is what he has come to be—turns slowly.

Sometimes he does turn when he sees the image of his own Togetherness projected back at him from Washington —the place he regards as the ultimate carrier of his inherited ideals. Washington is also, of course, the ultimate legatee of his departure from those ideals. The Joint Chiefs of Staff some years ago set up an intraservice team to produce a sort of package presentation of democracy to guide soldiers and civilians alike, under the heading "Militant Liberty" and complete with visual aids and lecturers. In some quarters the Pentagon collectivizers were thought to have gone too far. President Eisenhower himself, when with a lofty purpose in mind he called for a "People-to-People" program of get-together by American and foreign groups across the seas, soon found that many of the distinguished men appointed to its forty-odd committees preferred to do their getting-together privately and individually.

Togetherness begins by envisaging every couple, family, kindergarten, or idea as being simply the result of good committee work, and ends by producing a *reductio ad absurdum* of the same on top. Today, for instance, the President's office is served not only by a Cabinet and its several secretaries but by a National Security Council and *its* secretaries, an Operations Coordinating Board and *its* secretariat, and, most recently, by a committee of Special Assistants for Cabinet Coordination and *their* own additional secretariat. All are mechanisms for achieving unanimity between the Great White Father of the hour and the official offspring who multiply constantly according to Parkinson's Law. Togetherness could hardly go further, unless all the grouped co-ordinators and their chieftains were also asked, like a *McCall's* family, to dress alike.

RICHESSE OBLIGE

A short lecture to multimillionaires

By LUCIUS BEEBE

The editorial below appeared recently in one of the most unusual publications in the country, The Territorial Enterprise *of Virginia City, Nevada, once edited during the mining days by Mark Twain and currently published by Lucius Beebe, author and ex-columnist. A mixture of local news for Virginia City (population shrunken to 400) and articles on Western Americana for a large out-of-town audience, the weekly* Enterprise *accurately reflects the tastes of its owner, a man who laments the rococo past and never hesitates to lambaste what he regards as the more insipid present. In this editorial, reprinted by permission, Mr. Beebe examines the habits of the very, very rich and finds them sorely on the wane.*

Perhaps the saddest news story in recent weeks came to the world under a Texas date line when a Houston oil tycoon named James M. West at last encountered the old fellow with a scythe. Mr. West, who was described by the A.P. as a "multimillionaire rancher," left an estate of $100,000,000, take or leave a few dollars, $290,000 of which were squirrelled away in silver dollars in a secret cellar in his home, and a fleet of forty-one Cadillacs. His favorite occupation was riding night patrol with Houston policemen.

There you have it: the American archmillionaire of the Year of Our Lord 1958, forty-odd of the most offensive motor cars in the world, a taste for Skid Road adventure vicariously achieved, and so terrified of the times that he couldn't feel secure without a quantity of hard cash in the house.

If this were an isolated example of eccentricity and tastelessness in men of wealth, it would still be a matter for tears; but when you realize that it is, with slight variations on a witless theme, typical of the generation, it becomes a catastrophe of formidable proportions.

Forty-one Cadillacs. Not a Rolls or Bentley or Jaguar or Thunderbird or any car of real distinction or character among them. A taste for gutter squalor, but no mention of a library or an art gallery or the endowment of a chair of poetry among the dreadful football teams and drum majorettes of Texas. Nothing but first editions of *True Police Romances.*

What has become of the American generation of rich men worthy of the name or the possession of wealth? The J. P. Morgans, who ordered their chauffeurs to drive on the sidewalk when the street was blocked; Leland Stanford, who was overjoyed to learn that the endowment of Harvard University at the time was only $25,000,000 so that he too could endow a university, in California; the Vanderbilts, who thought nothing of building three or four entire Fifth Avenue blocks filled with French châteaux; even the

Ed Stotesburys, who announced that gold plumbing on their private cars was an economy because "it saved polishing."

Where are the August Belmonts, such as the first of that name, who spent an estimated $20,000,000 in ostentatious luxury in his New York home for the purpose of inducing apoplexy, as eventually it did, in his miserly neighbor James Lenox? Where even "Diamond Jim" Brady, who once arrived at Saratoga for the racing season in a private Pullman with solid silver trucks and brake rigging, thirty-five Japanese houseboys, and a gold-plated lady's bicycle belonging to Lillian Russell? Where Berry Wall, who changed his clothes forty times in an afternoon to achieve fame as "King of the Dudes," or the awful Bradley Martins, who gave a ball of such scandalous dimensions during bad times in New York that they had to live abroad the rest of their lives?

Here were people who, one way or another, had fun for their money, a laugh or so out of every million dollars they acquired. Their pleasures were various: mistresses, race horses, the endowment of universities, public bequests of Titians and Rembrandts, play actresses, seagoing yachts, or first folios of Shakespeare. Admirable or deplorable, at least they had character and the best, not the worst, that money could buy.

The wealth of these enviable and robust people was small change compared to the oil wealth of Texas, but somehow they managed to rise above Cadillacs, drum majorettes, television in million-dollar homes, and a taste for cola drinks instead of champagne. They didn't affect being "plain as an old shoe" or ready-made clothes or any of the infamies of spurious democratic conduct.

Forty-one Cadillacs! If the miserable man had owned forty-one Derby winners or maintained forty-one mistresses, he would have achieved some measure of worldly satisfaction in his wealth; some justification for having been around. As it is, no one need envy him. All he rated in the end was a Cadillac hearse.